TELEVISION, GLOBALIZATION AND CULTURAL IDENTITIES

Chris Barker

OPEN UNIVERSITY PRESS

Buckingham · Philadelphia

Open University Press
Celtic Court
22 Ballmoor
Buckingham
MK18 1XW

email: enquiries@openup.co.uk
world wide web: http//www.openup.co.uk

and
325 Chestnut Street
Philadelphia, PA 19106, USA

First Published 1999
Reprinted 2000

A catalogue record of this book is available from the British Library

ISBN 0 335 19954 2 (pbk)   0 335 19955 0 (hbk)

Library of Congress Cataloging-in-Publication Data
Barker, Chris, 1955–
    Television, globalization and cultural identities/Chris Barker.
        p.   cm.   (Issues in cultural and media studies)
    Includes bibliographical references and index.
    ISBN 0-335-19955-0 (hbk)   ISBN 0-335-19954-2 (pbk)
    1. Television – Social aspects.   2. Group identity.   I. Title.
    II. Series.
    PN1992.6.B352   1999
    302.23'45 – dc21   99-17601
                                                                CIP

Typeset by Type Study, Scarborough
Printed in Great Britain by Biddles Limited, www.biddles.co.uk

With love to Julie

CONTENTS

SERIES EDITOR'S FOREWORD

At a time when the cultural dynamics of television as a medium of mass communication are being decisively recast around the world, Chris Barker's *Television, Globalization and Cultural Identities* signals an important intervention into a number of pertinent debates in cultural and media studies.

In taking as its principal point of departure the issue of cultural identity, this book examines an extensive range of different conceptual approaches to the study of television within a global context. Barker dispenses with notions of cultural identity as a universal, fixed or essential entity in order to explore the socially contingent ways in which identities are culturally constructed. Special attention is given to understanding how relations of class, gender, sexuality, 'race' and ethnicity shape people's sense of who they are in relation to the world around them. Televisual representations, the author suggests, need to be recognized as a major resource for the construction of cultural identities within the lived experience of everyday life. That is to say, the profuse flow of televisual sounds and images provides viewers with a rich array of materials to enable them to refashion their individual 'identity projects' in highly complex, and typically contradictory, ways. This book thus makes for compelling reading as it succeeds in illuminating the key arguments being made about television in this regard while, at the same time, challenging many of the assumptions that underpin them.

The Issues in Cultural and Media Studies series aims to facilitate a diverse range of critical investigations into pressing questions considered to be central to current thinking and research. In light of the remarkable speed at which the conceptual agendas of cultural and media studies are changing, the authors are committed to contributing to what is an ongoing process of re-evaluation and critique. Each of the books is intended to provide a lively, innovative and comprehensive introduction to a specific topical issue from a fresh perspective. The reader is offered a thorough grounding in the most salient debates indicative of the book's subject, as well as important insights into how new modes of enquiry may be established for future explorations. Taken as a whole, then, the series is designed to cover the core components of cultural and media studies courses in an imaginatively distinctive and engaging manner.

Stuart Allan

ACKNOWLEDGEMENTS

Aspects of my research into soap opera viewing among young people have appeared in other forms as listed below. The author and publisher wish to thank the following for permission to use previously published material. *Young: Nordic Journal of Youth Research* for C. Barker and J. Andre (1996) Did you see? Soaps, teenage talk and gendered identity. *Young: Nordic Journal of Youth Research* 4(4) (Tidskriftsföreningen). *British Journal of Sociology* for C. Barker (1997) Television and the reflexive project of the self: soaps, teenage talk and hybrid identities. *British Journal of Sociology* 44(4) (Routledge). *Sociology* for C. Barker (1998) 'Cindy's a Slut': moral identities and moral responsibility in the 'soap talk' of British Asian girls. *Sociology* 32(1) (Cambridge University Press).

I would also like to thank Chris Pawling and Stuart Allan for reading and commenting on an earlier draft of this book.

Chris Barker

Introduction
TELEVISION, GLOBALIZATION
AND CULTURAL IDENTITIES

As you open this book I invite you to reflect on the fact that cosmopolitan-ism is fast becoming an aspect of day-to-day life in modern western societies. Diverse cultures which had once been considered 'alien' and remote are becoming accessible today (as signs and commodities) via our televisions, radios and shopping centres. As a consequence, we may choose to eat 'Indian', dress 'Italian', watch 'American' and listen 'African' (Hebdige 1990; Massey 1994). In contrast to this openness, consider the French government's longstanding hostility to American television summed up in former culture minister Jack Lang's fear of 'wall-to-wall Dallas' and Euro-pean attempts within the GATT (General Agreement on Tariffs and Trade) to sanction a protectionist wall against American audiovisual products. Consider also the fact that satellite dishes have been declared illegal in Saudi Arabia, Egypt, Bahrain and Iran, with the head of the Iranian Majlis (parlia-ment) committee on Islamic arts and guidance suggesting that 'This is a way of curbing the cultural assault . . . we showed the world that we are against foreign culture' (cited Tomlinson 1997: 127).

What do these apparently contradictory aspects of global culture tell us about the modern world? Are we growing together or further apart? Do we respect other cultures or fear them? Is **cultural identity** something to be kept 'pure' or something to be enlarged and enriched through mixing and match-ing? Questions about cultural identity, questions about television and ques-tions about the world we live in form the centrepiece of this book. Indeed, questions of cultural difference and cultural identity have become a central concern of contemporary cultural studies.

The search for identity

On the one hand, identity politics may be connected with the movement for justice, tolerance and solidarity, as in the US civil rights movement, the feminist movement and the anti-apartheid struggle in South Africa. On the other hand, questions of identity have been a haunting presence behind genocide in Rwanda and Bosnia. Further, the search for identity in an increasingly uncertain world is an aspect of religious movements and individual quests for meaning. In this context, cultural studies explores how we come to be the kinds of people we are, that is, how we are produced as subjects and how we identify with certain descriptions of ourselves as male or female, black or white, young or old, in short, what kinds of identities we adopt.

Indeed, as leading cultural studies theorist Stuart Hall argues, there has 'been a veritable discursive explosion in recent years around the concept of "identity", at the same moment as it has been subjected to a searching critique' (Hall 1996a: 1). Fuelled by political struggles, such as those involving feminism, gay rights and multiculturalism, as well as by philosophical and linguistic concerns, 'identity' has emerged as the central theme of cultural studies in the 1990s. Thus, the practices of feminism, post-colonial theory and queer theory, among others, have been high profile concerns intimately connected to the politics of identity. In turn, these struggles for and around identity necessarily raise the question, 'what is identity?'

Hall goes on to give a detailed and sophisticated account of identity, its 'impossibility' and its 'political significance'. The impossibility of identity is a reference to the mounting critique or deconstruction of the western notion of whole persons who possess a stable identity. That is, within western **cultures,** people have been thought of as unified agents who have a universal, fixed identity which belongs to them. In contrast, conceptions of identity within cultural studies have begun to stress the decentred subject, the self as made up of multiple and changeable identities. The plasticity of identity which such a view implies is one of the reasons why the concept has political significance, for the shifting and changing character of identities, and their theorizations, have intimate connections with social and political practices (see Chapter 1).

The globalization of television

While questions of identity have become the central theme of cultural studies, television, as the major form of communication in western societies, is one of its longstanding concerns. However, the case for exploring the economic and cultural significance of television is particularly acute at present because of changes in the patterns of global communications including a significant rise in transnational television. In turn, the **globalization** of the institutions of television raise crucial questions about culture and cultural identities. Thus, the globalization of television has provided a proliferating resource for both the deconstruction and reconstruction of cultural identities. That is, television has become a leading resource for the construction of identity projects.

By *identity project* is meant the idea that identity is not fixed but created and built on, always in process, a moving towards rather than an arrival. Such a project builds on what we think we are now in the light of our past and present circumstances together with what we think we would like to be, the trajectory of our hoped for future (Giddens 1991). It follows that the more resources that are available to us, the more complex the weave of our identities becomes and, I suggest, the processes of globalization provides us with just such an increased level of cultural resources.

Though television is not the only source of global cultural capital it is, I would argue, the major one. While the globalization of television will be discussed more fully in Chapter 2, we may note for the present that, through television, we can all be armchair global travellers 'subjected' to signs and **discourses** of and about other cultures. For example, last night on British television I watched *EastEnders* (British), *Fresh Prince of Bel Air* (American), *Holiday* (British, but covering Spain, the Caribbean and Blackpool), *Billy Connolly's World Tour of Australia*, *Soho Stories* (an insight into the lives of people in a famous location in London) and the *News* (covering among other things the personal life of US President Bill Clinton, the crisis over weapons inspections in Iraq and the development of Hong Kong under Chinese administration). These are, of course, mediated descriptions of the lives that other people lead and while those people may well want to challenge such descriptions, they remain a significant resource for my identity project.

Television is an asset open to virtually everybody in modern industrialized societies and one which is increasing its visibility across the planet. It is a site of popular knowledge about the world and increasingly brings us into contact, albeit in mediated fashion, with ways of life other than the one into which we were born. As Thompson has argued,

> We must not lose sight of the fact that, in a world increasingly permeated by the products of the media industries, a major new arena has been created for the process of self-fashioning. It is an arena which is

severed from the spatial and temporal constraints of face-to-face interaction and, given the accessibility of television and its global expansion,
is increasingly available to individuals world-wide.

(Thompson 1995: 43)

As people appropriate television's messages and meanings, suggests Thompson, they routinely incorporate them into their lives and their sense of themselves as situated in time and space. In other words, the meanings which
people produce interactively with television texts are woven into their identity projects. Thompson further submits that the detachment of a symbolic
form from its production context, and its re-embedding in new contexts, is
a central component of the experience of mass-mediated communication,
for example, the transplanting of the US soap opera *Melrose Place* on to
Australian TV screens. Consequently, identity work increasingly draws its
resources from a range of social practices which involve absent others and
necessarily engages with the social imaginary. Television is thus implicated
in 'the provision and the selective construction of social knowledge, of social
imagery, through which we perceive the "worlds", the "lived realities" of
others, and imaginary reconstruct their lives and ours into some intelligible
"world-of-the-whole" ' (Hall 1977: 140).

Simunye: the case of South Africa

Some of these abstract issues were made more concrete for me when I vis-
ited South Africa for a month during September 1996. South Africa,
described by its tourist board in the pithy sound-bite *A World in One Coun-
try*, is populated by Mandela's *Rainbow Nation* of Zulu, Xhosa, KhoiSan,
Swazi, Pedi, Venda, Ndebele, Tsonga, Tswana, South Sotho, Indian, Malay,
Cape Coloured, Afrikaner and British peoples. Or are they all South
Africans? Or perhaps we should regard the culturally diverse peoples of
South Africa as part of a common humanity?

In an attempt to aid the building of the 'new' post-apartheid South Africa,
the national television service South African Broadcasting Corporation
(SABC) promotes the idea of both cultural diversity and national unity.
Simunye is a Zulu word which translates into English as 'we are one'.
Against a background picture of black, brown, pink and white skinned
peoples in a variety of traditional and modern attire, the slogan *Simunye –
we are one* is continually emblazoned and sung across the SABC's three
channels.

Until recently, the people of South Africa were most definitely not 'one';

the system of apartheid based on a doctrine of racial difference separated the country economically, politically, socially and spatially into the 'haves' and 'have-nots'. How could peoples so divided now be one? Indeed, does it even make sense to talk of the black population of South Africa, the victims of apartheid, as *one* people? Go to Durban in KwaZulu/Natal and you will find that Inkhatha, a political party that claims to represent the Zulu people, is far from reconciled with the more strongly Xhosa based African National Congress (ANC), the government of the day. Needless to say, the cultural differences between various black African peoples was used as a divide and rule strategy by the white National Party's apartheid regime.

But what does it mean to say 'white' in South Africa? There is at the very least a cultural and political breach between the Afrikaans and British populations. The former have their cultural roots in ten generations of Dutch, German and Huguenot French ancestors whose Afrikaans language has developed entirely in Africa. The British are the British are they not? Well, not really, given that Britain's green and pleasant land, its sceptred isle, has at various moments in its history added Danes, Norwegians, Saxons, French, Italians, Greeks, Poles, Indians, Afro-Caribbeans and many more to its Celtic population. The English language is quite simply a polyglot of words from as diverse a set of languages as one could hope to find. Further, each of these national categories could themselves be deconstructed. Yet, we speak of Britain as a nation, and the British as a people, just as South African television seeks to blend the rainbow nation into one.

Simunye – we are one. It's not hard to be sympathetic to the intent of the slogan. Here is a diverse array of peoples segmented by **ethnicity**, tradition, language, history, **sex, gender**, power, wealth and poverty who one desperately hopes can live in peace and justice together in the new South Africa. South Africa is the name of a country, a nation, and it is under the sign of the nation that the South African government hopes to unite its disparate peoples. This is an act of imagination because such a nation will need to be built, created, for nationhood is not an a priori entity but a symbolic and communicative device around which people can imagine themselves to be one and to identify with their neighbours.

Simunye – we are one. How could one realistically believe that a slogan on television could create such a nation, such a utopia? The simple answer is that on its own it cannot; rather more is required in terms of political institutions, economic redistribution, social justice, tolerance and solidarity. No well intended slogan is going to bring that into being. And yet success in material terms depends in good measure on how people *think* about themselves and others, that is, how they are constituted culturally and use language as a guide to action. Imagining 'us' as 'one' is part of the process of nation building and there is no medium which has been able to speak to as many people in pursuit of that goal as television. If that seems fanciful or exotic because of its South African context, then consider Britain. The Football Association (FA) Cup Final, the Queen's speech at Christmas, the opening of Parliament, the Grand National, the *News*, *EastEnders* and *Coronation Street*, all address me in my front room as part of a nation and situate me in the rhythms of a national calendar, just as coverage of the Super Bowl, the President's State of the Union message, *CBS News* and *NYPD Blue* does for Americans.

However, just as we may consider the role of television in *constructing* **national identity** so we need also to engage in *deconstruction*, taking apart both the concept of national identity and the unifying role of television. National identity is only one kind of imagining, one form of cultural identity for, as we have already noted, black South Africans have different cultural identities based on language, history and traditions. We might also ask just how much black South African women have in common with black South African men when the language and practices of gender place women in subordinate positions. In my memory and imagination I see women walking for miles with bundles on their heads and children at their side. I see men working down the mines or sitting in the Shabeens drinking. On television I see evidence of a small but growing black business community as the ANC government encourages and demands that white owned business finds black partners. What does a relatively wealthy black businessperson have to say to unemployed shanty town dwellers? Or, for that matter, what do the rich white shareholders of South African diamond mines have to say to poor white farmers and labourers? For identity is as much a question of class and gender (and age and education and sexual orientation and so forth) as it is a matter of ethnicity and nation.

Television as unifier of the modern nation?

Perhaps, when there was only one channel on offer and 'we' all watched the same programmes, it was arguably the case that television unified the nation. But what about the present day when we have five channels, fifty channels or one hundred and fifty channels? How unifying a medium is television if we watch only what we have always liked and do so on segmented specialist channels – the sports channel, the movie channel, the music channel. Television, unifier of the nation, *Simunye – we are one*, how can that work when I have three TVs and you have none? Indeed, what is achieved by way of nation building when what is being watched on South African television is

Santa Barbara, Days of Our Lives, The Bold and the Beautiful and *The Young and the Restless*, all soap operas of American origin?

Thus, as the ordering impulse of modern television gives way to globalizing influences and postmodern cultural fragmentation, so the constitutive role of television in the production of cultural identities becomes increasingly complex and contradictory. Though this book is not about South Africa *per se*, it is concerned with the issues of television and cultural identity which any discussion of that country must involve. In this context, there are three core arguments which form the basis of the whole text and which I shall fill out in subsequent chapters. These arguments are summarized below.

Summary of arguments

First, television allows us all to be armchair travellers and experience something of the lives and cultural identities of others even as we stay at home. Consequently, television as it spreads across the globe is a major and proliferating resource for the construction of cultural identity. The concept of 'resource' is of considerable significance since, it will be argued, television is actively appropriated and deployed by audiences in making sense of their lives. Thus, television does not construct identities in the manner of a hypodermic needle but provides materials to be worked on. As Tomlinson (1991) has argued, the media are the dominant *representational* aspect of modern culture but its meanings are mediated by the 'lived experience' of everyday culture. The relationship between media and culture is therefore one of the subtle *interplay of mediations*.

Second, the concept of cultural identity does not refer to a universal, fixed or essential identity but to a contingent, historically and culturally specific social construction to which language is central. Though we commonly assume that we have a 'true-self', an identity which we possess and which can become known to us and others, we shall question the assumption that identity is a fixed thing to be owned or found and suggest instead that it is better understood as an ongoing description of ourselves marking a process of becoming. Further, cultural studies insists that questions of class, gender, sexuality, **race**, ethnicity, nation and age have their own particularities which cannot be reduced to any other dimension. Thus, issues of race should not be reduced to or explained solely in terms of class and so on. Equally, each *is* implicated in the other so that to explore the question of nationality, for example, is to understand how it has been gendered since nations are commonly spoken of as female and the notion of 'race' connected to the idea of the ascent of 'Man'. Further, young black women have different experiences from white women or black men or older black women, and so on. To grant the specificity of each element is to recognize the multiple experiences of people and the lived conditions of diverse cultural circumstances.

Third, identity is best thought of as the weaving of patterns of discourse into a centreless web and not as a set of attributes which a unified core self possesses. Such a conception of identity is premised upon an anti-representationalist view of language whereby words and sentences do not mirror an independent object world but are a resource in *lending form* to ourselves and our world out of the contingent and disorderly flow of everyday talk and practice (Wittgenstein 1953; Rorty 1989; Shotter 1993). In this view, it cannot be said that language directly *represents* a pre-existent 'I'; rather, language *constitutes* the 'I', brings it into being through the processes of **signification**. Further, since we lack an archimedian point outside of language from which to survey the relationship between the 'self' and sentences, we cannot be said to *have* an identity; rather, one *is* a centreless weave of beliefs, attitudes and identifications (Rorty 1991a). Indeed, identities are contradictory, they cross-cut or dislocate each other so that no single identity acts in an overarching organizing capacity. Instead, identities shift according to how subjects are addressed or represented. In contrast to our everyday usage of the word identity to designate an unproblematic self, this is a difficult and disturbing concept of identity which we shall explore more fully in Chapter 1.

1 | DISTURBING CULTURAL IDENTITIES

Before we can explore the place of television in the constitution and contestation of cultural identity we need to consider more fully what we mean by the term identity. Consequently, in this chapter we shall study debates about culture, subjectivity and cultural identity with a view to the question, 'What is cultural identity?' For the moment, we may take *culture* to refer to a variety of practices which generate meanings while the concept of *subjectivity* refers to the condition of being a person and the processes by which we become a person. As subjects (i.e. as persons), we are 'subject to' social processes which bring us into being as 'subjects for' ourselves and others. Subsequently, the descriptions we hold of ourselves, and with which we identify, we may call cultural *identity*. Thus, the question of subjectivity can be posed in terms of 'What is a person?' while the question of cultural identity can be posed as 'How do we see ourselves and how do others see us?'

The title of this chapter, 'Disturbing cultural identities', stems from two important aspects of cultural studies theory and practice.

First is the idea that cultural theory has disturbed the idea of a stable, fixed and universal identity which a person possesses, an assumption contained in the cultural repertoire of the self with which most people in the modern western world are familiar. For example, we tend to assume that we have a 'true-self', an identity which we own and which can become known to us. However, we shall question the assumption that identity is a fixed thing to be found and suggest that, rather than an entity to be possessed, identity is constituted through descriptions of ourselves with which we identify.

The second 'disturbance' lies in the connection between cultural identity and cultural politics. Cultural identity has emerged as a core political concern around which feminists, African Americans, British Asians and others have organized to 'disturb the peace' of white middle-class America or Middle England. As the hegemonic grip of unitary modern (and commonly white male middle class) identity is weakened and fragmented so the voices of modernity's marginalized 'others' – that is, the voices of women, gays, people of colour and those outside the west – have come to disturb the cultural peace. Indeed, the rise of **identity politics** and new social movements are among the distinguishing markers of contemporary global culture.

First person singular

While there is no culture known to western theory in which 'I' or its linguistic equivalent is not used, and which does not therefore have a conception of self and personhood, the manner in which this pronoun is used, what it means, does vary from culture to culture. Consequently, it is central to conceptions of subjectivity and identity within cultural studies that what it means to be a person is social and cultural 'all the way down'. That is, identities are wholly social constructions and are not entities which exist outside of cultural **representations** and **acculturalization**. By acculturalization is meant the social processes by which we are constituted in and by culture learning how to 'go on' as knowledgeable agents. Thus, acculturalization, which is centred on the family, peer groups, education, media and work organizations, is the process by which the helpless infant becomes a self-aware, knowledgeable person, skilled in the ways of the culture.

Formed through a lifelong relationship to cultural representations and discourses that constitute us, identity is wholly social and cultural in nature with no universal, transcendental or ahistorical elements to what it is to be a person. Identity is a *social* phenomenon in two crucial ways:

- First, the very notion of what it is to be a person is a cultural question. For example, individualism is a marker of modern western societies while in many other cultures people conceive of themselves as inseparable from family relations and their place in a network of social relationships rather more than as distinct individuals.
- Second, the very resources that form the material for an identity project are social in nature, language and social practices, so that what it means to be a woman, a child, Asian or elderly is formed differently in different cultural contexts.

In sum, identity is about sameness and difference, about the personal and the social, 'about what you have in common with some people and what differentiates you from others' (Weeks 1990: 89). Consequently, before we move on to the debate about identities, with particular reference to modern and postmodern identity formation, we need at least a provisional sense of what is understood by the concept of culture.

The idea of culture

The concept of culture is by definition central to cultural studies, yet there is no correct or definitive meaning attached to it. In describing it as 'one of the two or three most complicated words in the English language', Williams (1983) indicates the character of cultural studies as an arena of debate and contestation. That is, culture is not 'out there' waiting to be correctly described by theorists who keep getting it wrong. Rather, the concept of culture is a tool which is of more or less usefulness to us in understanding human beings as a life form. Consequently, its usage, and therefore meanings, continue to change.

Historically, the concept of culture within at least one strand of cultural studies has referred to *a whole way of life* (Williams 1981), or as Hall puts it, 'By culture, here, I mean the actual grounded terrain of practices, representations, languages and customs of any specific society. I also mean the contradictory forms of common sense which have taken root in and helped to shape popular life' (Hall 1996c: 439). Thus, culture is not a concept used in relation to individual meanings as such, for it is a collective term and refers to the idea of *shared meanings*. However, as we shall see in Chapter 2, the idea of culture as bounded by place is increasingly untenable in an era of globalization when any given place is permeated by cultural discourses from elsewhere. Thus, questions about culture are ones that ask which meanings are shared or contested by which persons in which places under which conditions.

While culture is concerned with the various ways we make sense of the world, meanings are not simply 'out there' waiting for us to grasp them, they are generated through signs, most notably language. Language is taken to be at the heart of culture and identity for two central and related reasons: first, language is the privileged medium in which cultural meanings are formed and communicated. Second, language is the means and medium through which we form knowledge about ourselves and the social world.

Increasingly, cultural studies has argued that language is not a neutral medium for the formation of meanings and knowledge about objects which exist in the 'real world' outside of language, but rather, that language is constitutive of those very values, meanings and knowledge. That is, language gives meaning to both material objects and social practices which are brought into view by language and made intelligible to us in terms which language delimits. These processes of meaning production are *signifying practices* and to understand culture is to explore how meaning is produced symbolically in language as a *signifying system*.

Signifying practices

According to the linguist Saussure (1960), a signifying system is constituted by a series of *signs* which are analysed in terms of their constituent parts, the signifier and the signified. A *signifier* is taken to be the form or medium of signs, for example a sound, an image, the marks that form a word on the page, while the *signified* has been understood in terms of concepts and meanings. Further, the relationship between the sounds and marks of language, the signifiers, and what they are taken to mean, the signified, is not held in any fixed eternal relationship. The relationship of signifiers to the signified is *arbitrary* in the sense that the animal we call a 'cat' as it sits on the 'mat' could equally be signified by *el gato* and *la estera* (in Spanish). Thus, Saussure's fundamental argument is that meaning in language is not produced by reference to an extra-linguistic reality, but rather is generated through a system of relational differences between signs (semiotic difference).

One of the classical illustrations of these semiotic arguments is the relation between colours as signs and their organization into the cultural code of traffic lights. Colours are breaks in the light spectrum which we classify in the paradigmatic field with signs such as red, green, amber and so forth. There is, as we have already noted, no universal reason why the sign 'red' should refer to a specific colour; rather, red is meaningful *in relation* to the difference between red and green (and so forth). These signs are then organized into a syntagmatic sequence which generates meaning through the cultural conventions of their use within a particular context. Thus, traffic lights deploy 'red' to signify 'stop' and 'green' to signify 'go'. This is the *cultural code* of traffic systems which temporally stabilizes and conventionalizes the relationship between colours and meanings. Thus, signs become naturalized codes whose operation reveals not the transparency of linguistic or visual codes, but the depth of *cultural habituation* of the codes in operation. Significantly, in the day-to-day usage of the code in traffic management, we are not referring to words on a page but to visual signs operating in cultural life. Thus, **semiotics** extends its reach from the language of words to cultural signs in general so that colours, material objects and images can all be analysed using semiotics as practices which work 'like a language'.

Consequently, given this view of culture, a good deal of cultural studies work is centred on questions of *representation*, that is, how the world is *socially constructed* and represented to us and by us through signification. Further, cultural representations and meanings are not floating around in the air waiting to be plucked out; they have a certain materiality, that is, they are embedded in sounds, inscriptions, objects and images, for example, in books, magazines and television programmes. In this context, cultural studies can be understood as the study of culture as the signifying practices of representation and their relationship with concrete human beings. This, as we shall see later in the chapter, includes identity as a form of representation to which language is central. However, at this stage of the argument our understanding of cultural identity under contemporary conditions will be structured by the work of Stuart Hall.

Modern and postmodern subjects

In a seminal article on 'The question of cultural identity' Hall (1992a) identified three very different ways of conceptualizing cultural identity which he called

- the Enlightenment subject
- the sociological subject
- the postmodern subject.

The purpose of the next section is to expand upon those conceptualizations of identity and to trace the development of the fractured, decentred or postmodern subject.

The Enlightenment subject

The notion of persons as unique, unified agents has been strongly connected with the philosophy of the Enlightenment, a philosophical movement which is associated with the idea that reason and rationality formed the basis for universal human progress. Thus, the *Enlightenment subject* 'was based on a conception of the human person as a fully centred, unified individual, endowed with the capacities of reason, consciousness and action, whose "centre" consisted of an inner core. . . . The essential centre of the self was a person's identity' (Hall 1992a: 275). Philosophically speaking, this is a view associated with Descartes and known as the Cartesian subject. Descartes's famous declaration 'I think therefore I am' places the rational, conscious *individual* subject at the heart of western philosophy. Here the mind is regarded as having inherently *rational* capacities which allow it to experience the world and make sense of it according to the actual properties of that world.

Conceiving of the subject in this way is not simply a matter of philosophy but of the wider cultural processes of subject and identity formation, for it is central to the current western account of the self to see persons as unified and capable of organizing themselves. For example, morality talk, which in western culture seeks to make intelligible and manageable the moral and ethical dilemmas that face us, is centrally concerned with questions of individual responsibility for actions. Indeed, such a view is embodied in the law which holds individuals to account, not withstanding certain exceptions such as the diagnosis of insanity (though this is also held to be the state of an individual). In addition, the organization of academic knowledge into discrete subjects embodies a view of the unified self in that the domain of psychology is held to be the workings of the individual mind, and, on the whole, western medicine treats individual ailments. Likewise, classical economic theory, though concerned with social processes, has the rational self-interested choice-making individual at its centre.

However, in contrast to the Enlightenment view of a universal self, identities can be regarded as social and cultural 'all the way down' because we are constituted as social creatures through the processes of acculturalization. This socialized self is what Hall calls the *sociological subject* where the 'inner core of the subject was not autonomous and self-sufficient, but was formed in relation to "significant others", who mediated to the subject the values, meanings and symbols – the culture – of the worlds he/she inhabited' (Hall 1992a: 275). Our first 'significant others' are likely to be family members from whom we learn, through praise, punishment, imitation and language, how to go on in social life. The key assumption of a sociological view of the subject is that people are social animals so that the social and the individual are mutually constitutive. Though the self is conceived as possessing an inner unified core, this is formed *interactively* between the inner world and the outside social world. Indeed, the internalization of social values and roles stabilizes the individual and ensures that individual persons 'fit' the social structure by being stitched or sutured into it. Thus, we may talk of self-identity and **social identity** in the manner of the sociologist Anthony Giddens.

The sociological subject: self-identity and social identity

For Giddens (1991), **self-identity** is the building up of a consistent feeling of biographical continuity including the ability to sustain a narrative about the self and to answer critical questions about 'What to do? How to act? Who to be?' The individual attempts to construct a coherent narrative which is the very basis of identity so that 'Self-identity is not a distinctive trait, or even a collection of traits, possessed by the individual. It is *the self as reflexively understood by the person in terms of her or his biography*' (Giddens 1991: 53). The argument put by Giddens conforms to a common sense notion of identity, for he is saying that our identity is, in one respect, what we as persons think it is. However, he is also arguing that identity is not a collection of traits that we possess, identity is not something we have, it is not an entity or a thing to which we can point. Rather, identity is a mode of thinking about ourselves. But, as we all know, what we think we are changes from circumstance to circumstance in time and space. That is why Giddens describes identity as a *project* by which is meant the idea that identity is created and built on, something always in process, a moving towards rather than an arrival.

Though self-identity may be conceived by us as *our* project it is a sociological truism to say that we are born into a world that pre-exists us, that we learn to use a language that was in use before we arrived and that we live our lives in the context of social relationships with others. In short, we are constituted as individuals in a *social* process using socially shared materials commonly understood as socialization or acculturalization. Without language, and without acculturalization, not only can we not be persons as we understand that notion in our everyday lives but also the very concept of personhood and identity would be unintelligible to us. Without having learned to use words, and without having learned what others expect of me, I could not think of myself as being a man, as being British, as being a friend, a partner, a son and so forth. Indeed, without language, a *social* resource, I could not even use the pronoun 'I'. Giddens further argues that,

> *Social identities* . . . are associated with normative rights, obligations and sanctions which, within specific collectivities, form roles. The use of standardised markers, especially to do with the bodily attributes of age and gender, is fundamental in all societies, notwithstanding large cross-cultural variations which can be noted.
>
> (Giddens 1984: 282–3)

Thus, the resources that we are able to bring to an identity project depend on the situational power and specific cultural contexts from which we derive our competencies. That is, it matters whether we are black or white, male or female, African or American, rich or poor, because of the differential cultural resources which have constituted us.

Thus far, the argument is that the intellectual movement from the 'Enlightenment' subject to the 'sociological' subject represents a shift from perceiving persons as unified wholes who ground themselves to seeing the subject as formed socially. Though the social subject is not the source of itself, nor is it a 'whole' by virtue of the truism that people take up a variety of social positions, nevertheless, the social subject is seen as having a core self able to reflexively coordinate itself into a unity. This is not so for the fractured postmodern subject.

The postmodern subject

According to Hall's schema the *decentred* or *postmodern* self involves the subject in shifting and fragmented identities so that persons are composed not of one but of several, sometimes contradictory, identities. Thus,

> The subject assumes different identities at different times, identities which are not unified around a coherent 'self'. Within us are contradictory identities, pulling in different directions, so that our identifications are continually being shifted about. If we feel that we have a unified identity from birth to death, it is only because we construct a comforting story or 'narrative of the self' about ourselves.
>
> (Hall 1992a: 277)

Hall goes on to argue that five major 'ruptures in the discourses of modern knowledge' have contributed to our understanding of the subject as decentred or fractured. These are located in

- Marxism
- psychoanalysis
- feminism
- the character of language and discourse
- the work of Foucault.

Thus, in order to grasp what Hall means by the decentred or postmodern subject, we shall briefly explore each of these in turn. The order of the discussion, though partly but not entirely chronological, allows us to end with the most significant of the 'ruptures', those connected with the so-called linguistic turn in cultural studies. That is, cultural studies has increasingly turned to language and linguistic analysis as being at the heart of culture, identity and the cultural studies project.

The historical subject of Marxism

Cultural studies writers have had a long, ambiguous, uneasy but productive relationship with Marxism. Cultural studies has not been a Marxist domain, but it has drawn succour from it while subjecting it to vigorous critique. Here, our concern with Marxism is its theoretical contribution to, and support for, the notion of the 'fragmented' self.

Marxism is, above all, a form of historical materialism which stresses the historical specificity of human affairs and the changeable character of social formations across times and places, while locating their core features in the material conditions of existence. Marx argued (see e.g. Bottomore and Rubel 1961) that the first priority of human beings is the production of their material means of subsistence through their labour, which transforms not only the material world but also themselves. As humans produce food, clothes and all manner of tools to shape their environment, so they also create themselves. Thus, labour and the form of social organization that material production takes, the mode of production, are central categories of Marxism.

Modes of production

The organization of a mode of production is not simply a matter of organizing 'things'; rather, it is inherently tied up with relations between people which, while social, that is, cooperative and coordinated, has also been a matter of conflict and power. Thus, the social class conflicts structured into relations of production, an intrinsic part of a mode of production, are regarded as the motor of historical change. For Marxism, history is not a smooth process of gradual change but is marked by significant breaks and discontinuities. Thus, Marx discusses an ancient mode of production, a feudal mode of production, a capitalist mode of production and the hoped for socialist/communist mode of production, each characterized by different forms of material organization, different social relations, and each superseded by another mode of production as internal contradictions, particularly those of class conflict, lead to transformation and replacement.

Marxism, Hall (1992a) argues, displaces any notion of a universal essence of personhood which is the possession of each individual because, to paraphrase Marx, 'people make history, but only on the basis of conditions not of their own making'. In other words, historically particular modes of production and social relations constitute subjects in specific ways so that what it is to be a person cannot be universal but is located in characteristics of the social formation of definite times and places. For example, a feudal mode of production is based on the power of barons who own land and serfs (or lease it to peasants), so that the identities of barons and serfs are quite different, not only from each other, but also from the social relations and identities formed within a capitalist mode of production, wherein capitalists (and share holders) employ and exploit the 'free' labour of the working class. What it means to be a baron, a serf, a capitalist and a worker are quite different because of the specific form of social organization of which they are a part.

Althusserian interpretation

Of particular significance for Hall is the Althusserian reading of Marx (Althusser 1971) in which the place of ideology in the constitution of subjects is central. In broad terms, by the concept of **ideology** is meant structures of signification or world-views which constitute social relations and mark the attempt to fix the fluid and relational character of meaning in ways which legitimize the interests of the powerful. Crucially, for Althusser, the subject formed in ideology is not a unified Cartesian subject but a shattered and fragmented one. For example, classes, while sharing certain common conditions of existence, do not automatically form a core unified class consciousness but are cross-cut by conflicting interests and are formed and unformed in the course of actual historical development. For example, though 'I' share similar working conditions with my neighbour, we do not share a homogeneous working-class identity because 'I' am male and 'she' is female, 'I' am black and 'she' is white, 'I' vote for the 'left' and 'she' for the 'right', 'I' am a liberal and 'she' is a nationalist.

The general point here is that subjects are formed through difference, marked by the play of signifiers, so that what we are is in part constituted by what we are not. In this context, Marxism points to the historically specific character of identity and to fractured subject formed in ideology. Indeed, this growing emphasis on difference in language and the social field is also pertinent to questions of psychoanalysis, especially in its Lacanian mode.

Psychoanalysis and subjectivity

For Hall (1996a), psychoanalysis has particular significance, for while discourse regulates the subjects it controls and enables some forms of identification yet excluding others; it is argued that psychoanalysis can shed light on how *identifications* of the 'inside' link to the regulatory power of the discursive 'outside'. Hall, along with many feminists, deploys psychoanalysis to illuminate the processes by which discursively constructed subject positions are taken up (or otherwise) by concrete persons through fantasy identifications and emotional 'investments' (Henriques *et al.* 1984). Indeed, this contention is central to Hall's whole conceptualization of 'identity' as

> the point of suture, between on the one hand the discourses and practices which attempt to 'interpellate', speak to us or hail us into place as the social subjects of particular discourses, and on the other hand, the processes which produce subjectivities, which construct us as subjects which can be 'spoken'. Identities are thus the points of temporary attachment to the subject positions which discursive practices construct for us.
>
> (Hall 1996a: 5–6)

Thus, to Freud, and his 'discovery' of the unconscious through psychoanalysis, Hall attributes the next of his decentrings. Psychoanalysis remains a hotly contested and controversial body of thought. For its supporters (Mitchell 1974; Chodorow 1978, 1989) the great strength of psychoanalysis is its rejection of the fixed nature of subjects and sexuality concentrating instead on the *construction* and formation of subjectivity, on not what a subject *is* but on how the subject *comes into being*. Thus, it is argued, psychoanalysis shows how psychic processes institute the humanization of infants in and through sexual difference. It can offer a deconstruction of the constitution of subjectivity in the psychic and symbolic domains which is always gendered and created through imaginary fantasies in patriarchal societies.

Self as ego, superego and unconscious

According to Freud, the self is constituted in terms of an ego, or conscious rational mind, a superego, or social conscience, and the unconscious or id, the source and repository of the symbolic workings of the mind which functions with a different logic from reason. Such a view of personhood immediately fractures the unified Cartesian subject. It suggests that we do things and think things which are not the outcome of a rational integrated self but of the workings of the unconscious which are normally unavailable to the conscious mind in any straightforward fashion. Further, since the self is by definition fractured into the ego, superego and unconscious, the unified narrative of the self is something we must acquire over time through entry into the symbolic order of language and culture. That is, through processes of *identification* with others and with social discourses we create an identity which embodies an illusion of wholeness.

Libido

According to Freud, the libido or sexual drive does not have any pre-given fixed aim or object. Rather, through fantasy, any object, which includes persons or parts of bodies, can be the target of desire. Consequently, an almost infinite number of sexual objects and practices are within the domain of human sexuality. However, Freud's work is concerned to document and explain the *regulation* and repression of this 'polymorphous perversity' through the resolution (or not) of the Oedipus complex into 'normal' heterosexual gendered relationships.

Oedipus complex

In classical Freudian thought, the Oedipus complex is the moment of formation of the ego and of gendered subjectivity since, prior to that time, we are unable to distinguish clearly between ourselves and other objects and have no sense of ourselves as male or female. That is, prior to the resolution of the Oedipus complex, infants experience the world in terms of sensory exploration and auto-eroticism as they seek physical satisfaction. The primary focus at this stage is the mother as a source of warmth, comfort and food. Consequently, an infant's first love object is its mother with whom it both identifies and desires, that is, the child both wants to 'be' the mother and 'possess' the mother. The resolution of the Oedipus complex involves the repudiation of the mother as a love object and the separation of the subject from the mother.

Incest taboo

For boys, the incest taboo symbolized by the power of the father as Phallus means that desire for the mother is untenable and threatened by punishment in the form of castration. As a consequence, boys shift their identification from the mother to the father and take on masculinity as the desirable subject form. This includes heterosexual relations with women as being both appropriate and an attempt to recapture the plenitude or oneness of the pre-Oedipal moment. For girls, the formation of heterosexual love objects and the separation from the mother are more complex and arguably never completed. Girls do not entirely repudiate mother identification nor do they take on father identification. However, they do recognize the power of the Phallus as something which they do not have but which the father does. Since they do not have a penis (or symbolic Phallus) they cannot ever be it and they cannot identify with it; however, they can set out to possess it, which they do by seeking to have a child by the father or more accurately other men, who stand in for the father as Phallus.

Lacanian interpretation

In Lacan's (1977) influential reading of Freud, the resolution of the Oedipus complex marks the formation of the unconscious as the realm of the repressed, the very possibility of subjects (established through entry into the subject positions of the symbolic order) and their constitution in gendered ways. The Lacanian reading of Freud is one which places language at its heart for it is through entry into the symbolic order, constituted primarily as language, that subjects are formed. Further, the unconscious is the site for the generation of meaningful representations which can be approached through language, or rather, in Lacanian terms, the unconscious is structured like a language. That is, the psychic mechanisms of condensation and displacement are equated with the linguistic functions of metaphor and metonymy.

Role of psychoanalysis in cultural studies

In so far as psychoanalysis appears as an ahistorical universal account of subjectivity marking the psychic processes of humankind across history and, furthermore, one which is inherently patriarchal and phallocentric, that is, focused on men where women become secondary and adjunct terms, it has proved to be unacceptable within cultural studies. However, more sympathetic critics (Mitchell 1974; Rose 1997) have suggested that psychoanalysis can be reworked as an historically contingent account, that is, one which describes subject formation only under specific historical circumstances. Consequently, changes in the cultural and symbolic order can lead to changes in subject formation and vice versa so that the subversiveness of psychoanalysis lies in its disruption of the social order, including gendered relations, by trying to bring new kinds of thinking and subjectivities into being. Thus, psychoanalysis could, it is argued, be stripped of its phallocentricism and made appropriate to understandings of femininity and the political project of feminism. Certainly, psychoanalysis does point to both the fractured subject (conscious–unconscious, and so on) and to the profoundly cultural character of even the deepest, most entrenched levels of our sexual identities. Indeed, though the exact forms vary and it remains a hotly contested field, it is common to find psychoanalysis deployed by feminists in their exploration of gendered identity.

Feminism: the politics of difference

Feminism, argues Hall, has had a decentring influence on conceptions of subjectivity and identity because of its challenge (through the slogan and practice of the 'personal is political') to the distinction between the outside and the inside, the public and the private. For example, domestic violence may occur in the private domain but is of public concern. Further, feminism has interrogated the question of how we are formed as gendered subjects in the context of gendered families so that the 'inside' of gender is formed by the 'outside' of the family. Thus, what it is to be a person cannot be universal or unified since at the very least identity is marked by sexual difference.

Feminism is a plural field of theory and politics which has competing perspectives and prescriptions for action. However, in the most general of terms, we may locate feminism as asserting that sex is a fundamental and irreducible axis of social organization which, to date, has subordinated women to men. Thus, feminism is centrally concerned with sex as an organizing principle of social life and one thoroughly saturated with power relations. The fact that the subordination of women is evident across a whole range of social institutions and practices, that is male power and female subordination are structural, has led feminists to describe our societies as a form of patriarchy with its derivative meanings of the male-headed family, mastery and superiority (Evans 1997).

Liberal feminism and socialist feminism

As a multiform movement, feminism has adopted a range of analyses and strategies of action which have been seen as liberal feminism, socialist or Marxist feminism, difference or radical feminism, black feminism, and post-structuralist and postmodern feminism. Thus, liberal feminism (Mackinnon 1987, 1991) tends to stress equality of opportunity for women and regards this as achievable within the broad structures of the existing legal and economic frameworks. In contrast, socialist feminism points to the interconnections between class and gender and the fundamental place of gender inequalities, including the dual roles (domestic work and paid work) of women, in the reproduction of capitalism (Oakley 1974).

Difference or radical feminism and black feminism

In contrast to liberal and socialist feminisms' stress on equality and sameness, difference or radical feminism asserts the essential differences between men and women. These differences are celebrated as representing the creativity of women and the superiority of their values over those of men (Rich 1986; Daly 1987). As such, radical feminism has developed a tendency towards separatism. One criticism of radical feminism, and indeed of the very concept of patriarchy, is that it treats the category of woman as an undifferentiated one (Rowbotham 1981). That is, all women are taken to share something fundamental in common, in contrast to all men. This is an assumption continually challenged by black feminists, who have argued that, in defining women as white, the movement has overlooked the differences between black and white women's experiences (Carby 1984).

Poststructuralist and postmodern feminism

Poststructuralist and postmodern feminism (Nicholson 1990; Weedon 1997) argues that sex and gender are social and cultural constructions which are neither to be explained in terms of biology nor reducible to the functions of capitalism. This is an anti-essentialist stance which argues that femininity and masculinity are not essential universal and eternal categories but are discursive constructions. As such, poststructuralist feminism is concerned with the cultural construction of subjectivity *per se* and with a range of possible masculinities and femininities. While poststructuralist feminism is the most far reaching perspective in its assertion of the cultural and linguistic character of sex and gender, all forms of feminism affirm that sexual difference is at the heart of the very formation of subjectivity. What distinguishes poststructuralism is its core emphasis on language, a stress that is central to Hall's account of fractured identity and the conception of identity around which this book is structured.

Language, discourse and identity

Contrary to our everyday assumptions, language is not best understood as a mirror which reflects an independent object world ('reality') but a resource in *lending form* to ourselves and our world out of the contingent and disorderly flow of everyday practice (Shotter 1993). Language and discourse do not *represent* objects or reality but *constitute* them, bring them into being, so that social reality and social relations are discursively constituted in and through language rather than represented by language. This approach is sometimes known as social constructionism.

In this view, identities are *discursive constructions* (that is, formed in discourse or regulated ways of 'speaking'); indeed, there can be no identity, experience or social practice which is not discursively constructed since we cannot escape language. That is, identities are constructions of language and not fixed eternal things. The idea that identities are discursive constructions is underpinned by a view of language in which there are no essences to which language refers and therefore no essential identities.

Thus, we have noted Saussure's argument that language generates meaning through underlying relations of difference between signs rather than to fixed universal referents in the material world. That is, signifiers do not refer directly in a one-to-one relationship to entities in an independent object world but generate meaning in relation to other signifiers. Thus, 'good' is meaningful in relation to 'bad', and a whole range of intermediaries such as evil-naughty-disagreeable/kind-worthy-virtuous, all of which generate meaning in relation to each other and not to a fixed entity or quality that 'exists' independently of language.

Derrida's interpretation

This relational character of language is underscored by the philosopher Derrida (1974), who argues that not even semiotic signs have stable meanings. Central to Derrida's project is the logic of the *supplement* as a challenge to the logic of identity. While the logic of identity takes the meaning of words to be identical with a fixed entity to which the word refers, a supplement adds to and substitutes for something else. For example, writing supplements speech by adding to it and substituting for it so that the meaning of a word is supplemented by the echoes or traces of other words in other contexts. The continual supplementarity of meaning, the continual substitution and adding of meanings through the play of signifiers, challenges the identity of noises and marks, words, with fixed meaning. Thus, meaning is always displaced and deferred.

For example, in *La Carte postale*, Derrida (1980) plays with the idea of postcards and postal systems which act as metaphors for the generation and circulation of meaning. This allows Derrida to challenge the idea that meaning operates within a closed circuit where intentions and messages are unambiguously sent and received. Rather, postcards may go astray, they may reach persons and generate meanings other than those which were intended, so that the idea of 'true' meaning or communication is displaced. Meanings circulate without any absolutely authorized source or destination and elude the power of reason to maintain the fixed controlled meaning of concepts. Overall, Derrida's arguments challenge the *identity of words with fixed meaning* and suggests that meaning is inherently unstable and constantly slides away. Thus, by **differance**, the key Derridian concept, is meant 'difference and deferral', so that the production of meaning is continually deferred and added to (or supplemented) by the meanings of other words. Consider, for example, when looking up the meaning of a word in a dictionary, the way in which one is referred to another word and onward to another word in a potentially endless search for a fixed meaning.

The view of language put forward in this section has important consequences for understanding the self and identity. It cannot now be said that language directly *represents* a pre-existent 'I', rather, language and thinking *constitute* the 'I', they bring it into being through the processes of signification. One cannot *have* an identity; rather, one *is* a centreless weave of beliefs, attitudes and identifications (Rorty 1991a).

Further, since identity is discursive, formed and enunciated in an unstable language (*differance*), then cultural identity is not, and cannot be, a reflection of a fixed, natural state of being but is a process of *becoming* and what we call identity is a necessary 'cut' or snapshot of the ever unfolding meanings of language. Thus, identities, as discursive constructions which do not refer to an already existent 'thing', are both unstable *and* temporarily stabilized by social practice and regular, predictable behaviour (Hall 1990, 1992a, 1996a).

To argue that identity is cultural 'all the way down', and therefore specific to particular times and places, suggests that identities are changeable and related to definite social and cultural conjunctures. The idea that identity is plastic and open to continual change is often referred to as **anti-essentialism**, an argument which depends, at least in a cultural studies context, on the understanding of language developed above in which signs have no fixed referents in the material world. The anti-essentialist argument is, in effect, a summary of Hall's position on cultural identity.

Though it has been argued that words are unstable because meaning is generated from relations between words and not to fixed entities, nevertheless, in social practice words gain conventional or *temporarily stabilized* or *regulated* meanings. That is, 'a cluster (or formation) of ideas, images and practices, which provide ways of talking about, forms of knowledge and conduct associated with, a particular topic, social activity or institutional site in society' (Hall 1997a: 6). These are regulated maps of meaning or ways of speaking which can, after Foucault, be called a **discursive formation**.

Foucault, discourse and the subject

The significance of Foucault for our discussion of the decentred self is that he attacks the 'great myth of the interior' and sees the subject as a historically

specific 'effect' of discourse with no transcendental continuity from one subject position to another. Foucault is said to have produced a 'genealogy of
the modern subject', that is, he has traced the lineage of subject formation
in and through history. He argues that we can locate particular kinds of
'regimes of the self' in specific historical and cultural conjunctures so that
different types of subject are the outcome of particular historical and social
formations. Thus, for Foucault the subject is radically historized, that is, the
subject is wholly and only the product of history.

In particular, Foucault describes a subject which is the product of **power**
through the individualization of those subject to power. For Foucault,
power is not simply a negative mechanism of control but is *productive* of
the self. The disciplinary power of schools, work organizations, prisons,
hospitals and asylums, not to mention the proliferating discourses of sexuality, *produce* subjectivity by bringing individuals into view and by fixing
them in writing or other forms of representation via the discourses of, for
example, medicine (Foucault 1977, 1979). The body is the site of disciplinary practices which bring subjects into being, these practices themselves
being bound up with the specific historical discourses of crime, punishment,
medicine, science, sexuality and so forth. In short, the subject and identity
is a historically specific construction of discourse and practice (discursive
practice).

For Foucault (1970, 1972), discourse concerns both language and practice and refers to the production of **knowledge** through language which gives
meaning to both material objects and social practices. Though material
objects and social practices 'exist' outside of language, they are given meaning and brought into view by language and are thus discursively formed.
Discourse constructs, defines and produces the objects of knowledge in an
intelligible way while at the same time excluding other ways of reasoning as
unintelligible. This includes the discursive production of subjects and 'identities'.

For example, the study of discourses of madness which Foucault (1973)
undertook included:

- statements about madness which give us knowledge about it
- the rules which prescribe what is 'sayable' or 'thinkable' about madness
- subjects who personify the discourses of madness (i.e. the 'madman')
- the manner in which discourses of madness acquire authority and truth at
  a given historical moment
- the practices within institutions which deal with madness
- the idea that different discourses about madness will appear at later

historical moments, producing new knowledge and a new discursive formation (i.e. patterns of meaning and practice)

(see Hall 1997a: 44–6)

Some critics fear that this stress on discourse and the constitutive character of language is a form of idealism. That is, a view which regards the world as formed by language and mind outside of any material considerations or that, in its extreme form, 'everything is discourse' and that there is no material world. However, this is not what is being argued for here. Rather than see language as divorced from the material, it is being suggested that material objects and social practices are given meaning and brought into view by language and are thus discursively formed. Consequently, as Butler (1993) argues, discourse and materiality are indissoluble. For example, not only is discourse the means by which we understand what material bodies are, but also, in a sense, discourse brings material bodies into view in particular ways. Thus, sexed bodies are discursive constructions, but indispensable ones, which form subjects and govern the materialization of bodies such that 'bodies will be indissociable from the regulatory norms that govern their materialization and the signification of those material effects' (Butler 1993: 2; see also Chapter 4).

Essentialism and anti-essentialism

In a line of argument which contrasts **essentialism** and anti-essentialism, Hall (1990) has usefully identified two poles or positions from which identity can be understood. In the first essentialist version, identity is regarded as the name for a collective 'one true self' and is thought to be formed out of a common history, ancestry and set of symbolic resources. Through such optics it is possible to speak of an 'American identity' expressed through the symbol of the 'Stars and Stripes', memories of the Second World War and collective rituals such as the Super Bowl, Thanksgiving and the nightly news. The underlying assumptions of this view are that identity exists, that in both its individual and collective forms it is 'a whole', and that it is *expressed* through symbolic representation. This account of identity is known as 'essentialism' because it assumes that social categories reflect an essential underlying identity. By this token there would be an essence of, for example, black identity.

By juxtaposing 'American' and 'black' as cultural identities, the assumptions of an essentialist argument are immediately made problematic since it might have been assumed that an American identity was a white Anglo-Saxon one. The presence of a substantial African American (and Hispanic, Jewish, Italian, Polish, and others) population makes such an assumption impossible to sustain and indeed redefines what it means to be American. Being American can involve being black with the capability to trace ancestry back to Africa. However, just as the concept of American identity is problematic so too is that of black identity since it is possible not only to argue for cultural identifications that *connect* black populations in Africa, America, the Caribbean and Britain but also to trace the lines of *difference*. Indeed, not only is being black American not the same as being black African or black British, but also the descriptor 'black' threatens to homogenize a diversity of experience and to *reduce* people to questions of race. As bel hooks (1990) has argued, a critique of essentialism allows African Americans to affirm multiple black identities and varied black experience in contrast to white supremacist views which reduce people of colour to race.

Thus, Hall's second anti-essentialist position from which to understand issues of cultural identity stresses that as well as points of similarity, cultural identity is constituted around points of difference. Above all, cultural identity is not seen as a reflection of a fixed, natural, state of being but as a process of *becoming*. There is no essence of identity to be discovered, rather cultural identity is continually being produced within the vectors of similarity and difference. Cultural identity is not an essence but a continually shifting position and the points of difference around which cultural identities form are multiple and proliferating. They include, to name but a few, identifications of class, gender, sexuality, age, ethnicity, nationality, morality and religion, and each of these discursive positions are themselves unstable.

The meaning of American-ness, Britishness, blackness, masculinity and so forth are subject to continual change since meaning is never finished or completed (*differance*). Identity then becomes a cut or a snapshot of unfolding meanings; it is a strategic positioning which makes meaning possible. This anti-essentialist position does not mean that we cannot speak of identity; rather, it points us to the *political* nature of identity as a discursive *production* and to the possibility of multiple and shifting identities where discourses of class, age, gender, nationality and race are 'articulated' together. **Articulation** suggests both expressing/representing and a joining together. Thus, representations of gender, which constitute what gender is, may join together with representations of race but in context specific and contingent ways which cannot be predicted before the fact.

Identities and the concept of articulation

Laclau (1977) has argued that there are no *necessary* links between discursive concepts and that those which are forged are essentially temporary and connotative, they are articulated together and bound 'by connotative or evocative links which custom and opinion have established between them'. That is, connections between discourses or identities are the work of culture rather than of 'nature'. For example, we commonly speak of the nation as 'one people' without pausing to consider its meaning. Yet, not only can this people never meet together, but also they are fundamentally *different* in terms of class, gender, sexuality, race, age, political persuasion and morality. The concept of articulation suggests that those aspects of social life which we think of as a unity (and sometimes as universals), for example, identity, or nation or society, can be thought of as the unique *historically specific* temporary stabilization or arbitrary closure of meaning. As Hall suggests,

> An articulation is thus the form of the connection that *can* make a unity of two different elements, under certain conditions. It is the linkage which is not necessary, determined, absolute and essential for all time. You have to ask, under what circumstances can a connection be forged or made? The so-called 'unity' of a discourse is really the articulation of different, distinct elements which can be rearticulated in different ways because they have no necessary 'belongingness'. The 'unity' which matters is a linkage between the articulated discourse and the social forces with which it can, under certain historical conditions, but need not necessarily, be connected.
>
> (Hall 1996b: 141)

Put in this way, it is possible to regard individuals (and social formations) as the unique, historically specific, articulation of discursive elements which are contingent but also socially determined. The argument is that there is no necessary or *automatic* connection between the various discourses of identity, be they class, gender or ethnically based. Thus, all working-class black women do not share the same identity and identifications any more than all middle-class white men do; rather, the various discourses that make up identity can be articulated together in different ways.

Hall gives an excellent illustration of this when he highlights the case of Clarence Thomas, a black judge with conservative political views who was nominated to the US supreme court by the then President George Bush. Thomas was accused of sexual harassment by Anita Hill, a black woman and former colleague of the judge. As Hall puts it,

> Some blacks supported Thomas on racial grounds; others opposed him on sexual grounds. Black women were divided, depending on whether their 'identities' as blacks or women prevailed. Black men were also divided, depending on whether their sexism overrode their liberalism.

White men were divided, depending, not only on their politics, but on how they identified themselves with respect to racism and sexism. White conservative women supported Thomas, not only on political grounds, but because of their opposition to feminism. White feminists, often liberal on race, opposed Thomas on sexual grounds. And because Judge Thomas is a member of the judicial elite and Anita Hill, at the time of the alleged incident, a junior employee, there were issues of social class position at work in these arguments too.

(Hall 1992a: 279–80)

Hall uses this example to make the point that identities are contradictory, they cross-cut or dislocate each other both in the context of the wider society and inside the heads of individuals. No single identity can, Hall argues, act as an overarching organizing identity; rather, identities shift according to how subjects are addressed or represented.

Shifting identities

Of course, multiple narratives of the self are not the outcome of the shifting meanings of language *alone* but are also the consequence of the proliferation and diversification of social relationships, contexts and sites of interaction (albeit constituted in and through language) so that discourse, identities and social practice form a mutually constituting set. For example, compared to the eighteenth-century peasant, modern persons have a much wider scope of relationships and spaces in which to interact. These may include not only spaces and relationships of work, family and friends, but also the global resources of television, email and travel. The proliferation and diversification of contexts and sites of interaction prevents easy identification of particular subjects with a given, fixed identity so that the same person is able to shift across subject positions according to circumstances. One such range of shifting identity positions is put by a young singer:

I rap in Bengali and English. I rap on everything from love to politics. I've always been into rapping . . . it was rebellious, the lyrics were sensational. I could relate to that, I could identify with it. Like living in the ghetto and that. . . . It's from the heart. It's: 'I'm Bengali, I'm Asian, I'm a woman, and I'm living here'.

(cited Gardner and Shukur 1994: 161)

To put this in Hall's more theoretical language, the subject positions of this young woman involve the articulation of positions drawn from a variety of discourses and sites. At the very least she has identifications with being Bengali, English, a woman, with youth culture and with Rap, an American-

Caribbean hybrid, now appropriated as Anglo-Bengali. She is involved not only in shifting identifications but also in enacting a *hybrid* identity (Chapter 3) which draws on multiplying global resources (Chapter 2).

Summary and conclusions

Thus far, it has been argued that identities are constituted in discourse or socially shared and regulated ways of speaking. That is, identities are discursive constructions. Indeed, there can be no identity, experience or social practice which is not discursively constructed since we cannot escape language. In this sense, identities are social and cultural 'all the way down', by which is meant that identities are wholly social constructions and cannot 'exist' outside of cultural representations. Thus, identities are, in a particular sense, not our own, for they are stories constructed from the intersubjective resource of language. Subjectivity does not produce intersubjectivity but the reverse. We form our selves in 'joint-action' (Shotter 1993) with others and using a social resource, language, which pre-exists us as individuals. Language is the tool by which we are 'made' and creatively 'make' ourselves, it is the pathway to identity.

Thus, the central argument of this chapter has been that 'identity' is not an already existent 'fixed thing', a possession of the self; rather, identity is a constitutive description of the self in language. Since the meanings of language are themselves unstable and fluid we can talk of 'identities-in-process' rather than identity. In short, there is a denial of fully separate, distinct and 'authentic' identities based on either a core self or on fully shared origins or experiences. Instead, there is a stress on multiple and fragmented identities.

Further, we do not *have* an identity; rather, we *are* a multiple weave of attitudes and beliefs, even though the historically specific and contingent cultural narratives of late **modernity** encourage us to see ourselves as a 'whole'. To talk of identity is to 'freeze' the unstable and proliferating meanings of language and to temporarily stabilize the narrative of the self in a cut or strategic positioning of meaning. While considerable stress has been placed in this summary on the significance of language and discourse, because it plays a very important part in Hall's schema which has structured this chapter, it was argued that Marxism, psychoanalysis and feminism also underpin the idea of a fractured or postmodern self.

The argument that identities are formed within and through representations is important to debates about culture, identity and television because TV is the major communicative device for disseminating those representations which are constitutive of (and constituted by) cultural identity. Thus, in Chapters 3 and 4, we shall consider the more specific questions of how race, nation, sex and gender are constructed as cultural identities and represented on television for there is an interplay between the construction and representation of identities on television and their formation in the wider social field. However, we first need to consider contemporary changes in the organization of social relationships, identities and television in an increasingly global context. Consequently, it is to issues of globalization and global television that we turn in Chapter 2.

Further reading

Giddens, A. (1991) *Modernity and Self-Identity: Self and Society in the Late Modern Age*. Cambridge: Polity Press.

Hall, S. (1992) The question of cultural identity, in S. Hall, D. Held and T. McGrew (eds) *Modernity and its Futures*. Cambridge: Polity Press.

Hall, S. (1996a) Who needs identity?, in S. Hall and P. Du Gay (eds) *Questions of Cultural Identity*. London: Sage.

Hall, S. (ed.) (1997) *Representation: Cultural Representations and Signifying Practices*. London and Thousand Oaks, CA: Sage.

Nicholson, L. and Seidman, S. (eds) (1995) *Social Postmodernism: Beyond Identity Politics*. Cambridge: Cambridge University Press.

Rabinow, P. (ed.) (1986) *The Foucault Reader*. New York: Pantheon.

2 | GLOBAL TELEVISION AND GLOBAL CULTURE

Identities, it has been argued, are narratives constructed from the intersubjective resource of language and, as such, are social and cultural 'all the way down'. That is, identities are constituted in and through cultural representations (including those produced by television) with which 'we' identify. However, our very notion of culture has begun to change, so that the image associated with the work of Raymond Williams of culture as an integrated, bounded and in-place 'whole way of life' is giving way to metaphors of fragmentation and plural, if overlapping, discourses which flow across established borders (Featherstone 1995). That is, cultures are no longer bounded by specific places but, through the migration of persons and the electronic transfer of ideas and images, transgress established boundaries. As Ang (1996) argues, 'in the increasingly integrated world-system there is no such thing possible as an independent cultural identity; every identity must define and position itself in relation to the cultural frames affirmed by the world-system' (Ang 1996: 145).

Consequently, in this chapter we focus on the character of globalization and the debates about global culture, including media and **cultural imperialism**, before exploring the globalization of the institutions and discourses of television. It will be argued that television, which needs to be understood in terms of **political economy**, representations and as a cultural relationship between texts and audiences, is an increasingly globalized set of institutions and cultural flows providing proliferating resources (representations) for identity construction. It will also be suggested that the outcome of globalization is a set of unpredictable, disjointed and multidirectional cultural flows rather than the simple expansion of western institutions and cultural formations to the rest of the world.

The concept of globalization

As a concept, globalization refers both to the time–space compression of the world and the intensification of consciousness of the world as a whole (Robertson 1992), that is, the ever increasing abundance of global connections and our understanding of them. By time–space compression is meant the processes that change the qualities of space and time that we experience and our conceptions of it. Compression refers to the speed-up in the pace of life and the overcoming of spatial barriers (associated with the history and spread of capitalism) and is clearly a relative term involving comparison with previous conditions. This 'compression of the world' has been understood in terms of the institutions of modernity, that is, the globalization of modern economic and cultural practices, which includes the institutions of television.

For Giddens (1990, 1991), the institutions of modernity, an historical period following the Middle Ages, consist of capitalism, industrialism, surveillance, the nation-state and military power. Subsequently, globalization is grasped in terms of

- the world capitalist economy
- the nation-state system
- the world military order
- the global information system.

In this view, modernity is a 'post-traditional' order marked by change, innovation and dynamism whose institutions are said to be globalizing because they allow for the *separation of time and space*, and the *disembedding*, or lifting out, of social relations developed in one locale and their re-embedding in different places. Though a number of factors can be seen to structure patterns of time–space distanciation (the processes by which societies are 'stretched' over shorter or longer spans of time and space), the commodification of time, so that it becomes separate from 'experience', and the development of forms of communication and information control which separate presence in time from presence in space, are, for Giddens, of particular significance. Thus, transactions may be conducted across time and space and any given place is penetrated and shaped by social influences quite distant from it. For example, the development of money and electronic communications allows social relations to be stretched across time and space in the form of financial transactions conducted 24 hours a day throughout the globe.

Global economic activity

On one level the processes of globalization are clearly economic in character and a relatively small number of transnational corporations dominate global networks of production and consumption. Thus, one-half of the world's largest economic units are constituted by a hundred transnational corporations who produce between one-third and one-half of world output (Giddens 1989). Indeed, in 1990, transnational corporations, of which Royal Dutch Shell, Ford and General Motors were the largest non-financial organizations, had 49 per cent of their assets and 61 per cent of their sales outside of the country of origin (Clarke 1996). Further, financial transactions can be conducted at any time of the day or night with the aid of electronic communication as witnessed by the rise of finance companies to the level of sizeable multinationals and the global significance of organizations like the World Bank and the International Monetary Fund. Globalization thus refers to economic activity on a planetary scale creating a world economy, though one which has grown in an *uneven* way.

Global economic activity is not a new phenomenon and since at least the sixteenth century there has been a growing expansion of western economic activity into Asia, South America and Africa. However, it is widely held that we are currently witnessing a new phase of *accelerated* globalization. In short, global recession hastened a renewed globalization of world economic activity involving the speed-up of production and consumption turnover assisted by the use of information and communication technology (Harvey 1989). In this sense, globalization refers to a set of related economic activities which are specifically to be understood as the practices of capitalism. Indeed, they are part of the restructuring of capitalism on a global scale which, for Lash and Urry (1987), is now a 'disorganized' set of global flows of capital, resources and people. That is, the effective *deconcentration* of capital through *globalized* production, financing and distribution giving rise to geo-planetary capitalism which is not organized through the mediation of any particular state. Their analysis stresses the global nature of capitalism, the power of transnational corporations and the difficulties faced by states trying to regulate their operations. Place remains significant as an intersection or nodal point of global flows but in unpredictable ways.

Globalization and modernity

Giddens's prime metaphor for modernity is that of a juggernaut, an uncontrollable engine of enormous power which sweeps away all that stands before it. However, this view of the relationship between modernity and globalization has been subject to the criticism that it is Eurocentric, envisaging only one kind of modernity, that of the west. Thus, Featherstone (1995) argues that modernity should be seen not only in temporal terms, that is, as an epochal social transformation, but also in spatial and relational terms. In other words, different spatial zones of the globe have become modern in a variety of ways so that we should speak of global modern*ies* in the plural. For example, Featherstone suggest that Japan does not fit neatly into a tradition–modernity–**postmodernity** linear development. Likewise, Morley and Robbins (1995) argue that Japanese technological development is now putting western modernity into question. As they argue, 'If the West is modern, Japan should be pre-modern, or at least non-modern. . . . What Japan has done is to call into question the supposed centrality of the West as a cultural and geographical locus for the project of modernity' (Morley and Robbins 1995: 160). In other words, the case of Japan suggests the uneven, non-linear character of contemporary economic and cultural flows.

Globalization and cultures

Of course, globalization is neither experienced nor to be understood solely in economic terms for it also concerns questions of cultural meaning and the intensification of a global consciousness. Thus, while the values and meanings attached to place remain significant, people are increasingly involved in networks which extend well beyond their physical locations. Though the scenario of a unitary world culture connected to a world state remains only at the level of the imagination, we can identify global cultural processes, of both cultural integration and disintegration, which are independent of inter-state relations. For example, as we noted in the introduction, cosmopolitanism in the west is an aspect of day-to-day life as diverse and remote cultures become accessible as signs and commodities via our televisions, radios, supermarkets and shopping centres.

According to Pieterse (1995), one can differentiate between a view of culture as bounded, tied to place and inward-looking, from one in which culture is seen as an outward looking 'translocal learning process'. Over all he argues that 'Introverted cultures, which have been prominent over a long stretch of history and which overshadowed translocal culture, are gradually receding into the background, while translocal culture made up of diverse elements is coming to the foreground' (Pieterse 1995: 62). Thus, patterns of population movement and settlement established during colonialism and its aftermath, combined with the more recent acceleration of globalization, particularly of electronic communications, have enabled increased cultural juxtapositioning, meeting and mixing. This suggests the need to escape from the model of culture as a locally bounded 'whole way of life'.

Travelling cultures

Consequently, Clifford (1992), among others, has argued that culture and cultural identities can no longer be adequately understood in terms of place, but are better conceptualized in terms of *travel*. This includes peoples and cultures which travel and places/cultures as sites of criss-crossing travellers. In one sense this has always been the case; for example, Britain has a population drawn from Celts, Saxons, Vikings, Normans, Romans, Afro-Caribbeans, Asians and others, so that the 'English' language is a hybrid of words from all over the world. Likewise the USA, whose diverse peoples have a heritage derived from native American Indians, the English, French, Spanish, African, Mexican, Irish, Polish and too many more to mention. However, the accelerated globalization of late modernity has increased the relevance of the metaphor of travel because *all* locales are now subject to the influences of distant places. This includes television, whose institutions and products have increasingly been subject to the processes of globalization. But what sort of culture is globalization creating? For some critics the vision is one of western domination of global culture and the production of homogenization, or sameness, across the world. For other writers, the image of the globe which is forming is more unpredictable, chaotic and fragmented in its cultural flows.

Homogenization and fragmentation

One strand of the cultural homogenization argument stresses the global reach of capitalist consumerism, for which global television is the vehicle par excellence. Thus, according to Hamelink, 'the principal agents of cultural synchronisation today are the transnational corporations' (Hamelink 1983: 22). This perspective highlights a loss of cultural diversity and the growth of 'sameness' attaching a negative evaluation to the process. The grounds for being critical of cultural synchronization being posed in terms of a loss of cultural autonomy and diversity in a process dubbed cultural imperialism.

Central to the concept of cultural imperialism is the domination of one culture by another. In one rendition, cultural imperialism is understood in terms of the imposition of one *national* culture upon another with the media seen as central to this process, that is as carriers of cultural meanings which penetrate and dominate the cultures of subordinate nations. Other versions assert that cultural imperialism is represented by a set of economic and cultural processes which are implicated in the reproduction of global *capitalism*. Thus, for Robins, homogenization is regarded primarily as the spread of western capitalism and culture so that,

> For all that it has projected itself as transhistorical and transnational, as the transcendent and universalizing force of modernization and modernity, global capitalism has in reality been about westernization – the export of western commodities, values, priorities, ways of life.
>
> (Robins 1991: 25)

Put in its boldest form, this argument suggests that global media are in the service of American capitalism. Thus, Herbert Schiller (1969, 1985) emphasizes both the systematic and integrated nature of modern global capitalism and the critical role of the multinational and transnational corporations within it. He points to the global domination of the international communications industries by US controlled corporations and to the interlocking between US television networks, defence sub-contractors and the Federal government. Consequently, many commentators have feared that the increased global market for television programmes would be dominated by the Americans, who hold the top three positions in terms of global turnover for both traditional television companies and the world film industry.

Problems with globalization as cultural imperialism

There are three central difficulties with the 'globalization as cultural imperialism' argument. Thus,

- it is not necessarily the case that the global flows of cultural discourse are any longer constituted as one-way traffic from the 'west-to-the-rest'
- in so far as the predominant flow of cultural discourse is from west to east and north to south, this is not necessarily to be understood as a form of domination
- it is unclear that globalization is simply a process of homogenization since the forces of fragmentation and **hybridity** are equally as strong.

There is little doubt that the first waves of globalization, economic, military and cultural, were part of the dynamic spread of western modernity. In so far as these institutions originated in Europe, and have spread outward from this base, we would have to say that modernity is a western project and that early phases of globalization involved western interrogation of the non-western 'other'. The expansion of European military and economic power also involved the imposition of its cultural forms as mercantile expansion gave way to a phase of more direct rule. Colonial control entailed military dominance, cultural ascendancy and the origins of economic dependency as occupied lands were turned into both a protected market for selected commodities from the imperial power and a provider of raw materials. Though the early twentieth century saw a series of successful anti-colonial struggles and independence movements, by this time the economies of these countries were integrated into the world economic order as subordinate players (Wallerstein 1974).

The South African example

The cultural legacy of this European colonialism is still evident on a global scale. For example, it is the divisive legacy of European power that South African television is trying to overcome with its slogan *Simunye – we are one* (see Introduction). The consequences of European might and cultural superiority is nowhere more compelling and obvious than in the doctrine and practice of apartheid where God and the sword combined to create and justify white domination in the most crude of forms. It is no accident that in a country with many different languages, it is English which provides the most common shared point of translation, as indeed it increasingly does over the entire planet. European culture is evident in South Africa not only in terms of language but also in architecture, music, food, painting, film, television, and the general sense among whites that European culture represents 'high' culture.

However, two musical forms encountered among the black South African community complicates the idea of simple cultural imperialism. First is a black male quartet from Soweto who play European chamber music underpinned by more African rhythms. Second is the prevalence and popularity of American inspired Hip-Hop and Rap music among black South Africans epitomized by the Soweto based 'Prophets of Da City'. Both take non-African musical forms and give them an African twist to create a form of hybridization which is now being exported back to the west. Further, Rap, which was described here as American, can of course trace its roots/routes back to the influence of West African music and the impact of slavery. South African Rap is therefore part of the cultural exchanges of the 'Black Atlantic' (Gilroy 1993) rather than a representative of American cultural imperialism.

These musical examples, in highlighting the uneven and multidirectional character of cultural flows, complicate a concept of cultural imperialism which depends at heart on a notion of force, for in what sense can it be argued that the popularity of Rap in South Africa represents coercion? Does not the music of 'Prophets of Da City' represent a form of diasporic identification and identity rather than imposition? If Africans listen to some forms of western music, watch some forms of western television and buy western produced consumer goods, which they enjoy, this cannot easily be maintained as domination without resort to arguments that rely on 'false' consciousness. In addition, it should not be assumed that the consumption of western consumer goods has the same meanings or the same outcomes in Africa as it does in the west.

Uneven development of globalization

Indeed, contemporary accelerated globalization is increasingly less one-directional for it is 'a process of uneven development that fragments as it co-ordinates – introduces new forms of world interdependence, in which, once again there are no "others", involving "emergent forms of world interdependence and planetary consciousness"' (Giddens 1990: 175). As Giddens puts it, 'the point is not only that the other "answers back", but that mutual interrogation is possible' (Giddens 1994: 25). Indeed, for Appaduria, existing centre–periphery models are inadequate in the face of a new 'complex, overlapping, disjunctive order' in which,

> for people of Irian Jaya, Indonesianisation may be more worrisome than Americanisation, as Japanisation may be for Koreans, Indianisation for Sri Lankans, Vietnamisation for Cambodians, Russianisation for the people of Soviet Armenia and the Baltic Republics.
> (Appaduria 1993: 328)

Appaduria (1993) argues that globalization is far from an even process of western expansion driven by economic imperatives. Instead, contemporary global conditions are best characterized in term of the disjunctive flows of ethnoscapes, technoscapes, finanscapes, mediascapes and ideoscapes. That is, globalization involves the dynamic movements of ethnic groups, technology, financial transactions, media images and ideological conflicts which are not neatly determined by one harmonious 'master plan'; rather, the speed, scope and impact of these flows are fractured and disconnected.

Chaos culture

In this way, the idea that the institutional and economic aspects of modernity are driving the cultural and ethnic in a linear fashion is challenged. Not only does the cultural shape the economic, and indeed our very models of globalization, but also metaphors of uncertainty, contingency and 'chaos' replace those of order, stability and systemacity. Rather than conceptualize global culture in terms of one-way determinations, either from the 'west to-the-rest' or from economics to culture, we might see their operation as 'rhizomorphic'.

> To be rhizomorphous is to produce stems and filaments that seem to be roots, or better yet connect with them by penetrating the trunk, but put them to new uses. We're tired of trees. We should stop believing in trees, roots and radicles. They've made us suffer too much. All of aborescent culture is founded on them, from biology to linguistics.
>
> (Deleuze and Guattari 1988: 15)

In other words, globalization and global cultural flows should not necessarily be understood in terms of a set of neat linear determinations, but instead viewed as a series of overlapping, overdetermined, complex and 'chaotic' conditions which, at best, can be seen to cluster around key 'nodal points'. This has led, 'not to the creation of an ordered global village, but to the multiplication of points of conflict, antagonism and contradiction' (Ang 1996: 165) arising from unpredictable overdeterminations of which television forms a part.

The fact that capitalist modernity does involve an element of cultural homogenization seems undeniable since modernity increases the levels and amount of global coordination. However, it is being argued here that mechanisms of fragmentation, hetrogenization and hybridity are also at work so that, as Robertson argues, 'It is not a question of *either* homogenisation or hetrogenisation, but rather of the ways in which both of these two tendencies have become features of life across much of the late-twentieth-century world' (Robertson 1995: 27).

The global and the local

Bounded cultures, ethnic resilience and the re-emergence of powerful nationalistic sentiments coexist with cultures as 'trans-local learning processes' (Pieterse 1995). Indeed, the global and the local are mutually constituting, leading Robertson (1992) to argue that much which is considered to be local, and counterpoised to the global, is the outcome of translocal processes. Thus, nation-states were forged within a global nation-state system and the contemporary rise in nationalist sentiment can be regarded as an aspect of globalization, not just as a reaction to it. Further, it may be that the global spread of consumer capitalism encourages limitless needs/wants and the pleasures of constant identity transformation so that heterogeneity arises in part as a result of the globalizing forces of consumer capitalism (Ang 1996).

Thus, the global and the local are relative terms. The idea of the local, specifically what is considered local, is produced within and by a globalizing discourse which includes capitalist marketing and its increasing orientation to differentiated local markets. In any case, an emphasis on particularity and diversity can be regarded as an increasingly global discourse so that 'the expectation of identity declaration is built into the general process of globalisation' (Robertson 1992: 175). Robertson adopts the concept of *glocalization*, in origin a marketing term, to express the global production of the local and the localization of the global.

In this view, the impact of Anglo-American television in a global context may be understood as the creation of a layer of western capitalist modernity which overlays, but does not necessarily obliterate, pre-existing cultural forms. Modern and postmodern ideas about time, space, rationality, capitalism, consumerism, sexuality, family and gender are placed alongside older discourses, setting up ideological competition between them. The outcome may be both a range of hybrid forms of identity and the production of traditional, 'fundamentalist' and nationalist identities. Nationalism and the nation-state continue to coexist with cosmopolitanism and the weakening of national identities (Chapter 3).

Reverse flow

To question the idea that globalization is constituted as a monolithic one-way flow from the west-to-the-rest is to raise the issue of 'reverse flow', the impact of non-western ideas and practices on the west. For example, the global impact of Reggae, Rap, Hip-Hop and 'World Music' and the export of telenovelas from Latin American to the USA and Europe. It would also include the creation of ethnic **diaspora** through population movement from 'developing' nations into the west, the influence of Islam, Hinduism and other world religions within the west and the commodification and sale of 'ethnic' food and clothing. All of which adds up not only to a general decentring of western perspectives about 'progress' but increasingly to the deconstruction of the very idea of homogenous national cultures.

Thus, Ashcroft *et al.* (1989) argue that the critique of essentialism and the physical meeting and mixing of peoples throws the whole notion of national or ethnic literatures and cultures into doubt. Thus, hybridization and creolization of language, literature and cultural identities is a common theme of *post-colonial literature* and marks a certain meeting of minds with **postmodernism**. That is, neither the colonial nor colonized cultures and languages can be presented in 'pure' form, nor separated from each other. This gives rise to *hybridity* which challenges not only the centrality of colonial culture and the marginalization of the colonized, but also the very idea of centre and margin as being anything other than representational effects. For example, the idea of the Creole continuum has gained in significance in a Caribbean linguistic context, that is, a series of overlapping language usages and code switching which deploys not only the specific modes of other languages, say English and French, but also invents forms peculiar to itself. Creolization stresses language as a cultural practice over the abstractions of grammar or any idea of 'correct' usage.

In short, it is being argued that claims about cultural homogenization are not a strong basis for the arguments of cultural imperialism:

- Processes of reverse flow, fragmentation and hybridization are quite as strong as the push towards homogenization.
- While arguments against 'sameness' can be sustained as a value judgement, one has to say in exactly what sphere sameness is a bad thing and why. Overall, as Tomlinson suggests,

> Globalisation may be distinguished from imperialism in that it is a far less coherent or culturally directed process. For all that it is ambiguous between economic and political senses, the idea of imperialism contains, at least, the notion of a purposeful project; the intended spread of a social system from one centre of power across the globe. The idea of globalisation suggests interconnection and interdependency of all global areas which happen in a far less purposeful way. It happens as the result of economic and cultural practices which do not, of themselves, aim at global integration, but which nonetheless produce it. More importantly, the effects of globalisation are to weaken cultural coherence in all individual nation-states, including the economically powerful ones – the imperialist powers of a previous era.
>
> (Tomlinson 1991: 175)

However, these criticisms of the cultural imperialism thesis should not lead us to abandon its core concern, namely ideas of power and inequality. Thus, Massey argues that what is at stake in what she calls the 'power geometry' of globalization is the fact that 'some people are more in charge of it than others; some initiate flows and movements, other don't' (Massey 1994: 149).

The power geometry of globalization

In the context of discussions about power, the idea of cultural imperialism does have strength, especially in relation to television, where people are *denied* a cultural experience as a result of homogenization, or fail to be adequately represented as a result of the homogenization of production. Thus, if the economics of global television lead to certain kinds of programmes not being produced (for example local drama), or certain socio-economic groups not being adequately represented (such as a particular ethnic group), that is legitimate grounds for criticism. Further, Tomlinson (1991) makes the case for seeing the spread of western modernity as cultural *loss* in that the culture of modernity stresses the western concept of development as 'more of everything', particularly more material goods, at the expense of growth as personal and meaningful experience, even spiritual experience in its broadest sense.

Recognition of imbalance or loss is not the same as viewing the process of globalization as any longer a one-way process of domination and it has been argued that the concept of globalization is more adequate than that of cultural imperialism because it suggests a less coherent, unified and directed process. However, the fact that power is diffused, or that commodities are subversively used to produce new hybrid identities, does not displace power or our need to examine it, for, as Pieterse (1995) argues,

> Relations of power and hegemony are inscribed and reproduced *within* hybridity for wherever we look closely enough we find the traces of asymmetry in culture, place descent. Hence hybridity raises the question of the terms of the mixture, the conditions of mixing and melange. At the same time it's important to note the ways in which hegemony is not merely reproduced but *refigured* in the process of hybridisation.
>
> (Pieterse 1995: 57)

For example, the hybridity of the cultural forms produced by the black African diaspora does not obscure the power that was embedded in the moment of slavery nor the economic push–pull of migration. As Hall (1992a) argues, diaspora identities are constructed within and by cultural power. 'This power', he suggests, 'has become a constitutive element in our own identities' (Hall 1992a: 233). Consequently, the cultural identities of rich white men in New York are of a very different order from those of poor Asian women in rural India. Nevertheless, while we remain unequal participants and globalization an uneven process, we are all part of a global society in the sense that no one can escape its consequences (Giddens 1990).

Global television

Having set out the broad parameters of what is at stake in debates about globalization and global cultural change we need to consider more specifically the place of television within these wider economic and cultural flows. The concept of global television suggests three related phenomena:

- On an *institutional* level, the term implies all the various configurations of public and commercial television which are regulated, funded and viewed within the boundaries of nation-states and/or language communities.
- Global television refers to television which in its technology, ownership, programme distribution and audiences operates across the boundaries of nation-states and language communities. Global television in this sense means *transnational* television.
- The idea of global television is concerned with world-wide flows of discourses and *cultural representations* which, in turn, raise issues of power and cultural identity within the context of a global electronic culture.

Globalizing the television market

There is little doubt that television is a global phenomenon in its production, dissemination and viewing patterns. According to *Screen Digest* (February 1995) there are in excess of 850 million television sets in more than 160 countries watched by 2.5 billion people every day. Between 1984 and 1994 the number of television households grew most quickly in the developing world, with marginal growth in Europe and North America compared with Africa and Asia, where the number of television sets trebled, or Central America where the figure doubled.

The globalization of the institutions of television is an aspect of the dynamic logic of capitalism, which stems from the pursuit of profit as the primary goal. This requires the constant production of new commodities and new markets so that capitalism is inherently expansionist and dynamic. While there is money to be made from the production and sale of television programmes these are also a means to sell the technological hardware of television, from satellites to sets, and to deliver audiences to advertisers so that television stands at the core of wider commercial activities and is central to the expansion of consumer capitalism. Thus, to understand the globalization of television, we need to grasp the changing character of its economic and organizational facets.

The changing economies of world television

The British Broadcasting Corporation (BBC) is one of the world's oldest and largest vertically integrated television organizations and, as such, makes, sells and transmits programmes. Funded primarily from a licence fee, the BBC has stood like a colossus across the British television landscape, both technically and artistically, making it one of the most famous and respected television companies in the world. In contrast, BSkyB is a relatively recent satellite channel manager transmitting from the Luxembourg-registered Astra satellite; it takes between 5 and 8 per cent of the UK television audience with its mix of sport, news, movies and archive programmes. Sky makes few programmes other than news, preferring to buy them in, and relies heavily on its coverage of football to secure itself a foothold in the market. On the face of it, one would not rush to buy shares in Sky nor imagine it is going to give the executives of the BBC much in the way of sleepless nights.

However, appearances can be deceptive and, in comparative terms, it is not the BBC which is the colossus but Sky; or rather, it is a segment of a colossus, the gigantic News Corporation owned by the ubiquitous Rupert Murdoch. Indeed, during 1996 Murdoch removed the BBC from his Asian satellite system Star TV, apparently because BBC news was irksome to the Chinese government. Further, the BBC supplies programmes for UK Gold, a satellite channel which operates under the Sky umbrella, is dependent on a deal with Sky for its football coverage and looks set to play second fiddle to Murdoch's digital television plans. Given that Murdoch has already dented the American networks by establishing the cable system Fox-TV as a virtual fourth network, one would not bet against the success of his projected satellite venture in the US market either.

In the mid-1980s, such a scenario was unthinkable, except perhaps by Murdoch himself, which prompts the question, how is it that the television order could be turned upside down? Explanations for such changes in world television require attention to a number of interrelated factors which include ownership, technology, political decision-making and social/cultural contexts.

Ownership matters

The significance of television ownership lies with issues of constraint and independence related to diversity or monopoly control so that, it is argued, diversity of programmes is related to diversity of ownership and control. Murdock and Golding (1977) have argued that the ownership of communications by private capital is subject to a *general* process of concentration via conglomeration. This produces multimedia and multi-industry corporations who are part of a wider process of capital conglomeration. Thus, many commercial television companies have investment interests in both media and non-media activities or are part of organizations who do. On the basis of their core activities, Murdock (1990) distinguishes three basic kinds of conglomerates operating in the global communications field:

- industrial conglomerates
- service conglomerates
- communications conglomerates.

Any contemporary exploration of television technology and ownership needs to be placed in the context of wider changes in the global communications industries. Radical changes in telecommunications have been constituted by a combination of technological developments and market change which has contributed both to the creation of global communications giants and to the **convergence** (or erosion of boundaries) between sectors. Thus, technological developments such as the unfolding of fibre-optic cable, satellite technology and digital switching technology have opened up commercial possibilities that have led telecommunications to be hailed by corporation and state alike as *the* industry of the future. Of particular significance are the processes of synergy, convergence and deregulation (or re-regulation) (Dyson and Humphreys 1990).

Synergy and convergence in global television

From the mid-1980s onwards there has been a good deal of diversification by financial, computer and data processing companies into telecommunications, creating multimedia giants dominating sectors of the market. Companies need the financial power that can come from mergers to undertake the massive investment needed to be a player in the global market. For example, the 1989 merger of Time and Warner created the largest media group in the world with a market capitalization of $25 billion. This was followed in 1995 by Time-Warner's acquisition of Turner Broadcasting (CNN). In late 1993 the merger of Paramount communications and Viacom, owner of MTV, saw the emergence of a $17 billion company, making it the fifth largest media group behind Time-Warner, News Corporation, Bertelsmann and Walt Disney.

One of the prime reasons for these developments is the search for **synergy**. In effect, synergy means the bringing together of the various elements of television and other media at the levels of both production and distribution so that they fit together and complement each other to produce lower costs and higher profits. No communications organization represents that synergy better than Rupert Murdoch's News Corporation.

News Corporation

The acquisition by News Corporation of the Hong Kong based Star TV for $525 million has given Murdoch a satellite television footprint over Asia and the Middle East with a potential audience of 45 billion viewers. When allied to his other television interests – BSkyB (UK) and Fox-TV (USA and Australia) – his organization's television interests alone have a global reach of some two-thirds of the planet. What is significant in looking at the News Corporation dominion is not just the spatial breadth of ownership but the potential link-ups between its various elements. In Twentieth Century Fox and Star TV, Murdoch acquired a huge library of film and television products which he can channel through his network of distribution outlets. He clearly hopes to create a lucrative global advertising market. At the same time, Murdoch can use his newspapers to promote his television interests by giving space in his press holdings to the sporting activities covered by his television channels. Thus does News Corporation make the gains accruing to synergy whose intertextual link-ups are paralleled by technological and organizational convergence.

Television and computers

It is estimated that by the year 2005 there will be 25 million interactive cable households in the USA and some 22 million in Europe (*Screen Digest* October 1994). This expansion of the Internet and interactive cable is said to be laying the foundations for a 'super information highway', that is, television with built-in personal computers (PCs) linked to cable which allow us to order and pay for shopping, transfer e-money, keep an eye on our bank account, call up a selection of films, and search the world-wide web for information. The idea of PC-TV highlights the issue of technological *convergence*, that is, technologies which had been produced and used separately are beginning to merge into one. Thus, convergence refers to the breakdown of boundaries between technologies, which is paralleled by organizational convergence, as documented above, so that synergy is sought through mergers and take-overs giving rise to multimedia corporations.

Digital technology

To a considerable degree such technological convergence is enabled by digital technology, which enables information to be electronically organized into bytes, or discrete bundles of information, which can be compressed during transmission and decompressed on arrival. This allows a good deal more information to travel down any given conduit, be that cable, satellite or terrestrial signals (it also opens up previously unusable zones of the spectrum to use) and at greater speed over larger distances. Indeed, the impact of new technologies in general, and digital processes in particular, can be summed up in terms of speed, volume and distance, that, is more information at greater speed over larger distances. Alongside the development of digital television, it is becoming apparent that the technologies having the most impact are those concerned with distribution – cable and satellite. Organizations which control the distribution mechanisms are eclipsing the power of producers because no one wants to commit expensive resources to a project which has not secured a distribution agreement.

Satellites

Satellites are able to offer a much increased number of TV signals, either directly or via head stations of cable systems and, despite high start up costs, have the potential to offer high quality picture and sound on a much increased scale. Of course, the impact of satellite technology has been distinct in different parts of the world. In India, the development of commercial satellite television threatens state owned television's (Doordarshan) dominance (forcing the government to entertain commercial broadcasting) whereas in Britain, though the satellite channels of BSkyB have had some success in creating a niche for themselves, especially in relation to sport, the audience share of 8 per cent has some way to go before it can be seen to dislodge the BBC or Independent Television (ITV) channels. A similar contrast can be made between the Netherlands, where the Luxembourg based Radio Télévision Luxembourg 4 (RTL4) satellite station has made decisive inroads into the Dutch market, and the USA, where Direct Broadcasting by Satellite (DBS) has had little impact having been eclipsed by cable (though News Corporation's intervention in the market may change this).

Cable systems

Most of the present cable systems are based on the copper coaxial specification. However, its future will lie with the use of fibre-optic cable with its far greater capabilities in terms of channel capacity and the potential for interactive programmes. Unsurprisingly, there is still extremely unequal development of cable across the globe with, for example, nearly 70 per cent of television households having access to cable in North America, some 23 per cent in the European Union, 20 per cent in Asia and only 7 per cent in South America. World levels of cable penetration of television households stands at about 23 per cent, which represents about 189 million households (*Screen Digest* April 1995).

In the USA, cable expanded at a considerable rate during the early 1980s (indeed Fox-TV is effectively a fourth network) though the latter part of the decade saw a considerable slowing of penetration rates. In contrast, cable struggled in the UK, which has one of the lowest cable density rates in Europe despite the government's attempts to encourage its development. However, during the 1990s a new wave of American investment in British cable, combined with its use as a carrier for satellite programmes, has prompted a gradual expansion of cable though it is a long way from the 95 per cent penetration level enjoyed by the Netherlands – the most densely cabled country in Europe.

Industry and government

The kinds of *synergy* and *convergence* described above have been made to happen by the captains of industry and allowed to happen by politicians. For, though multimedia conglomerates have existed for many years, the scope of their activities has been permitted to widen by governments who have relaxed the regulations that restricted cross-media ownership and the entry of new players. That is, the media have been undergoing a period of deregulation.

Deregulation and re-regulation in global television

The mid-1980s and early 1990s witnessed a significant period of deregulation in television or, to be more accurate, re-regulation. These new regulations, which are considerably less stringent than their predecessors, have been occasioned by a number of factors including

- the growth of 'new' communication technologies which have invalidated the natural monopoly argument since digital technology allows frequencies to be split and alternative delivery systems employed
- the establishment by court rulings in various countries of the legal right to communicate and the adoption of diversity as a key public principle (Porter 1989)
- governmental enthusiasm (particularly in the USA and UK) for the market, including a preference for the funding of television by commercial means rather than through taxation.

Thus, it was the relaxation of television and newspaper ownership rules that allowed Murdoch to launch Fox cable TV in the USA and to own newspapers and television companies in the UK. Similarly, deregulation has allowed AT&T, the biggest telephone operator in the USA, to participate in the television market from which it had previously been excluded by law. In the UK, the privatization of British Telecom (BT) and the deregulation of the telecommunications industries has led BT, best known for its telephone business, to seek new global partners, which will let it into the cable television market and allied services.

New European tele-landscapes
Deregulation and commercial expansion have prompted widespread discussion about the emerging shape of the new tele-landscapes. In Europe, the 'old order' was marked by the subordination of broadcasting to public service goals set in the context of a broadly political process of regulation. Television was of a largely national character and was generally non-commercial in principle. The 'new order' in television is marked by the coexistence of public and commercial broadcasting, the deregulation of commercial television, the increasing emergence of multimedia transnational companies and pressure on public service television to operate with a commercial logic (McQuail *et al.* 1992).

Public television viewing figures
Data from Sanchez-Tabernero (1993) certainly suggests a decline, though not as yet a terminal one, in the viewing figures for public television in Europe. For example, in France and Germany, public television which in 1975 accounted for 100 per cent of viewers took only 33 and 60 per cent respectively in 1990. The decline was somewhat less dramatic in the UK where the percentage move was from 52 (1975) to 48 per cent (1990). Nevertheless, public service broadcasting has proved surprisingly resilient in the face of competition. For example, in Australia the nationally funded Australian Broadcasting Commission (ABC) has achieved its highest ratings for decades, in Italy the public Radiotelevisione Italiana (RAI) channels rate better than their combined commercial rivals, in India the state owned Doordarshan is fighting back against commercial opposition and in Britain the BBC looks set to remain a major player for the foreseeable future. However, though they have survived, public service organizations are now simply *one* player, instead of being *the* player, in the more plural and fragmented global television landscape which has sedimented itself in the 1990s and looks set to grow into a new century.

Globalization and technology
Overall, the technologies of cable, satellite, digital technology and international computer networks enable media organizations to operate on a global scale by assisting in the process of internal organizational communication and in allowing media products to be distributed across the world. Both functions of new technology are intimately bound up with the globalization of media in general and television in particular which, it can be argued, are laying the foundations of a global electronic culture.

Global electronic culture

In the context of globalization, culture can be seen to span time and place so that in the age of *electronic* reproduction, culture comes to us via the screen, video and radio, rather than requiring us to explore it in the context of ritualized spaces. Cultural artefacts and meanings from different historical periods and geographical places can mix together and be juxtaposed so that, while the values and meanings attached to place remain significant, the networks in which people are involved extend far beyond their physical locations. In this context, the debate about the impact of television is in part a reprise of the cultural homogenization/imperialism debate for, as both technology and cultural form, television is a western originated project and continues to be dominated economically by western, and particularly American, economic powers.

Media imperialism?

Thus, Schiller (1969, 1985) makes the case that the media fit into the world capitalist system by providing ideological support for capitalism and transnational corporations in particular. The media are seen as vehicles for corporate marketing, manipulating audiences to deliver them to advertisers. This is allied to the assertion of a general ideological effect by which media messages create and reinforce audience attachment to the status quo.

US dominance in television trade

Concerns about media imperialism have been fuelled by a limited number of studies of the global television trade which have concluded that programming flows are dominated by the USA (Varis 1974, 1984). Certainly the USA is the major exporter of television programmes, a position enabled by the economics of the industry which allow US producers to cover much of their costs in the domestic market, leaving exports as profit. This enables US producers to sell their programmes at a level borne by the market rather than being determined by production costs. Thus, an episode of a programme costing $1.5 million to produce can be sold in France for $50,000 and in Zimbabwe for $500. Of course the world-wide familiarity with, and popularity of, Hollywood narrative techniques also plays a part.

However, while 44 per cent of all imported television hours to western Europe came from the USA, Sepstrup (1989) argues that what is more relevant is that 73 per cent of the total national supply in all of western Europe was domestically produced. Further, 'more and more nations are producing an increasing proportion of their own programming', a significant number of which are 'doing over half of their own programming, both in the total broadcast day and during primetime' (Straubhaar 1997: 293).

Of course, not only are gross import–export figures open to various interpretations, but they tend to obscure the differences between large and small nations (the latter tend to import more), between programme types (American programme supply is heavily concentrated in fictional pro- grammes) and levels of consumption (US programmes seem to be heavily concentrated in prime-time hours). Further, while the USA can claim 'at least 75% of the world-wide television programme exports' (Hoskins *et al.* 1995), there has been a distinct move towards *regionalization* of markets on the basis of shared language, culture and historic trade links.

Geo-cultural television markets

Thus, during the 1980s, 80 per cent of US overseas distribution was going to seven countries – Australia, Canada, France, Germany, Italy, Japan and the UK (Waterman 1988). Indeed, Straubhaar (1997) argues that there are a number of 'geo-cultural' markets emerging including those based on west- ern Europe, Latin America, the Francophone world of France and its former colonies, an Arabic world market, a Chinese market and a South Asian market. Further, these markets are not necessarily bounded by geographical space, but involve diaspora populations distributed across the world. For example, the Indian film industry serves not only the Indian sub-continent but also areas of Africa, Malaysia, Indonesia and Europe.

While television does play a direct role in the penetration of some cultures by meaning systems from another, rather than obliterating local conceptions it may be more accurate to see the process as the overlaying of local mean- ings by alternative definitions, so relativizing both and creating new senses of ambiguity and uncertainty (Ferguson 1990). What we are seeing is a set of economic and cultural processes dating from different historical periods, with different developmental rhythms, being overlaid upon each other to create global disjunctures as well as new global connections and similarities (A.D. Smith 1990; Appaduria 1993).

The Chinese example

Above all, the US media imperialism argument does not take on board the contradictory, unpredictable and heterogeneous meanings that audiences are able to take from television (see Chapter 5). That television is uneven and contradictory in its impact is illustrated by Lull's research in China. Here, according to Lull (1991, 1997), is a television system introduced by a government keen to use it as a form of social control and cultural hom- ogenization but which has turned out to be quite the opposite. Although the

Chinese government have attempted to use television to re-establish social stability after Tiananmen Square, and preserve the authority of the party, it has instead become a central agent of popular resistance. Television has amplified and intensified the diversity of cultural and political sentiments in China by presenting alternative views of life. For example, commercial and imported dramas have been juxtaposed to China's own economic difficulties as television, driven by the need to attract larger audiences, becomes a cultural and ideological forum of competing ideas. Further, not only are programmes themselves polysemic, but also audiences have become adept at reading between the lines of official pronouncements. For Lull, the challenge to autocratic rule raised by the Chinese resistance movement, with its stress on freedom and democracy, could not have happened without television. In short, though television may circulate discourse on a global scale, its consumption and use as a resource for the construction of cultural identities always take place in a local context.

Television as global and local

Television can be said to be global in its circulation of similar *narrative forms* around the world; soap opera, news, sport, quiz shows and music videos can be found in most countries.

Soap opera
Soap opera, for example, is a global form in two senses:

- it is a narrative mode *produced* in a variety of countries across the globe
- it is one of the most exported forms of television *viewed* in a range of cultural contexts.

The global attraction of soap opera can be partly attributed to the apparently universal appeal of particular open-ended narrative forms, the centrality of the personal and kinship relations and in some circumstances the emergence of an international style embedded in the traditions of Hollywood. However, the success of the soap opera can also reflect the possibilities offered to audiences of engaging in local or regional issues and problems located in recognizable 'real' places. For example, while South African television screens a good deal of American and Australian soap opera, it is also possible to watch the locally produced *Generations*.

The tensions between the poles of the global and the local are highlighted by, on the one hand, the enormous global popularity of soaps like *Neighbours* and *Dallas,* and on the other, the failure of these very same soaps in particular countries (e.g. *Neighbours* in the USA, *Dallas* in Japan). As Crofts

(1995) has pointed out, the global success, and failures, of soap opera depends on both the specificities of soap opera as a televisual form and the particularities of the conditions of reception. While we have witnessed the emergence of an international primetime soap opera style, including high production values, pleasing visual appearances and fast paced action-oriented narrative modes, many soaps retain local settings, regional language audiences and slow paced story telling.

News

Similar arguments can be put in relation to the genre of news, which shows both global similarities and local differences. The general case for regarding news as a global phenomenon rests on the establishment of news exchange arrangements whereby subscribing news organizations exchange news material with a particular emphasis on the sharing of visual footage. Consequently, Straubhaar (1992) concluded (based on a cross-cultural study involving the USA, former USSR, Japan, former West Germany, Italy, India, Colombia and China) that 'what is news' is 'fairly consistent' from country to country and that the format of 20–40 minute programmes anchored by presenters was a common feature. Likewise, data collected by Gurevitch *et al.* (1991) about the Eurovision News Exchange and the 36 countries which regularly use it suggest that the availability of common news footage and a shared professional culture has led to 'substantial, but not complete' convergence of news stories.

That Straubhaar should have found similarity over difference may reflect 'the drift towards an international standardization of basic journalistic discourses' (Dahlgren 1995: 49) and the domination of global news agendas by western news agencies. News is gathered, selected and controlled by western transnational corporations who treat news as a commodity to be bought and sold. For example, two large western services, Visnews and Worldwide Television News (WTN), are powerful forces within television news. Further, there is also an emerging direct supply of finished news product to audiences via satellite television, most notably by Cable News Network (CNN), the BBC and News Corporation. However, the fact that western news agencies tend to supply 'spot news' and visual reports without commentary allows different interpretations of events to be dubbed over the pictures, leading to what Gurevitch *et al.* (1991) call the 'domestication' of global news which is regarded as a 'countervailing force to the pull of globalisation'.

Electronic bricolage

Beyond specific genres like soap opera and news, the global multiplication of communications technologies has created an increasingly complex semiotic environment in which television produces and circulates an explosive display of competing signs and meanings. This creates a flow of images which fuses news, views, drama and reportage so that a variety of juxtapositions of images and meanings creates a sort of electronic bricolage. By bricolage is meant the recombination and resignification of previously unconnected elements into a new 'whole'. Thus, the globalization of television has contributed to the construction of a collage of images from different times and places which has been dubbed postmodern.

Global postmodern culture

Lash (1990) identifies the shift from the 'discursive' to the 'figural' as core to the postmodern turn by which he means that the signifying logics of the modern and postmodern work in different ways. For Lash, the modernist 'regime of signification' prioritizes words over images, promulgates a rationalist world-view, explores the meanings of cultural texts and distances the spectator from the cultural object. In contrast, the postmodern 'figural' is more visual, draws from everyday life, contests rationalist views of culture and immerses the spectator in his/her desire in the cultural object. In short, the globalization of the essentially *visual* medium of television forms a central part of the postmodern cultural turn.

The stylistic markers of the postmodern in television have been seen as

- aesthetic self-consciousness/self-reflexiveness
- juxtaposition/montage/bricolage
- paradox
- ambiguity
- uncertainty
- the blurring of the boundaries of genre, style and history.

Techniques include montage, rapid cutting, non-linear narrative techniques and the decontextualization of images so that programmes which have commonly been identified with the postmodern decentre the importance of linear narrative in favour of a new look and feel in which image takes preference over story telling (Kellner 1992).

Intertextuality

Also postmodern is the growth of a self-conscious intertextuality (i.e. citation of one text within another) involving both explicit allusion to particular programmes and oblique references to other genre conventions and styles, for example, explicit reference to *Thelma and Louise* and *The Graduate* in *The Simpsons* or to *Twin Peaks* in *Northern Exposure*. This intertextuality is an aspect of enlarged cultural self-consciousness about the history and functions of cultural products including television.

Twin Peaks *as genre blurring*

An example of postmodern genre blurring in television was the US series *Twin Peaks*, which mixed the conventions of police series, science fiction and soap opera. Sometimes this was to be taken seriously while on other occasions it was to be treated as humorous ambivalent parody. This was accompanied by a series of tonal variations including pathos and camp, seriousness and humour which encouraged a shifting of subject positions and oscillation of emotional involvement (Collins 1992). Further, *Twin Peaks* was 'double coded' (Jencks 1986), involving a combination of codes which enabled it to engage both with a 'concerned minority' familiar with an 'expert' language and a wider popular audience. Finally, *Twin Peaks* was a prime example of the postmodern 'semiotics of excess'. That is, the series was brimming over with meanings many of which seem to be 'irrelevant' to the solving of the central crime or the forward movement of the narrative, but were part of a spectacle or a diversion.

Consumer culture

Globalization, consumer culture and postmodernism are closely allied phenomenon. First, globalization has involved the 'displacement' of the west and its philosophical categories from the centre of the universe; indeed, some have seen the collapse of western classifications as *the* marker of postmodernism. Second, the rise in visibility and status of popular culture, hastened by electronic media like television, has meant that the distinction between high and low culture is no longer viable. As Chambers (1986: 194) puts it, 'High culture becomes just one more sub-culture, one more opinion, in our midst', a view which is characteristically postmodern. Third, the blurring of the boundaries between art, culture and commerce, allied to the rising prominence of the postmodern 'figural', has resulted in a general aestheticization of everyday life (Featherstone 1991, 1995) to which television is central.

The development of global television as a fundamentally commercial form has placed that core activity of consumer culture, visual based *advertising,* in the forefront of its activities. Consequently, television is pivotal to the production and reproduction of a *promotional culture* focused on the use of visual imagery to create value added brands or commodity signs. Indeed, Wernick argues that cultural phenomena which serve to communicate a promotional message of some type or another have become 'virtually co-extensive with our produced symbolic world' (Wernick 1991: 184). The phrase

Coca Cola culture encapsulates the global reach of this promotional culture and highlights the alleged link between global capitalism, advertising and cultural homogenization. That is, for some critics these global processes are argued to represent a form of cultural homogenization particularly in the field of consumer culture, so that *Coca Cola, McDonald's, Nike* and *Microsoft's Windows* circulate world-wide. However, the global circulation of consumer goods should not lead us to assume that their impact is the same the world over. Indeed, it is the juxtaposition of *Microsoft's Windows* and ox-drawn carts, *The Simpsons* and *Hum Log* (an Indian soap opera), Hollywood and Bollywood, *The Prodigy* and traditional dance music that suggests the idea of a global postmodern.

Summary and conclusions

This chapter has sought to map in a general way the changing and expanding contours of television on a global scale. In particular, it was argued that the search for synergy in the context of a deregulated television landscape was leading to corporate mergers and take-overs. These developments advance the formation of multimedia transnational media corporations able to shape the global production and distribution of television. The globalization of the institutions of television is paralleled by the world-wide circulation of key television narratives and genres, including news, soap opera, music television, sport and game shows, set within an advancing 'promotional' culture. It was further suggested that television across the globe was developing a postmodern cultural style marked by bricolage, intertextuality and genre blurring.

However, it was suggested that the globalization of television is not best understood in terms of cultural imperialism and the homogenization of world culture. Rather, it was argued that while forces of homogenization are certainly in evidence, of equal significance is the place of heterogenization and localization. Consequently, globalization and hybridity are preferred concepts to imperialism and homogeneity as we approach the end of the twentieth century. Nevertheless, it was also suggested that decentring conceptions of cultural imperialism in favour of the idea of globalization did not negate the necessity to explore issues of economic and cultural power; indeed, hybrid cultures and identities are themselves embroiled in questions of power.

These arguments are of significance because they illustrate the scope of television and its cultural representations as a major and proliferating resource for the construction of cultural identity. Considering the arguments of Chapters 2 and 3 together, we may say that:

- Identity is not a fixed 'thing' but a description of ourselves, a *representation*, with which 'we' identify.
- Television is the major disseminator of representations in contemporary global culture.
- The globalization of television has enabled the dislocation of 'culture' from place leading to the juxtapositioning of a variety of global discourses.
- The global electronic bricolage of representations that television circulates are constitutive of increasingly complex cultural identities.

The relationship between globalization, television and cultural identities is a complex one which may give rise to absolutist ethnic identities, fundamentalist religious identities, hybrid cross-cultural identities, fragmented **multiple identities**, postmodern neo-tribes, 'third cultures' of transglobal workers and intellectuals and the understanding that while our planet is a finite bounded space, it is composed of diverse cultures and peoples with complex local and global cultural identities. Thus, armed with a theoretical understanding of cultural identity (Chapter 1) in the context of increasing cultural globalization (Chapter 2), we can now turn to the formation of specific cultural identities using race (Chapter 3) and gender (Chapter 4) as our prime examples.

Further reading

Barker, C. (1997b) *Global Television: An Introduction*. London: Blackwell.

Giddens, A. (1994) Living in a post-traditional society, in U. Beck, A. Giddens and C. Lash, *Reflexive Modernisation*. Cambridge: Polity Press.

Murdock, G. (1990) Redrawing the map of the communications industries: concentration and ownership in the era of privatisation, in M. Ferguson (ed.) *Public Communication: The New Imperatives*. Newbury Park, CA and London: Sage.

Robertson, R. (1995) Glocalization: time–space and homogeneity–hetrogeneity', in M. Featherstone, S. Lash and R. Robertson (eds) *Global Modernities*. Newbury Park, CA and London: Sage.

Tomlinson, J. (1991) *Cultural Imperialism*. London: Pinter Press.

3 | # THE CONSTRUCTION AND REPRESENTATION OF RACE AND NATION

In this chapter we shall follow up the theoretical discussion which constituted Chapter 1 with a closer look at race and nation as organizing points of cultural identity in contemporary global culture. We shall first distinguish between biological discourses of race and cultural discourses of 'racialization', that is, between the argument that racial subordination is the outcome of biology and the argument that social groups are *culturally constructed* as subjected races. This will be followed by a discussion of ethnicity as a cultural concept marking the boundaries between social groups. After briefly considering the related question of national identity, we will note the blurring of boundaries between the categories of race, nation and ethnicity which is marked by the formation of new hybrid identities.

Having established, in the first half of the chapter, that race is a social construction, the second half will be devoted to an exploration of the cultural representation of race with particular reference to television. That is, we shall explore the **stereotypes** that commonly constitute race as a form of identity and refer to examples from both television and the wider cultural domain. As with other forms of representation, television generates meaning through a set of signifying practices which constitute the objects of knowledge. These selective and value laden significations are neither 'accurate' nor inaccurate representations of the world but the site of struggles over what counts as meaning and truth.

The concepts of race and ethnicity

The concept of race continues to bear the traces of its origins in biological discourses and a form of social Darwinism which stresses 'lines of descent'

and 'types of people' based on alleged biological and physical characteristics. The most obvious of these distinctions is skin pigmentation, an
attribute that is frequently linked with 'intelligence' and 'capabilities' so that
'racial' groups are marked by a hierarchy of superiority and subordination.
Such a conception of race is at the root of racism whereby racial classifications are constituted by and constitutive of power and the forced social and
material ranking of 'racialized' groups.

Racialization or race formation

The idea of 'racialization' or 'race formation' has been deployed to illustrate
the argument that race is a social construction and not a universal or essential category of either biology or culture. Races do not exist outside of representation but are formed in and by it in a process of social and political
power struggle. Observable characteristics are transformed into signifiers of
race including the spurious appeal to essential biological and cultural difference. As Gilroy argues,

> Accepting that skin 'colour', however meaningless we know it to be, has
> a strictly limited material basis in biology, opens up the possibility of
> engaging with theories of signification which can highlight the elastic-
> ity and emptiness of 'racial' signifiers as well as the ideological work
> which has to be done in order to turn them into signifiers of 'race' as an
> open political category, for it is struggle that determines which defi-
> nition of 'race' will prevail and the conditions under which they will
> endure or wither away.
>
> (Gilroy 1987: 38–9)

The historical formation of 'race' has been one of power and subordination
so that in Britain and the USA, for example, people of colour have occupied
structurally subordinate positions in relation to almost every dimension of
'life-chances'. That is, in broad terms, African Americans, Aboriginal Aus-
tralians and British Afro-Caribbeans have occupied positions of lower paid,
less skilled jobs, have been disadvantaged in the housing market, at school
and in media and cultural representations. Consequently, race formation or
racialization is inherently racist at a structural level for it involves forms of
social, economic and political subordination which are lived through the
categories of race.

Differential racialization

As a discursive construct, the meanings of 'race' can change and are struggled over within a given social formation so that different groups are 'differentially racialised' (Brah 1996) and the target of different racisms. For

example, British Asians have historically been subject to different forms of stereotyping and have occupied a different place in the social and racial hierarchy in Britain from Afro-Caribbeans. As one '31 year old black electronics engineer' put it, 'There's a lot of love in Handsworth, black, white and Asian. But the Asians are second-class citizens, and we're the lowest of all. We're the third' (*Observer*, 15 September 1985, cited Gilroy 1987: 238). Further, the meanings of race differ over time and across space. For example, it has been argued (M. Barker 1982) that the 'new racism' in Britain does not rely on biological discourses of superiority, as in South African apartheid, but on cultural differences which are said to exclude black people from being fully a part of the *nation*.

National difference

In addition, the meanings of race differ across distinct cultures, say the USA and Britain. In Britain, the relatively homogeneous white character of the *in situ* population was disturbed in the 1950s by arrivals from the Caribbean and Indian sub-continent, making questions of national identity a crucial category through which racialization operated. However, as West (1992) has argued, the history of the modern United States begins with the dispossession and genocide of native American peoples and continues through the long history of slavery so that questions of race are posed at the very inception of the USA in ways which are more longstanding, but less concerned with nationality, than in Britain.

Ethnicity

While 'race' is a cultural construct masquerading as biological science, ethnicity is a distinctively cultural concept centred on the sharing of norms, values, beliefs, cultural symbols and practices. The formation of 'ethnic groups' therefore relies on shared cultural signifiers which have developed under specific historical, social and political contexts and which encourage a sense of belonging often based, at least in part, on a common mythological ancestry. However, following the anti-essentialist arguments of Chapter 1, it is clear that ethnic groups are not based on primordial ties or universal cultural characteristics as such, but are formed through discursive practices. Ethnicity is a relational concept concerned with categories of self-identification and social ascription. Consequently, ethnicity is not best understood in terms of cultural characteristics *per se*, but as a process of *boundary* formation which are constructed and maintained under specific socio-historical conditions (Barth 1969). Of course, to suggest that ethnicity is not about pre-given cultural difference but a process of boundary formation and maintenance, does not mean that such distinctiveness cannot be socially constructed around signifiers which do connote universality, territory and purity. For example, metaphors of blood, kinship and homeland have been much in evidence in the television news reporting of events in Serbia, Bosnia and Croatia.

A culturalist conception of ethnicity is a valiant attempt to escape the racist implications which are inherent in the very concept of race as it has been forged historically so that, as Hall writes,

> If the black subject and black experience are not stabilised by Nature or by some other essential guarantee, then it must be the case that they are constructed historically, culturally and politically – the concept which refers to this is 'ethnicity'. The term ethnicity acknowledges the place of history, language and culture in the construction of subjectivity and identity, as well as the fact that all discourse is placed, positioned, situated, and all knowledge is contextual.
>
> (Hall 1996d: 446)

Usage problems with ethnicity
The concept of ethnicity is not without its problems of usage and it remains a contested term. For instance, white Anglo-Saxons frequently use the concept of ethnicity to refer to *other* people, usually with different skin pigmentation, so that Asians, Africans, Hispanics and African Americans are ethnic groups but somehow the English or white Anglo-Saxon Americans are not. However, it is important to maintain that white English, American or Australian people *do* form ethnic groups, where the concept is used as a constitutive descriptor and not as the basis of an exclusionary nationalism. Consequently, as Dyer has argued, studying whiteness 'is about making whiteness strange rather than treating it as a taken for granted touchstone of human ordinariness' (Dyer 1997). Of course, as Dyer (1997) again notes, the recognition that whiteness is a historical invention does not mean that it can simply be wished away.

One problem with the concept of ethnicity, especially in the context of discussions about multiculturalism, is that questions of power and racism are too often sidelined. Ethnicity can be deployed to suggest that a social formation operates with plural and equal groups rather than hierarchical racialized groups. Consequently, hooks (1990) and Gilroy (1987) prefer the concept of 'race', not because it corresponds to any biological or cultural absolutes, but because it connotes, and refers investigation to, issues of power.

Redefining ethnicity

In contrast, Hall looks to a reworking of the concept of ethnicity and to its rearticulation in terms of the exploration of cultural practices within specific historical and political conjunctures so that we are *all* ethnically located (Hall 1996d). As such, ethnicity must concern itself with the relations between groups which define each other in the context of power so that ethnicity is concerned with questions of relations of marginality, of the centre and the periphery, in the context of changing historical forms and circumstances. However, questions of the centre and the margin have to be grasped as issues of the politics of representation, which includes television, for as Brah argues, 'It is necessary for it to become axiomatic that what is *represented* as the "margin" is not marginal at all but is a *constitutive effect of the representation itself*. The "centre" is no more a centre than is the "margin" ' (Brah 1996: 226).

Discourses of centrality and marginality are the common route by which questions of race and ethnicity are articulated with issues of national identity. Thus, history is littered with examples of how, within a given nation-state, one ethnic group is defined as central and superior to another. While Nazi Germany, apartheid South Africa and 'ethnic cleansing' in Bosnia are the most obvious examples (places and events which most of us know about only through television) the core metaphor of superiority and subordination is no less applicable to contemporary Britain, the USA and Australia. Indeed, national identity is often allied to a conception of the nation as a shared culture requiring that ethnic boundaries should not cut across political ones, though of course they do.

National identities

The nation-state

The modern nation-state is a relatively recent invention and most of the human beings who have ever walked the earth did not participate in any kind of state nor identify with one. The nation-state and national identity as collective forms of organization and identification are not 'naturally' occurring phenomenon, though we often think of them as such; rather, they are particular contingent historical-cultural formations. The nation-state is a fundamentally *political* concept which refers to an administrative apparatus deemed to have sovereignty over a specific *space* or territory within the nation-state system. National identity is a form of imaginative identification with that nation-state as expressed through symbols and discourses. Thus, nations are not only political formations but also systems of *cultural representation* so that national identity is continually reproduced through discursive action. The nation-state as a political apparatus and a symbolic form has a *temporal* dimension in that political structures endure and change while the symbolic and discursive dimensions of national identity often narrates and creates the idea of origins, continuity and tradition.

Imagined communities

For Benedict Anderson (1983), the nation is an 'imagined community' and national identity a construction assembled through symbols and rituals in relation to territorial and administrative categories.

> It is *imagined* because the members of even the smallest nation will never know most of their fellow members, meet them, or even hear of them, yet in the minds of each lives the images of their communion. . . . The nation is imagined as *limited* because even the largest of them, encompassing perhaps a billion living beings, has finite, if elastic boundaries, beyond which lie other nations. . . . It is imagined as *sovereign* because the concept was born in an age in which Enlightenment and Revolution were destroying the legitimacy of the divinely ordered, hierarchical dynastic realm. . . . Finally, it is imagined as a *community* because, regardless of the actual inequality and exploitation that may prevail in each, the nation is always conceived as a deep, horizontal comradeship. Ultimately, it is this fraternity that makes it possible, over the past two centuries, for so many millions of people, not so much to kill, as willingly to die for such limited imaginings.
>
> (Anderson 1983: 15–16)

Print capitalism

For Anderson, communication is of central importance to the rise of national identity and the nation-state. Thus, the mechanized production and commodification of books and newspapers, the rise of 'print capitalism', allowed vernacular languages to be standardized and disseminated providing the conditions for the creation of a national consciousness. For the first time it was possible for the mass of people within a particular state to understand each other through a common print language. The processes of print capitalism thus 'fixed' a vernacular language as *the* 'national' language and made possible a new imagined national community, hence, nation and communication are inescapably linked together. In addition, the media encourage us to imagine the simultaneous occurrence of events across wide tracts of time and space which contributes to the concept of nation and to the place of states within a spatially distributed state system. However, in contemporary global conditions (Chapter 2), it is not just a matter of the print media, but of the electronic dissemination of cultural representations and the rhythms of life connected to the television.

Thus, Scannel (1988) has argued that broadcasting is 'profoundly implicated in the temporal arrangements of modern societies'. In particular, television sustains routines which are significant aspects of the reproduction of social life. Thus broadcasting brings major public events into the private worlds of viewers and in doing so constructs a kind of national calendar which organizes, coordinates and renews a national public social world. Such events would include, in a British context, sporting events such as the FA Cup Final, the Grand National and Wimbledon but might also include political events like the opening of Parliament, party conferences and royal birthdays. In other words, television connects representations with domestic routines to facilitate the production of national identity.

Telenovelas

In a Latin American context, Martin-Barbero (1988, 1993, 1995) argues for the key role played by television in general, and telenovelas (Latin soap opera) in particular, in the construction of national identity through the circulation of national symbols and myths together with the creation of feelings of solidarity and simultaneous activity. He argues that during the first stage of television's development in Latin America its decisive role was to convey the challenge and appeal of populism, metamorphosing an unnamed mass into a people and subsequently into a nation. In particular, television helped to transform the political idea of the nation into a form of everyday experience and feeling. This included the national landscape, the typical looks, gestures and habits of people, national cultural stereotypes, local modernization and the feeling of simultaneous viewing even as one remains at home.

Likewise, Lopez (1995) argues that telenovelas have created a televisual 'national' allowing audiences to 'live' the nation in everyday life through a sense of simultaneous viewing and the weaving of national themes and symbols into the narratives. For example, she suggests that Colombian telenovelas have 'provided the beleaguered nation with a self-image that differs markedly from the violent narco-trafficking for which it is known throughout the rest of the world' (Lopez 1995: 263). In the case of the US Spanish speaking market 'the telenovelas is making "nation" where there is no coincidence between nation and state' (Lopez 1995: 266). Through the Spanish language networks, Univision and Telemundo, telenovelas have helped promote a shared sense of Hispanic or Latino cultural identity among the US based Spanish diaspora.

However, telenovelas do not unambiguously promote national identity and Martin-Barbero highlights a developmental tension within the telenovela between national, Latin American and international themes. On the one hand, the introduction of a realist strand into telenovelas allowed for the representation of specific places; notably characteristics of particular nation-states – Brazil, Peru, Argentina, Mexico – while, on the other, there has been a trend towards Latin American integration through the use of standardized sounds, rhythms and icons which promoted the export of telenovelas throughout the continent. The internationalization of the telenovela through its export to Portugal, Spain, Italy, Poland, Japan and other countries furthered a 'progressive neutralisation of the characteristics of Latin American-ness' since 'production for a global market implies the generalisation of narrative models and the thinning out of cultural characteristics' (Martin-Barbero 1995: 283).

Shortcomings in Anderson's interpretation

Useful though Anderson's (1983) aforementioned account is in linking forms of national identity with modes of communication, his work falls short, as Thompson (1995) points out, of specifying exactly how new print forms give rise to national sentiments. At best, Anderson shows how print media established the necessary conditions for the nation-state and national identity. Nor does he deal adequately with the various ways in which divergent social groups use media products and decode them in different ways. Thus, Anderson overstates the unity of the nation and the strength of national identities which covers over differences of class, gender, ethnicity and so forth. While we often assume that the nation-state is one entity, it is useful and necessary to uncouple the concepts of nation and state since cultures and national cultural identities are not coterminous with states. The presence of various global diaspora – African, Jewish, Indian, Polish, Irish – attest to forms of national and ethnic cultural identity which span the borders of nation-states. Further, within nation-state boundaries one is likely to find diverse cultural and ethnic identifications so that few states have ethnically homogeneous populations. For example, A.D. Smith (1990) distinguishes between *civic*/political conceptions of nations and *ethnic* ones and is able to list over 60 civic states which are constituted by more than one national or ethnic culture.

Cultural diversity and discursive unity

Since cultures consist of changing practices and meanings, which operate at different social levels, they are not static entities. Any given national culture is understood and acted upon by different social groups in divergent ways, thus, governments, ethnic groups, classes and genders may perceive it differently. At which level then should a national culture be identified? Which set of values within those groups are the 'authentic' ones? For any ethnic group or nation will be marked by lines of difference (Tomlinson 1991). Consequently, any representation of a national culture is a snapshot of symbols and practices which have been foregrounded at specific historical conjunctures for particular purposes by distinctive groups of people. In effect, national identity is a way of unifying cultural diversity so that, as Hall argues,

> Instead of thinking of national cultures as unified, we should think of them as a discursive device which represents difference as unity or identity. They are cross-cut by deep internal divisions and differences, and 'unified' only through the exercise of different forms of cultural power.
>
> (Hall 1992a: 297)

The unity of the nation is constructed in *narrative* form by which stories, images, symbols and rituals represent 'shared' meanings of nationhood (Bhabha 1990). National identity is a constitutive representation of shared experiences and history told through stories, literature, popular culture and, of course, television. For example, at the moment of writing my television screen is full of national imagery – flags, logos, songs – associated with the football World Cup. Indeed, televised sport is currently one of the prime promoters of national discourses and sentiments. Such narratives emphasize the traditions and continuity of the nation as being 'in the nature of things', though they may be 'invented' traditions including the foundational myth of a collective point of origin. This, in turn, both assumes and produces the linkage between national identity and a pure, original people or 'folk' tradition (Hall 1992a).

Thus far, it may have been assumed that, even though they are cultural constructions, race, ethnicity and nation are constitutive of *discrete* and stable identities which appear as 'natural' and taken for granted. However, globalization has increased the range of sources and resources available for identity construction, allowing for the production of *hybrid* identities in the context of a post-traditional global society, where bounded societies and states, though still with us, are cut across by the circulation of other global cultural discourses. Indeed, the proliferation and diversification of contexts and sites of interaction, constituted in and through discourse, prevents easy identification of particular subjects with a given, fixed identity so that the same person is able to shift across subject positions according to circumstances. In this context, it is significant that new prominence is being given to the old concept of diaspora.

Diaspora and hybrid identities

The idea of diaspora is concerned with issues of travel, journey, dispersion, homes and borders in the context of questions about who travels, 'where, when, how and under what circumstances' (Brah 1996: 182). Thus, 'diasporic identities are at once local and global. They are networks of transnational identifications encompassing "imagined" and "encountered" communities' (Brah 1996: 196). Diaspora is a fundamentally *relational* concept referring to 'configurations of power which differentiate Diaspora internally as well as situate them in relation to one another' (Brah 1996: 183). Since diaspora is a relational concept it follows that,

> Diaspora space as a conceptual category is 'inhabited' not only by those who have migrated and their descendants, but equally by those who are constructed and represented as indigenous. In other words, the concept of *Diaspora space* . . . includes the entanglement, the intertwining of the genealogies of dispersion with those 'staying put'. The Diaspora space is the site where *the native is as much a Diaspora as the Diaspora is a native*.
>
> (Brah 1996: 209)

While the idea of diaspora does indeed point to a dispersed network of related peoples, it is one which, as Gilroy remarks, is

> characteristically produced by forced dispersal and reluctant scattering [which] connotes flight following the threat of violence [in which] Diaspora identity is focused less on the equalising, proto-democratic force of common territory and more on the social dynamics of remembrance and commemoration defined by a strong sense of the dangers involved in forgetting the location of origin and the process of dispersal.
>
> (Gilroy 1997: 318)

Black Atlantic

As a means of comprehending cultural identity in the context of diaspora, Gilroy (1993) introduces the concept of the Black Atlantic. Black identities cannot be understood, he argues, in terms of being American or British or West Indian, nor can they be grasped in terms of ethnic absolutism (that there is a global essential black identity), but rather should be understood in terms of the black diaspora of the Atlantic. Cultural exchange within the black diaspora produces hybrid identities and cultural forms which are to be grasped in terms of similarities and differences between the various locales of the diaspora for black 'self-definitions and cultural expressions draw on a plurality of black histories and politics' (Gilroy 1987: 125). Thus, Rap and Hip Hop, itself an American-Caribbean hybrid, have become prominent musical forms of the black diaspora and a point of identification within the Black Atlantic. In addition, in Britain, Asian youth have produced their own hybrid forms of Banghra-reggae-rap cross-overs. In this sense, the concept of diaspora helps us to think about identities not in terms of absolutes of nature or culture but in terms of contingency, indeterminacy and conflict, of identities in motion, routes rather than roots. Thus, the 'changing same' of the diaspora involves 'creolized, syncretized, hybridized and chronically impure cultural forms' (Gilroy 1997).

Structural and cultural hybridization

Though the concept of hybridity has proved useful in highlighting cultural mixing and the emergence of new forms of identity we do need to differentiate between *types of hybridity* and to do so with reference to the specific circumstances of particular social groups. Thus Pieterse (1995) has suggested that we make a distinction between structural and cultural hybridization. Structural hybridization refers to a variety of social and institutional *sites* of hybridity, for example border zones, while cultural hybridization distinguishes between *cultural responses* ranging from assimilation, through forms of separation, to hybrids that destabilize and blur cultural boundaries. Pieterse goes on to argue that structural hybridization, which increases the range of organizational options to people, and cultural hybridization, which involves the opening up of 'imagined communities', are signs of increased boundary crossing. However, they do not represent the erasure of boundaries and we need to be sensitive to both cultural *difference* and to forms of identification that involve recognition of *similarity*.

This requires us to recognize the *range* of cultural, ethnic and national identities which are formed and unformed over time and across a variety of spaces. For example, we might think of at least six different kinds of identifications which range from ethnic absolutism to new forms of cultural hybridity (C. Barker 1997a, 1997b). Thus,

- Two distinct cultural traditions are thought of as separate in time and/or space. We would define ourselves as Asian *or* British. This is the domain of nationalism and ethnic absolutism.
- Two separate cultural traditions are juxtaposed and meet in time and space. We would define ourselves as Asian *and* British and move between them as situationally appropriate.
- Cultures are translocal and involve global flows. Hybridization occurs out of recognition of difference and produces something new. We are 'British Asian'.
- Cultural traditions develop in separate locales but develop identifications based on perceived similarity and commonalty of tradition and circumstance. For example, an essentialist version of pan-global Black or Asian nationalism or, in its more contingent form, the Black Atlantic.
- One cultural tradition absorbs or obliterates the other and creates effective similarity. This could involve assimilation (my parents are Asian but I am British) or cultural domination and imperialism (one tradition is wiped out).
- New forms of identity are forged out of shared concerns along the axis of class, ethnicity, gender, age, and so on. This is an anti-essentialist position in which similarity is strategic and created, for example, a strategic alliance in which black and Asian people share a common anti-racist strategy. Equally, strategic identifications and alliances occur on other axes such as gender or age.

The concept of hybridity remains problematic in so far as it assumes or implies the meeting of completely distinct and autonomous cultural spheres. For example, the idea of British–Asian hybrid forms thought of as two separate traditions mixing in time and space overlooks the fact that neither British nor Asian cultures are homogeneous in the way that the phrase implies. Anything that could be called British or Asian is already a hybrid form and both are divided along the lines of religion, class, gender, age, nationality, and so forth. Thus hybridization is the mixing of that which is already a hybrid. Nevertheless, the concept of hybridity enables us to recognize the production of the new, for example in the phrase 'British Asian' or in Ragga and British Banghra as musical forms. Consequently, as with the very notion of cultural identity, the concept of hybridity is acceptable provided that it is recognized as a discursive device, a way of capturing cultural change by way of a strategic cut or temporary stabilization of cultural categories. For the purposes of illuminating these arguments about hybridity I shall explore the example of British Asian young people. Such persons form the subjects of the audience research reported in Chapter 5.

Hybridity and British Asians

In the context of the migration patterns of 'accelerated globalization', Ballard (1994) documents the emergence, since the early 1950s, of *Desh Pardesh*, a phrase with the double meaning of 'home from home' and 'at home abroad'. He emphasizes the determination of arrivals from South Asia to pursue their own self-determined goals, the diverse and heterogeneous character of South Asian ethnicities in Britain, and the changing dispositions involved in the settlers' adaptive strategies. Some idea of the complex nature of South Asian settler cultural identities can be grasped by realizing that the vast majority of direct migrants came from three distinct geographical areas, the Punjab, Gujarat and Sylhet, which are cross-cut by religious differences, stratified by cast, social class and gender as well as by an urban–rural distinction. To this already complicated picture we may add the presence of 'twice migrants' who arrived in Britain by way of East Africa.

According to Ballard, migrants from South Asia to Britain went through a process involving the move from 'sojourners to settlers', that is, from a temporary entrepreneurial disposition involving the primacy of earning and saving money, to becoming permanent settlers involving the construction of families, houses, businesses and cultural institutions. However, even when settler status was taken on board, clear boundaries were drawn between themselves and their white neighbours. In particular, the maintenance of *izzat*, or personal honour, required them to keep some distance from a culture which seemed to have little sense of family, of sexual morality, of respect for elders or personal hygiene. 'Those who mimicked English ways too closely began to be accused of being *be-izzat* – without honour' (Ballard 1994: 15).

However, the emergence of British-born young 'Asians' gave rise to a generation which was much more deeply involved in transactions across ethnic boundaries than were the original migrants. Young British Asians went to school with white and Afro-Caribbean Britons, shared leisure sites, watched television and were frequently bilingual. Though they share aspects of a parental South Asian cultural identity, they are fundamentally British in cultural outlook. Young Asians in Britain have often been categorized as being 'between two cultures' (Watson 1977) or embedded in a process of 'cultural conflict'. However, we would do better to see these young people as skilled operators of cultural code switching. This is so for six main reasons:

- The notion of two cultures is incorrect because both 'British' and 'Asian' cultures are in themselves heterogeneous and stratified
- There is no reason to see cultural meetings as necessarily involving clashes or conflicts

- The relationship between 'British' and 'Asian' cultures is multidirectional, not a one way process
- While some Asians may experience dissonance, there is no evidence to suggest that this is widespread
- Intergenerational difference should not be conflated with conflict
- Above all, these Asian-British young people have developed their own home-grown political and cultural discourses of 'British Asian-ness' and syncretic or hybrid cultural forms.

(Brah 1996)

Of course, by definition, hybrid identities cannot be seen as 'essential' identities but as part of a widespread 'cut 'n' mix' of cultural forms in the context of globalization. Indeed, according to Hall, the end of essentialism 'entails a recognition that the central issues of race always appear historically in articulation, in a formation, with other categories and divisions and are constantly crossed and recrossed by the categories of class, of gender and ethnicity' (Hall 1996b: 444). Thus, identities are never either pure or fixed but formed at the *intersections* of age, class, gender, race and nation. This may be considered to be so in three fundamental ways:

- through the capability of persons to move across discursive and spatial sites of activity which address them in different ways, for example, from work to home to sites of leisure activity
- in terms of the multiple identities of the postmodern subject, that is, the ability to weave the patterns of identity from the discourses of class, race, gender
- through the construction of one discourse in terms of metaphors drawn from another, that is, the construction of nation through gendered metaphors or of race in terms of class; for example, the idea of 'race' is connected to the idea of the ascent of 'Man', ethnic groups may be derided as effeminate, nations are gendered as female and absolute ethnic differences are premised on the idea of blood lines and thus women's bodies.

To critique spurious biological arguments, to highlight the radical contingency of race and to accept the idea of hybridity which this entails helps to combat the *reduction* of people to race, which as we shall see later television is all too fond of doing, and enables us to regard all persons as multifaceted. As bell hooks has argued,

Employing a critique of essentialism allows African-Americans to acknowledge the way in which class mobility has altered collective black experience so that racism does not necessarily have the same impact on our lives. Such a critique allows us to affirm multiple black

identities, varied black experience. It also challenges colonial imperialist paradigms of black identity which represent blackness one-dimen-
sionally in ways that reinforce and sustain white supremacy. . . . When
black folks critique essentialism, we are empowered to recognise multiple experiences of black identity that are the lived conditions which
make diverse cultural productions possible. When this diversity is
ignored, it is easy to see black folks as falling into two categories:
nationalist or assimilationist, black-identified or white-identified.

(hooks 1990: 28–9)

Further, as hooks goes on to argue, the benefits of casting off essentialism,
and thus black absolutism or nationalism, means that black women do not
have to subsume their critique of aspects of black masculinity. It is not a
betrayal of black people to put forward a black feminist critique of black
male macho (Wallace 1979) nor a betrayal of women to critique white
feminism from the perspective of black women (Carby 1984; hooks 1986),
rather, these are the processes of articulation and coalition building which
are core to cultural politics. Thus, race is articulated to gender and both are
social constructions, not biological essences.

Thus far, it has been argued that race and nation as cultural identities can
be understood as descriptions or representations with which we identify or
emotionally invest in. As Hall argues, identity emerges 'in the dialogue
between the meanings and definitions which are *represented to us* by the discourses of a culture, and our willingness (consciously or unconsciously) to
respond to the summons of those meanings' (Hall 1997b: 219). Consequently, while we have explored race, ethnicity and nation as concepts, we
need to consider the manner in which they are represented both in the wider
culture and more specifically on global television. Such cultural representations, including those on global television, are constitutive of what, for
example, race 'is' and the audience for television will 'respond to the summons' differently according to the way they are located in the global and the
local (see Chapter 5).

Television, race and representation

Racism is not simply a matter of individual psychology or pathology, but of
patterns of cultural representation deeply ingrained within discourses, practices and subjectivities of western societies. Consequently, the representations of race and ethnicity which global television disseminates cannot be
separated from these wider cultural stereotypes.

Types and stereotypes

As Dyer (1977) argues, there is a distinction to be made between types and *stereotypes*. The former act as general and necessary classifications of persons and roles according to local cultural categories, while the latter are regarded as vivid but simple representations which *reduce* persons to a set of exaggerated, usually negative, character traits. Thus, 'stereotyping reduces, essentializes, naturalizes and fixes "difference" ' (Hall 1997c: 258). That stereotyping commonly involves the attribution of negative traits to persons who are different from ourselves points to the operation of *power* in the process of stereotyping and to its exclusionary role within the social, symbolic and moral order. Thus, Dyer suggests that 'types are instances which indicate those who live by the rules of society [social types] and those who the rules are designed to exclude [stereotypes]' (Dyer 1977: 29). Consequently, stereotypes focus on those 'abjected' or thrown out from the 'normal' order of things and simultaneously establishes who is 'us' and who is 'them'. Stereotyping is thus a staple mechanism of racism.

Images of black people

In a variety of ways, cultural representations within the west construct images of people of colour as a series of *problems,* objects and victims (Gilroy 1987). That is, black people are represented as the object rather than subject of history. They are designated as unable to effectively think or act for themselves. In this view, people of colour do not initiate activity or seek to control their own destiny, but are represented by others or act in response to others, notably white people. Subsequently, as objects and aliens from another place, black people pose a series of difficulties for white people, for example, as a foreign contaminating cultural presence, the perpetrators of crime or the passive victims of family disintegration. Too often, as we shall see, this is precisely how television represents people of colour.

In charting the transformations of racism in Britain, Gilroy (1987) argues that in the 1950s anxiety about black criminality within the police, judiciary and press was relatively low and concerned only the alleged association of black people with prostitution and gambling. This imagery of sexual squalor was combined throughout the late 1950s and early 1960s with the theme of housing shortages and overcrowding. During the late 1960s and the 1970s, racial discourse centred on immigration, the 'alien presence' in Britain and the 'threat' to national culture and law which this was claimed to pose. Subsequently, the idea that there was something intrinsically criminal about black culture began to take hold and the imagery, circulated through the press and television, of black youth as dope smoking muggers and/or urban rioters came to the fore. Thus, the alleged hedonism, evasion of work and criminality of black culture, and its implied difference from white culture, became the closely entwined motifs of British racism in the media.

Hall *et al.* (1978) have argued that in covering stories about 'mugging', journalists reproduce the assumption that street crime is solely the work of young black men. Further, journalists seek the views of the police, politicians and judges who declare that not only is street crime on the increase, but also something must be done about it in the form of heavier policing and harsher sentences. The news media report such comments as common sense concerns about rising crime and its association with black youth. The circle becomes complete when judges subsequently cite news coverage of crime as the expression of public concern and use it to justify the very much harsher sentences and increased police activity which they and politicians had called for. In so far as such increased police activity is directed to areas in which young black men live, because they have been seen as the perpetrators of such crime, this is liable to fuel confrontation between the police and black youth.

Racist stereotypes: colonial and plantation
Many of the more obvious racist stereotypes to be found in Britain and the USA echo colonial and slave history respectively, both of which are aspects of globalization. As Hall (1997c) argues, a central component of British imperial representations of black people was the theme of non-Christian savages in need of civilizing by British missionaries and adventurers. These images were subsequently transformed into what Hall calls 'commodity racism' whereby 'Images of colonial conquest were stamped on soap boxes . . . biscuit tins, whisky bottles, tea tins and chocolate bars' (McClintock cited Hall 1997c: 240). Such representations of white colonial power and black 'savagery' were gendered in that the 'heroes' of imperial Britain were male while the commodities on which such images appeared were frequently domestic and targeted at women. For example, Hall argues that,

> Soap symbolized this 'racializing' of the domestic world and the 'domestication' of the colonial world. In its capacity to cleanse and purify, soap acquired, in the fantasy world of imperial advertising, the quality of a fetish object. It apparently had the power to wash black skin white as well as being capable of washing off the soot, grime and dirt of the industrial slums and their inhabitants – the unwashed poor – at home, while at the same time keeping the imperial body clean and pure in the racially polluted contact zones 'out there' in the Empire. In

the process, however, the domestic labour of women was often silently erased.

(Hall 1997c: 241)

American plantation images share the British concern with the binary of white civilization and black 'naturalness' and 'primitivism'. Black people were represented as naturally incapable of the refinements of white civiliz-ation, they were by nature lazy and best fitted for subordination to whites. Thus, the social and political inferiority of black people was represented as part of the inescapable God-given order of the universe. Not that US racial stereotypes were exactly the same as those in Britain. On the contrary, we need to recognize the existence and emergence of different historically specific forms of racism across the globe and of the subtle typologies within given cultural contexts. In the American context, Bogle (1973) argues that five distinct stereotypes are to be found in US films having their origin in plantation and slave images:

- *Toms:* good blacks, submissive, stoic
- *Coons:* slapstick entertainers, gamblers, 'no-account' 'niggers'
- *Tragic Mulattos:* beautiful, sexy, exotic mixed race women forever 'stained' with black blood
- *Mammies:* female house servants, big, strong, bossy but devoted and sub-servient to the white family
- *Bad Bucks:* big, strong, violent, oversexed male renegades.

Of course, what is the case for film is no less so for television, though the precise form of representation may differ somewhat.

Race and television

Ignoring people of colour
The first point to make regarding the representation and construction of race on western television is that members of ethnic groups other than whites have for a long time simply been ignored. Thus, in the USA, it was not until the late 1960s and early 1970s that we begin to find any black families in television drama (Cantor and Cantor 1992). Further, the Kerner Commis-sion, set up to examine the unrest that spread across urban USA in the 1960s, argued that the US news media 'has too long basked in a white world, looking out of it, if at all, with whitemen's eyes and a white perspec-tive' (Kerner Commission 1968: 389) reflecting what the commission called 'the indifference of white America'.

In 1980s Britain, the Commission for Racial Equality (1984) noted that while in the USA black people were being seen more frequently on television, in the UK this was still not the case, with only 5 per cent of dramatic characters being black and only 3 of 62 non-white appearances being in leading roles. For example, one criticism of British soaps has been the representation of community as, on the whole, exclusively white, heterosexual and working class. For the majority of its existence *Coronation Street* has had few black characters, somewhat odd for a programme with realist pretensions located in multicultural Manchester. Nor have US soaps from *Dallas* and *Dynasty* to *Melrose Place* and *Pacific Heights* much of a track record in terms of the representation of the American multi-ethnic population. Of course, the invisibility of black people within the media not only is incompatible within any kind of democratic role that it may be assumed to have, but also arguably promotes white ignorance about black people and black cultures. Media coverage which ignores black people places them outside of mainstream society, to be regarded as peripheral and irrelevant.

Kinds of representations

The second critical issue is focused on the kinds of representations which are constitutive of ethnicity and race as cultural identities. While the colonial and plantation images of 'savages' and 'sambos' are no longer common within British media, current stereotypes carry echoes or traces of those meanings. For example, black people in Britain are frequently represented as a problem, so that black youth in particular is associated with crime and civil disorder, or in terms of images drawn from a colonial past suggesting stupidity and ignorance. In the 1970s sitcom *Mind your Language*, set in an English language class, every single non-white community was reduced to a stereotype and the one 'these-foreigners-are-hilarious-because-they-all-talk-funny-don't-they' 'joke' (Medhurst 1989).

In the USA, the first television programme to feature black people was *Amos 'n Andy*, a so called comedy which has subsequently become a symbol for the way in which black people are degraded through the use of humour based on stereotypes. Indeed, the US film and television industry has a long history of presenting stereotypical images of black people drawn from the plantation tradition of the 'sambo' and 'brute' slave through the smooth liberals of the 1960s to the 'superspade' detectives of the mid-1970s. As Leab argues,

Yet whether Sambo or Superspade, the black image on screen has always lacked the dimension of humanity. With all too few exceptions this human dimension has been lacking in the movie treatment of the black ever since the 1890s, when the first motion picture was produced.

(Leab 1975: 5)

Historical legacy

The historical legacy of the representation of race is not to be lightly dismissed. However, if we are to understand the representation of race in the 1990s and beyond, then we must recognize that aspects of it have changed. For example, Campbell (1995) reports that in a study of 40 hours of US local news 'there was no evidence of intentional, blatant bigotry' and few examples of what he calls 'old-fashioned racism' (but a good deal of more subtle modern racism). Indeed, since the mid-1970s there have been some more positive attempts to construct discourses of Britain and the USA as multicultural societies. In these representations, a more pluralistic society is depicted in which the cultures and customs of different ethnic groups add to the richness and variety of society. In Britain, for example, *Empire Road* at least tried to centre on black family life and be funny without the use of racist humour and in the USA the black Huxtable family (*The Cosby Show*) stars in one of the most popular primetime comedies. Further, during the 1980s and 1990s there has been some expansion of the boundaries of representation in soaps. For example, the British serial *EastEnders* has tried to portray a wider cross-section of ethnic communities and characters.

Negative representations

This is not to say that such representations have not been without their justified criticisms, for example treating racism as a personal issue of illiberality rather than structured inequality or giving insufficient attention to the specificity of black culture. Indeed, modern representations of race in television continue to associate black people, specifically young men, with crime and social problems. According to Martindale (1986) and Campbell (1995), the most common portrayal of African Americans in newscasts is as criminals associated with guns and violence. Poor blacks in particular are constructed as a 'menace to society' having moved beyond the limits of acceptable behaviour through their association with crime, violence, drugs, gangs and teenage pregnancy. For H. Gray (1996), this is typified by the CBS documentary *Vanishing Family: Crisis in Black America*. This programme, he argues, associated normalcy with the (white) nuclear family and turned African American families into problems, while failing to attend to the more general transformation of family life occurring across the social spectrum.

More particularly, Gray argues that the documentary focused on the contrast between a number of caring and conscientious young African American women struggling to raise young children and a breed of feckless men hanging around on street corners. Though the programme contained references to what the television presenter called 'successful strong black families in America', these merely functioned to shift blame away from the structural and systematic character of racial inequality in the USA and redirected blame on to alleged individual weakness and moral deficiencies of poor black people.

It is useful to note Gray's argument that what might be regarded as 'positive' representations of African Americans do not always function positively, particularly when placed alongside other images of black people in the wider context of representations of race. In other words, the meanings associated with the representation of black people are both cumulative and *intertextual*. For example, the association of black people with crime and their depiction as a constant social problem is contrasted with, and arguably reinforced by, the more positive *assimilationist* imagery of contemporary sitcoms.

Assimilationist strategies

The Cosby Show's Huxtable family (along with talk show hosts such as Oprah Winfrey) represent black middle-class success and social mobility. Since the American dream dictates that success is open to all who are talented and work for it, an argument which, in circular fashion, *The Cosby Show*'s successful black family suggests is 'true', then, African American poverty must be at best an outcome of individual weakness and at worst a collective aspect of African American culture (since why else would black people be over represented in all the statistics of poverty and urban deprivation in the USA?). As Jhally and Lewis argue, 'The Huxtables' success implies the failure of a majority of black people . . . who have not achieved similar professional or material success' (Jhally and Lewis 1992: 137). Accordingly, while middle-class black American sitcoms stress not only material success but also the values of hard work, honesty, responsibility, and so forth, they obscure the argument that 'many individuals trapped in the underclass have the very same qualities but lack the options and opportunities to realise them' (H. Gray 1996: 142).

Entman (1990) argues that similar assimilationist strategies in local news, notably the use of black anchors, contributes to the idea that racism no longer exists in the USA. Not only does the presence of black authority figures on the screen suggest that racism is a thing of the past, but also their adoption of majority cultural views and common sense lends credence to the assimilationist vision. This view is supported by Campbell (1995) by way of his qualitative analysis of local American news coverage of the Martin Luther King holiday celebrations. This coverage, with one notable exception, depicted racism as a thing of the past and the holiday a celebration of King's success, rather than a reminder of the very failure of his historic vision to be materialized in the day-to-day reality of American life.

Ambiguities in the representation of race

It is apparent that contradictions are inherent in the imagery of black America and Britain, for black people are, at one and the same time, represented as at the poles of criminality and middle-class success. Race is held to be a current 'problem' and yet racism is held to be a thing of the past. As Hall (1997c) remarks, not only does racism often take this binary form – failure/success, good/bad, civilized/primitive – but also black people are required to be both things at the same time. In a sense, there is always an element of ambiguity in the representation of race.

Ambiguity and ambivalence in the representation of black people can be seen even when the effort is made to construct 'positive' images. For example, the prominence given to African American and black British sports men and women in the Olympics or in basketball and football is double edged. On the one hand this is a celebration and acceptance of black success, while on the other it can be seen as part of a process by which black success is *confined* to sport and black people depicted in stereotypical fashion as primarily physical rather than mental beings.

Similar ambiguity can be seen in a series of African American films which are closely associated with rap music, although more obviously positioned in the mainstream. These include the work of Marion Van Peebles (*New Jack City*) and John Singleton (*Boys N the Hood*), which Jacquie Jones (1996) describes as forming 'the new ghetto aesthetic'. On the one hand, these films are significant simply for the fact that they are Hollywood films made by African Americans; they have also been praised for their representation of the shocking life circumstances of some African Americans. On the other hand, they arguably 'codify a range of behaviours as uncharacteristic of the black experience as those represented in films made by whites' (Jones 1996: 41). Two facets of these films might be regarded as problematic:

- the depiction of black communities as racked by crime and violence whose causes are represented as lying with individual pathologies and whose solution is either more police or strong father figures
- the portrayal of women in the standard Bitch/Ho mode so that few if any can be defined apart from their relationships with men.

Too often in these films we get to know the men in terms of their personal histories and emotional torments whereas the women are *reduced* to being only tough and/or sexy. Of significance is the gendered character of the representation of race so that an exaggerated male macho style is held to be symbolic of black resistance to white power (hooks 1990). While for some black men the adoption of a hard and excessive form of masculinity has been a form of response to white power, since it offers a sense of self-worth and strength in the face of continual social disempowerment, this does not negate the undesirability of the Bitches/Ho binary or of 'Black Macho' (Wallace 1979).

It is important to consider the ambiguities of representation in relation to race and not to reduce the debate to a simple good/bad binary which elicits knee jerk accusations of 'racism' or demands for only positive images. After all, positive images, useful and desirable though they are in the context of so many stereotypes, do not necessarily undermine or displace negative representations. Indeed, it is not uncommon to find that what is considered to be a 'positive' image by some is attacked by others. For example, both the British series *EastEnders* and the US series *I'll Fly Away* consciously attempted to engage with realistic and positive representations of black people but have, nevertheless, been seen by some commentators as problematic.

EastEnders
EastEnders contains, as a consequence of deliberate policy, an array of black and Asian characters rarely seen on British television. The series goes beyond the representation of blackness as 'a problem' to allow black characters to take up active and significant dramatic roles. *EastEnders* does represent a multi-ethnic community and in a way which does not reduce black and Asian characters to one-dimensional representatives of 'the black experience'. Further, the programme contained the sympathetic representation of a mixed race relationship/marriage which, according to Bramlett-Solomon and Farwell (1996), is virtually absent from US soaps. However, the serial has also been attacked for stereotyping, for example representing British Asians as doctors and shopkeepers, and for ignoring the wider structural forms of racism by reducing it to individual character traits. It is also argued that the centrality of the white Beale family (and other traditional white East End characters) displaces black and Asian characters to the margins of representation so that they can never be a part of the core of the drama (see Daniels and Gerson 1989).

I'll Fly Away
The debate about *I'll Fly Away* centres on the representation of the central character Lily Harper and her relationship both to other characters, and to

the politics of the civil rights movement. For Karen Smith (1996), the series offered a character who, though a maid, was most definitely not a 'mammy'. Rather, Lily Harper was portrayed as an independent minded and wise woman who was active in the civil rights movement and not subordinated to the white family for whom she worked. Though Smith points out that other writers have indeed seen Lily Harper as a mammy, her core criticism is of the network who promoted the series with 'out-of-context' images suggesting that Lily *was* a stereotyped black maid. In other words, the Lily Harper character became, through the intertextual array of representations for different purposes, a site of contradictory and ambiguous meaning construction.

Representing difference and diversity

The demand for unambiguously positive images can be understood in terms of the need to show that black people are 'really as good as' or 'really as human as' white people in the context of the circulation of negative stereotypes and assimilationist expectations (West 1993). However, this strategy involves three problems.

- it rests on an essentialist version of black identity and promotes a homogenization of black people, obliterating differences of class, gender, sexuality, etc.
- it is difficult to know what an unambiguously positive image of black people, one that could not be accused of unrealistic stereotyping, would be
- it rests on reflectionist or realist conceptions of representation by which it would be possible to bring representations closer to 'real' black people. This is impossible for the 'real' is always already representation (see Chapter 1).

These arguments form part of a wider debate about what representation 'does'. A common call is for more accuracy and realism in relation to the representation of race. However, this is to employ a realist epistemology by which television mirrors the real world and is able, for better or worse, to illuminate our understanding of that world. However, as the discussion of language in Chapter 1 suggests, there are great difficulties with the realist **epistemology** which underpins the argument since television is not an objective or universal representation of the world, but a specific cultural construction. Representation is *constitutive* of race as cultural identity and is not a mirror or a distortion of it. No criteria can assess the accuracy of the representation of race, not least because there is no neutral archimedian point from which to assess either what race 'actually' is or whether representations are a distortion of what is 'really' the case.

Thus, Hall (1996d) has looked towards a 'politics of representation', which registers the arbitrariness of signification and seeks the recognition and willingness to live with difference. That is, rather than demand positive images alone, the politics of representation promotes representations which themselves explore power relations and deconstruct the black–white binary. Hall has seen such a politics in Kureishi's *My Beautiful Laundrette*, the photography of Robert Mapplethorpe, and the work of film maker Isaac Julien.

Such arguments revolve around the social and political consequences of constructing and disseminating specific discursive constructions of the world. The role of criticism becomes the development of a more profound understanding of our cultural and symbolic processes and the way in which they are connected to social, political and economic *power*. This would include evaluative criteria based on *difference* and *diversity* as political *values*, so that criticism becomes centred on questions of discourse, social relationships, power and its consequences. Such criticism does not require universal epistemological justification since it is made from within a tradition of cultural pluralism, which values equality and democracy, and is based on pragmatic comparison with other forms of social organization, and not on notions of universal reason or representation of the 'real world'. In other words, judgements are based on political/value justifications rather than on epistemological/universal truth claims. Consequently, once we have rid ourselves of the worst and most viscous of stereotyped representations, the issue may not be so much a question of positive images, but of the representation of the *difference* and *diversity* of peoples. Of course, such a claim is rarely made about whiteness *per se* where diversity is assumed.

Summary and conclusions

It has been argued that race, ethnicity and nationality are forms of identity which do not refer to fixed entities but are shifting and unstable discursive constructions. Nationality, for example, can be seen as a symbolic device, and an imagined community, which represents difference as unity. It was further suggested that, in the context of globalization, both the physical movement of peoples and the electronic distribution of 'culture' contributed to the development of hybrid identities. The concept of diaspora was explored as both a symbolic representation of hybridity and as the embodiment of the real experiences of actual peoples. Of significance is the way that global television marks a point of diaspora identification through the circulation of, for example, Rap videos.

Subsequently, we examined a number of representations of people of colour in British and US television. We noted a range of different stereotypes of black people including colonial and plantation images, the marginalization and criminalization of black communities, especially young black men, and a variety of assimilationist discourses. Though television does still produce and circulate clearly racist discourses, there have, nevertheless, been changes in approach to the question of race and I argued that representations of black people on television are frequently and fundamentally ambiguous and ambivalent. Such ambiguities are the site of cultural struggle over meaning rather than the fixing of definitive meanings for audiences. These struggles over the meaning of race as cultural identity take place within the context of globalization marked by the migration of peoples and the electronic circulation of cultural representations by television.

Further reading

Brah, A. (1996) *Cartographies of Diaspora*. London: Routledge.

Gilroy, P. (1993) *The Black Atlantic*. London: Verso.

Gray, H. (1996) Television, Black Americans, and the American dream, in V. Berry and C. Manning-Miller (eds) *Mediated Messages and African American Culture*. Thousand Oaks, CA and London: Sage.

Hall, S. (1996d) New ethnicities, in D. Morley and D-K. Chen (eds) *Stuart Hall*. London: Routledge.

hooks, b (1990) *Yearning: Race, Gender, and Cultural Politics*. Boston, MA: South End Press.

4

SEXED SUBJECTS AND GENDERED REPRESENTATIONS

Just as it was suggested in Chapter 3 that race is a social construction, so, it will be argued here, are sex and gender even though we may feel them to be deeply embedded in our psyches and naturalized in our cosmos. Traditionally, sex has been taken to be a stable biological marker over which the cultural expectations of gender are laid. However, it will be suggested here that both sex and gender are discursive productions. This will be argued through a body of work which brings together discourse theory and psychoanalysis.

Overall, it will be argued that identities based on sex and gender are socially produced descriptions with which we identify and not universal categories of nature or metaphysics. Of course, some of the most widely disseminated cultural representations of sex and gender are to be found on television, a discussion of which forms the second half of the chapter, wherein we explore both the stereotyping of women and attempts to destabilize this imagery. The representations of gender which television produces and circulates are themselves constitutive of gender as a cultural identity. Or, to put it another way, the two halves of this chapter – on the social construction of sexed subjects and the representation of gender (including on television) – are constitutive of each other.

The social construction of sex and gender

For most people, though not all, the identification of oneself as female or male, based on particular bodies and their attributes, is a foundation stone of self-identity. This common sense view can encourage a form of biological determinism which suggests that the biochemical and genetic structures of human beings determine the behaviour of women and men in quite definite and specific ways. Thus, men may be regarded as 'naturally' more aggressive, domineering, hierarchically oriented and power hungry while women are seen as nurturing, child rearing and domestically oriented. However, few within the field of cultural studies would disagree with Connell's conclusion that 'there is no evidence at all of strong determination in this sense. . . . And the evidence of cross-cultural and historical diversity in gender is overwhelming' (Connell 1995: 229).

Accordingly, a good deal of sociological, cultural and feminist (Chapter 1) writing has sought to challenge biological determinism through the conceptual division between sex and gender, where sex represents the biology of the body and gender the cultural assumptions and practices which govern the social construction of women, men and their social relations. It is subsequently argued that it is the social, cultural and political discourses and practices of gender which lie at the root of women's inequality. Nicholson (1995) calls this the 'coat-rack' view of self-identity by which the body is viewed as a rack upon which cultural meanings are thrown. As she argues, 'one crucial advantage of such a position for feminists was that it enabled them to postulate both commonalities and differences among women' (Nicholson 1995: 41). Further, it is argued that since gender is a cultural construct, it is open to change in ways that biology may not be. What is important about this displacement of biological essentialism is the struggle over 'gender as sign', that is, the cultural representation of gender (including on television). Debates about biology, signification, essentialism, difference and equality within feminism have cohered around the question 'What is a woman?'.

Essentialism: women's difference

An essentialist answer to the question 'What is a woman?' would take the category 'woman' as reflecting an underlying identity based on either biology or universal patterns of culture. Some feminist work, for example Collard and Contrucci's (1988) ecofeminist *Rape of the Wild*, does seem to rely on a form of biological essentialism in its arguments that all women are linked by childbearing bodies and innate ties to the natural earth and to egalitarian, nurturance-based values. Likewise Rich (1986), who celebrates women's difference from men and locates its source in motherhood, which is condemned in its historical modes of oppression, but celebrated for its female power and potentialities.

However, most of the arguments which celebrate women-cultures and push towards seeing women as fundamentally different from men are linguistic and cultural, even as they are based on signifiers of the female body. For example, Daly (1987) again links women to nature stressing not only the material and psychological oppression of women but also the radical celebration and separation of woman-culture. Nevertheless, since much of her argument revolves around the language used to describe women and its power over them, her arguments appear closer to a form of cultural rather than biological essentialism. A clearly culturally founded argument for women's difference comes from Gilligan (1982) and her study of moral reasoning in which she argues that while men are concerned with an 'ethic of justice', women are more centred on an 'ethics of care'. Women, it is argued, develop, for cultural reasons, *a Different Voice* from men which stresses contextual and specific forms of argument in contrast to the more abstract thinking of men.

Luce Irigaray's interpretation

An alternative, psychoanalytic and philosophical route to women's difference comes from Irigaray, who theorizes a pre-symbolic 'space' or 'experience' which is unavailable to men. This is constituted by a feminine *jouissance* or sexual pleasure, play and joy, which is outside of intelligibility. Indeed, Irigaray (1985a, 1985b) has been at the forefront of attempts to write the unwritable, to inscribe the feminine through *écriture feminine* (woman's writing) and *le parler femme* (womanspeak). Irigaray proceeds by means of a deconstructive reading of western philosophy which for her seeks to guarantee the masculine order and its claims to self-origination and unified **agency**. In this context, Irigaray tries to read philosophical texts for their absences, the feminine that is excluded. Of course, she is faced with a problem, namely of trying to critique philosophy for its exclusions while using the very language of that philosophy and in doing so enacting what she seeks to expose. Her strategy is to 'mime' the discourse of philosophy, to cite it and talk its language but in ways which are not a reiteration of the original but a questioning of the very capacity of philosophy to ground its own claims. Womanspeak mimes phallogocentrism (male centred language) only to expose what is covered over (Irigaray 1985b). For Irigaray's supporters she represents a bold attempt to

- assert the specificity of the feminine
- break with the logic of identity and of masculinity
- celebrate the undefinable *jouissance* of women
- tactically and successfully mime and expose phallocentric thinking.

As such, Irigaray can be seen as offering a challenge to a masculine symbolic order through poetic writing. However, critics have accused her of essentialism, either in the assertion of the primacy of female biology or a distinct female imaginary which undermines the very attempt to explore the *construction* of sexuality and subjectivity. Here, the positing of women as imaginative, poetic, feeling and so on could be said to mirror patriarchal discourse itself which sees reason as male and emotion as female.

In contrast to Irigaray's apparent essentialism there is another strand of feminism which, in forwarding arguments about sex equality in the institutions and practices of social formations, rejects any form of essential difference between the capabilities of men and women. Here it is argued that no essential sex differences exist and that those which are apparent are insignificant in relation to arguments for social equality. That is, femininities and masculinities are regarded as solely and only social constructions.

Anti-essentialism: the construction of femininity

In contrast to Daly or Irigaray, Alcoff (1989) regards any emphasis on a special and benign female character as wrong not only because there is a lack of evidence for innate difference, but also on the political grounds that 'it is in danger of solidifying an important bulwark for sexist oppression: the belief in innate "womanhood" to which we must all adhere lest we be deemed either inferior or not "true" women' (Alcoff 1989: 104). Equality, rather than difference, is also stressed in the work of Catherine Mackinnon (1987, 1991), who regards a woman-culture as 'making quilts'. In doing so, Mackinnon upholds the sex–gender distinction, arguing that the latter is fundamentally a matter of social power founded on men's dominance of institutionalized heterosexuality. Thus, gender is a hierarchical social construct which overlays biological distinctions and, though not all men have equal power and not all women are subject to the same forms of oppression, her view of feminist arguments as 'we're as good as you. Anything you can do, we can do. Just get out of the way' (Mackinnon 1987: 32) stresses equality.

However, as Scott has argued, the equality–difference debate relies on a false binary since it is possible for equality and difference to coexist, for 'equality is not the elimination of difference, and difference does not preclude equality' (Scott 1990: 137–8). Further, just as Scott deconstructs the equality–difference binary, so the very distinction between sex as biology and gender as a cultural construction is being broken down within a good deal of contemporary cultural theory on the grounds that there is in principle no access to biological 'truths' which lie outside of cultural discourses. That is, sex, like gender, is a discursive construction so that the boundary between the two categories breaks down. In this view, the body does not disappear:

Rather, it becomes a variable rather than a constant, no longer able to ground claims about the male/female distinction across large sweeps of history but still there as always a potentially important element in how the male/female distinction *gets played out in any specific society.*

(Nicholson 1995: 43–4; my emphasis)

Michel Foucault's work

A good deal of these anti-essentialist arguments about subjectivity, femininity and masculinity take their inspiration from the work of Foucault (see Weedon 1997) for whom, as we saw in Chapter 1, subjectivity is a discursive production. Alongside hospitals and the penal system, the body and sexuality were major themes in Foucault's work. Sexuality is regarded by Foucault as the central power locus for the production of subjectivity in western societies, for subjectivity is coterminous with sexuality as subjects are constituted through the production of 'sex' and the control of the body. Foucault is concerned with the way in which sex is 'put into discourse' and, far from arguing that a 'natural' sexuality is repressed and prohibited, Foucault suggests that discourses of polymorphous sexualities have proliferated and been disseminated through medicine, the church, psychoanalysis, education programmes and demography. In particular, the confessional, developed by Catholicism, has been adapted and taken over by other institutions and has become the basis of discursive 'subjection'. For example, in contemporary culture, the 'therapy TV' of television talk shows such as *Springer* and *Oprah* not only is based on the confessional but also plays a significant role in regulating the boundaries of gender and delineating the morality of relationships.

For Foucault, the proliferating discourses of sexuality analyse, classify and regulate it in ways which not only produce particular kinds of sexed subjects but also make sexuality a cornerstone of subjectivity. For example, Foucault argues that from the early eighteenth century onwards women's bodies were subject (to become a subject and to be subjected) to the discourse of modern science which produced them as hysterical and nervous while reducing them to their reproductive system. Thus, there was,

a three fold process whereby the feminine body was analysed – qualified and disqualified – as being thoroughly saturated with sexuality; whereby it was integrated into the sphere of medical practices, by reason of a pathology intrinsic to it; whereby, finally, it was placed in organic communication with the social body (whose regulatory fecundity it was supposed to ensure), the family space (of which it had to be a substantial and functional element), and the life of children (which it produced and had to guarantee, by virtue of a biologico-moral responsibility lasting through the entire period of the children's education): the mother, with her negative image of 'nervous women', constituted the most visible form of this hysterization.

(Foucault 1979: 104)

Foucault's work has been subject to feminist criticism for, paradoxically, neglecting 'to examine the gendered character of many disciplinary techniques' (McNay 1992: 11). Foucault, it is argued, treats bodies as gender neutral with little specificity beyond a male norm since he does not explore how men and women are related differently to the disciplinary institutions he describes. Further, Foucault's early description of subjects as 'docile bodies' has been a cause for concern to feminists in so far as it robs subjects of the agency central to feminism as a politics. However, it is also arguable that Foucault's (1984, 1986, 1987) later work which is centred on notions of 'techniques of the self' does reintroduce agency and the possibility of resistance and change. That is, ethical considerations may provide the basis of a self-fashioning and a route for feminist political activity. Significantly, in Chapter 5 I argue that talk about soap opera is frequently centred on questions of relationship and gender ethics. That is, television provides resources for audiences to discuss and regulate what it means to be a man or a woman.

Deconstructing sexual identity

Overall, what is being argued for here is the, in principle, infinite plasticity of human sexuality and gender which is moulded and regulated into specific forms under particular historical and cultural conditions. Of course, most societies have deployed, and continue to operate with, a binary male–female distinction to which is attached cultural expectations which are detrimental to women. Indeed, as we shall see later, television plays a significant part in the regulation of gender. However, the cultural variations that exist between women (and between men), based, for example, not only on differences of class, ethnicity or age but also on differences about what it means to be a woman, suggest that there is no universal cross-cultural category of 'woman' (or 'man') that is shared by all. That is, there are multiple modes of femininity (and masculinity) which are enacted not only by different women, but also, potentially, by the same woman under different circumstances. As such, 'women are constantly confronted with the cultural task of finding out what it means to be a women, of marking out the boundaries between the feminine and unfeminine' (Ang 1996: 94). This question has been approached by, amongst others, Julia Kristeva and Judith Butler.

Julia Kristeva: sexual identity as representation

Kristeva holds a firmly anti-essentalist view of sexual identity, that is, there is no essence that defines a woman/man or the feminine/masculine. Thus, Kristeva has argued that 'To believe that one "is a woman" is almost as absurd and obscurantist as to believe that one "is a man" ' (cited Moi 1985: 163). Of course, we may identify with gendered identities, we may act as if gendered categories were essential and we may find it necessary for political reasons to continue to campaign as women (i.e. **strategic essentialism**) but one cannot *be* a woman for sexual identities as opposites can come into being only after entry into the *symbolic* order. That is, sexual identity is not an essence but a matter of representation.

Mother identification and father identification

According to Kristeva, a small child faces the choice of mother identification and subsequent marginality within the symbolic order, or father identification giving access to symbolic dominance, but wiping out pre-Oedipal mother identification. These choices face *both* male and female infants and, though the resolution of the Oedipus complex leads boys more easily and commonly to father identification/masculinity and girls to femininity, nevertheless, degrees of masculinity and femininity exist in biological men and women. Femininity then is a condition or *subject position* of *marginality* which some men, for example avante garde artists whose writing disrupts the symbolic order, can also occupy. Indeed, it is the patriarchal symbolic order that tries to fix all women as feminine and men as masculine and thus position all women as the marginal 'second sex'.

Given that sex and gender are relational social and historical constructs, both representations of women and the subject positions and identifications available to women are open to change. Indeed, Kristeva suggests not only that women occupy a range of subject positions but that a new symbolic space and subject position is opening itself up to women. In particular, she explores the idea that a new generation of feminists is emerging who seek to reconcile the linear time of history and politics with the cyclical gestation time of motherhood. That is, the space is now available for women to intermingle motherhood (and difference) with the politics of equality and the symbolic order. In this, Kristeva advocates a third position in which the very dichotomy man/woman as an opposition between two rival entities may be understood as belonging to *metaphysics*. What can 'identity', even 'sexual identity', mean in a new theoretical and scientific space where the very notion of identity is challenged? . . . What I mean is, first of all, the demassification of the problematic of *difference*, . . . in order that the struggle, the implacable difference, the violence be conceived in the very place where it operates with the maximum intransigence, in other words, in the personal and sexual identity itself, so as to make it disintegrate in its very nucleus.

(Kristeva 1986: 209)

Balancing femininity and masculinity within the individual

Kristeva is suggesting that the struggle over sexual identities takes place within each individual, rather than between two opposing male–female masses, and concerns the balance of masculinity and femininity within specific men and women. This struggle, she suggests, could result in the deconstruction of sexual and gendered identities understood in terms of marginality within the symbolic order. This stresses the singularity and multiplicity of persons as well as the relativity of symbolic and biological existence. 'The time has perhaps come to emphasise the *multiplicity* of female expressions and preoccupations' (Kristeva 1986: 193; my emphasis).

Judith Butler: between Foucault and psychoanalysis

The attempt by Kristeva to deconstruct the very idea of sexual identity is one shared by Judith Butler. Though Foucault rejected psychoanalysis as yet another network of disciplinary power, Butler has attempted to work with and between the work of Foucault and psychoanalysis. She accepts the Foucauldian argument that regulatory power produces the subjects it controls working as a normative ideal by which subjects are formed. However, she also suggests a return to psychoanalysis in order to pursue 'the question of how certain regulatory norms form a "sexed" subject in terms that establish the indistinguishability of psychic and bodily formation' (Butler 1993: 22).

Butler reads psychoanalysis in a way which opens up a space in which to discuss how regulatory norms are invested with psychic power through processes of identification which are never perfect, complete nor exclusive. In Foucauldian fashion, Butler argues that discourse is the means by which we understand what bodies are; in a sense, discourse brings bodies into view in particular ways. Thus,

The category of 'sex' is, from the start, normative; it is what Foucault

has called a 'regulatory ideal'. In this sense, then, 'sex' not only functions as a norm, but is part of a regulatory practice that produces the
bodies it governs, that is, whose regulatory force is made clear as a kind
of productive power, the power to produce – demarcate, circulate,
differentiate – the bodies it controls. Thus, 'sex' is a regulatory ideal
whose materialisation is compelled, and this materialisation takes place
(or fails to take place) through certain highly regulated practices. In
other words, 'sex' is an ideal construct which is forcibly materialised
through time. It is not a simple fact or static condition of a body, but a
process whereby regulatory norms materialise 'sex' and achieve this
materialisation through a forcible reiteration of those norms.

(Butler 1993: 1–2)

To put this another way, the discourses of sex are ones which, through repetition of the acts they guide, bring sex into view as a necessary norm. Sex is
a construction, but an *indispensable* one which forms subjects and governs
the materialization of bodies. This view does not mean that 'everything is
discourse'; rather, as Butler argues, discourse and the materiality of bodies
are indissoluble.

Citational performativity
Butler conceives of sex and gender in terms of citational **performativity**
where the performative is 'that discursive practice which enacts or produces
that which it names' (Butler 1993: 13) through citation and reiteration of the
norms or conventions of the 'law' (in its symbolic, Lacanian sense). A performative in speech act theory would be the statement within a marriage ceremony 'I pronounce you . . .' which puts into effect the relation that it
names. By way of further example, Butler argues that judges in criminal and
civil law do not originate the law or its authority but cite the conventions of
the law which is consulted and invoked. However, this is an appeal to an
authority which has no origin or universal foundations; rather, the very
practice of citation produces the authority which is cited and thus reconsti-
tutes the law. Consequently, the maintenance of the law is a matter of
reworking a set of already operative conventions and involves iterability,
repetition and citationality.

In the same way, Butler argues that 'sex' is always produced as a reiteration of hegemonic norms which can be read as a kind of performativity which
is always derivative. The 'assumption' of sex, which is not a singular act or
event but an iterable practice, is secured through being repeatedly performed.
Thus, the statement 'it's a girl' initiates a process by which 'girling' is compelled. That is, 'Femininity is thus not the product of choice, but the forcible

citation of a norm . . . this citation of the gender norm is necessary in order to qualify as a "one", to become viable as a "one" ' (Butler 1993: 232). Not only is performativity not a singular act, for it is always a reiteration of a set of norms, but also it should not be understood as a performance given by a self-conscious intentional actor; rather, the performance of sex is compelled by a regulatory apparatus of heterosexuality. Indeed, the very idea of an intentional sexed actor is a discursive production of performativity itself, thus, 'gender is *performative* in the sense that it constitutes as an effect that very subject it appears to express' (Butler 1991: 24). Of course, the regulatory apparatus of heterosexuality is one which is constantly recited and reiterated on television in a variety of adverts, dramas, news reports, serials, and so on.

Instability of identity
Butler combines the reworking of discourse and speech act theory with psychoanalysis to argue that the 'assumption' of sex is also a question of identification with the normative phantasm of 'sex'. Sex is a symbolic position assumed under threat of punishment (for example, of symbolic castration or abjection). Here, the symbolic is rethought as a series of normative injunctions which secure the borders of sex through the threat of psychosis and abjection (an exclusion, a throwing out, a rejection). Identification may be understood as a kind of affiliation and expression of emotional tie with an idealized fantasized object (person, body part) or normative ideal. It is grounded in fantasy, projection and idealization. However, identification is not an intentional imitation of a model or conscious investment in subject positions, but is indissoluble from the very formation of subjects. It is coterminous with the emergence of an ego. Further, like Rose (1997), psychoanalysis highlights for Butler the very *instability of identity*. Since identification is with a fantasy or idealization, it can never be coterminous with 'real' bodies or gendered practices; there is always a gap or slipping away of identification. Further, identifications can be multiple and need not involve the repudiation of all other positions.

The role of drag
Butler is perhaps best known for her argument that forms of drag can destabilize and recast gender norms through a resignification of the ideals of gender (Butler 1990). Through a miming of gender norms, drag can be subversive to the extent that it reflects on the performative character of gender. That is, drag suggests that all gender is a form of performativity and as such destabilizes the claims of hegemonic heterosexual masculinity as the origin which is imitated. Rather, hegemonic heterosexuality is itself an imitative performance which is forced to repeat its own idealizations. The fact that it must

reiterate itself suggests that heterosexuality is beset by anxieties that it can never fully overcome. That is, the need for reiteration underlines the very insecurity of heterosexual identifications and gender positions, for why else would they need to be continually repeated? However, we should take Butler's argument only as indicative of one kind of possible subversive activity for, as she points out, drag is at best always ambivalent and can be itself a reiteration and affirmation of the Law of the Father and heterosexuality. Indeed, for Butler, *all* identity categories are necessary fictions which, though we have to continue using them, should simultaneously be interrogated.

Infinite plasticity of gender

Butler, Kristeva and others have argued for the, in principle, infinite plasticity of human sexuality and gender which is moulded and regulated into specific forms under particular historical and cultural conditions. Consequently, there are multiple modes of femininity (and masculinity) which are enacted not only by different women, but also, potentially, by the same women under different circumstances. As Ang and Hermes (1996) have argued,

> What we have tried to clarify, then, is the importance of recognising that there is no prearticulated gender identity. Despite the force of hegemonic gender discourse, the actual content of being a woman or a man and the rigidity of the dichotomy itself are highly variable, not only across cultures and historical times, but also, at a more micro-social and even psychological level, amongst and within women and men them-selves. Gender identity, in short, is both multiple and partial, ambiguous and incoherent, permanently in process of being articulated, disarticulated and rearticulated.
>
> (Ang and Hermes 1996: 125)

Needless to say, television plays a part in the reiteration of the heterosexual ideal through representations of women and men which attempt to fix the fluidity of meanings which surround femininity and masculinity. That is, television is constituted by, and constitutive of, gendered identities in quite specific mythic ways while simultaneously drawing from the wider cultural repertoire of gender representations.

Gender, representation and television

A good deal of feminist writing in the field of culture has been concerned with the representation of gender and of women in particular. As Evans

(1997) comments, in the first place there was a concern to demonstrate that women had played a part in culture, and in literature in particular, in the face of their omission from the canon of good works. This was coterminous with a concern for the kinds of representations of women which were made by men. That is, 'the thesis that gender politics were absolutely central to the very project of representation' (Evans 1997: 72).

In the earlier feminist studies an assumption was commonly made that representation was a direct expression of social reality and/or a potential and actual distortion of that reality. That is, representations of women reflected male attitudes and the position of women in society, often through the misrepresentation of 'real' women. This is sometimes known as the 'images of women' perspective.

Images of women

In this approach the concept of the stereotype occupies a prominent place. A stereotype, as we noted in Chapter 3, involves the reduction of persons to a set of exaggerated, usually negative, character traits. Thus, 'stereotyping reduces, essentializes, naturalizes and fixes "difference"' (Hall 1997c: 258) and through the operation of *power* marks the boundaries between the 'normal' and the 'abjected', 'us' and 'them'. In this context, Meehan (1983) analysed the stereotypes into which women are commonly cast on US television. Her study combined a quantitative analysis, which counted the number and kind of representations of women, with a qualitative interpretation of women's roles and power(lessness) within those representations. Overall, she suggests that representations on television cast 'good' women as submissive, sensitive and domesticated while 'bad' women are rebellious, independent and selfish. More specifically, Meehan (1983) identifies the following as common stereotypes:

- *the imp:* rebellious, asexual, tomboy
- *the goodwife:* domestic, attractive, home-centred
- *the harpy:* aggressive, single
- *the bitch:* sneak, cheat, manipulative
- *the victim:* passive, suffers violence or accidents
- *the decoy:* apparently helpless, actually strong
- *the siren:* sexually lures men to a bad end
- *the courtesan:* inhabits saloons, cabaret, prostitution
- *the witch:* extra power, but subordinated to men
- *the matriarch:* authority of family role, older, desexed.

Meehan concludes that 'American viewers have spent more than three decades watching male heroes and their adventures, muddied visions of boyhood adolescence replete with illusions of women as witches, bitches, mothers and imps' (Meehan 1983: 131).

Affirmation and denial

Of course, it is not simply US television that represents women in this way. Indeed, Gallagher's (1983) survey of women in the media suggests a consistent *global* depiction of women as commodified and stereotyped into the binary images of 'good' and 'bad' women. For example, Krishnan and Dighe (1990) argue that two main trends were evident in their study of the representation of women on Indian television, those of affirmation and denial. Affirmation of a limited definition of womanhood as passive and subordinate being tied to housework, husbands and children. Denial of the creativity, activity and individuality of women, particularly in relation to work and the public sphere.

In relation to television fiction, they report that men were the principle characters in much larger numbers than women (105 men to 55 women) and while men were represented in a range of occupations, most women (34) were depicted as housewives. Each of the principle characters were described on the basis of 88 polar opposite personality attributes and analysis revealed that the most common characteristics ascribed to men and women were:

Male characters	*Female characters*
self-centred	sacrificing
decisive	dependent
self-confident	emotional/sentimental
seeing a place in the larger world	anxious to please
conniving	defining the world through family
dignified	relations
dominant	maternal

Women were further stereotyped into the idealized and deviant. The ideal woman was caring and maternal. She was supportive of men in their ambitions but had none of her own, being sacrificing, empathic and home-centred. As a passive wife/daughter she accepted male control and was devoted to the men in her life, for example, defending even the most reprehensible of husbands in an unquestioning and submissive fashion. On the other hand, deviant women were domineering of their husbands and did not remain at home to look after the family. Rather, in having personal ambitions, they broke up family ties, disrupted male bonding and were not understanding or accommodating enough.

Epistemological problems

Illuminating though such studies are, the 'images of women' approach faces an epistemological problem in so far as it asserts the truth and falsity of representations. For example, Gallagher (1983) describes the world-wide representation of women as demeaning, damaging and *unrealistic*. As Moi comments, an 'images of women' approach 'is equivalent to studying *false* images of women constructed by both sexes because the "image" of women in literature is invariably defined in opposition to the "real person" whom literature somehow never quite manages to convey to the reader' (Moi 1985: 44–5). The central problem is, as was argued in Chapter 1, that the 'real' is always already a representation and there is no archimedian point from which to juxtapose the real with representations.

Later studies informed by poststructuralism regard all representations as cultural constructions and not as reflections of a real world. Consequently, studies became centred on how representations are produced in the context of social power and what the potential consequences for gender relations, and women in particular, might be. That is, not on the basis of representational adequacy, but on a *politics of representation* in which the marginality or subordination of women can be understood as a constitutive effect of representation realized or resisted by living persons. This approach explores 'women as a sign' (Cowie 1978) and the *subject positions* constructed for women by representations.

Subject positions of femininity

A subject position is that perspective or set of regulated discursive meanings from which the text or discourse makes sense. It is that subject with which we must identify in order for the discourse to be meaningful. In identifying with this subject position the text subjects us to its rules, it seeks to construct us as a certain kind of subject or person. For example:

> Addressing us in our private personae, ads sell us, as women, not just commodities but also our personal relationships in which we are feminine: how we are/should be/can be a certain feminine woman, whose attributes in relation to men and the family derive from the use of these commodities . . . a woman is nothing more than the commodities she wears: the lipstick, the tights, the clothes and so on are 'woman'.
>
> (Winship 1981: 218)

Thus, Winship argues that advertising constructs subject positions for women which place them in the patriarchal work of domesticity, child care, beautification and 'catching men'. Women are to be mothers, housewives, sexually attractive and so forth.

The slender body

Among the more powerful and influential representations of women that western television, and advertising in particular, promotes is the 'slender body' as a disciplinary cultural norm (Bordo 1993). That is, slenderness and a concern with diet and self-monitoring is a preoccupation of western media culture and its interest in a 'tighter, smoother, more constrained body profile'. Consequently, adverts target bulge, fat or flab and the desirability of flat stomachs and cellulite management. Of course, as Bordo (1993) goes on to argue, the slender body is a gendered body for the image, and subject position, of the slender body is usually female. Slenderness is a contemporary ideal for female attractiveness and girls and women are culturally more prone to eating disorders than men.

Paradoxically, television offers us images of desirable foods while proposing that we eat low calorie items and buy exercise equipment. In the face of this contradiction, Bordo argues, the capacity for self-control and the containment of fat is posed in moral as well as physical terms. That is, the choice to diet and exercise is regarded as an aspect of self-fashioning and the production of an appropriate form of gendered identity with a firm body as a symbol of the 'correct' attitude. The failure to exert such control, symbolically manifested in obesity and anorexia, is disciplined through, among other things, television talk shows which feature portrayals of 'eating-disorders' or the struggles of the obese to lose weight. The *Oprah Winfrey Show*, for example, has placed the presenter's struggle with weight gain at the centre of its strategy to humanize her.

The independent mother

In arguing that texts construct stereotypes and subject positions about and for women, we should not imagine that these representations remain static. For example, Woodward (1997) discusses the changing representation of motherhood in contemporary culture and notes the emergence of a new 'independent mother' representation which is not an idealized domesticated figure concerned only with child care but is supportive of independence and work for women/mothers. Woodward argues that the pleasures of this subject position lie in the fantasy of being a mother *and* having a career *and* being able to explore one's individuality *and* looking attractive.

Post-colonial women

It might be argued that the subject position of women assumed in much of the discussion above is that of white women. However, globalization in conjunction with the influence of black feminism and post-colonial theory has placed the intersection of ethnicity and gender more firmly at the centre of debates, even within the western academy. In a post-colonial context, not only are women important as images of the purity and reproduction of the nation, they carry a double burden of being colonized by imperial powers and subordinated by colonial and native men.

Said (1978) has argued that Orientalism is a set of western discourses of power that have constructed an Orient, have orientalized the Orient, in ways which depend on and reproduce the positional superiority and hegemony of the west. Orientalism is a general group of ideas that are shot through with European superiority, including racism and imperialism, elaborated and distributed through a variety of texts and practices. It is a system of representations that brought the Orient into western learning and includes Flaubert's encounter with an Egyptian courtesan, which produced an influential image of the Oriental woman who never spoke for herself, never showed her emotions and lacked agency or history. That is, the sexually beguiling dark maiden of male power-fantasy.

In this context, Spivak (1993) has argued that the 'subaltern cannot speak', by which she means that poor women in colonial contexts neither have the conceptual language to speak nor the ear of colonial and indigenous men to listen. It is not that women cannot literally open their mouths, but that there are no subject positions within the discourse of colonialism which allow them to speak. They are thus condemned to silence.

According to Krishnan and Dighe (1990), the representation of the idealized woman on Indian television as subservient wife is embedded in and drawn from the Hindu *dharma shastras* or sources of tradition and right conduct such as the *Ramayana* and *Mahabharata*. These texts also provide the ideal moral universe and ideological structure for a whole series of popular Hindi films produced in Bombay that transform and rework their narratives and value systems (Mishra 1985). Not only are such films shown on television (and the *Ramayana* and *Mahabharata* were themselves serialized on Indian TV) but Gillespie (1995) reports that they are widely watched within the British Indian diaspora. Thus, they are likely to have been seen by the British Asian girls discussed in Chapter 5 so that representations of women in *EastEnders* and *Neighbours* (western soap operas) are juxtaposed with those of *Suhagg, Ek Hi Bhool* or *Dilwale Dulhania Le Jayenge* (Hindi movies).

Bollywood Wives
The title of one Hindi film, *Suhaag*, connotes a symbol of marriage that is a continuing motif of the movie, which acts as a guide to what constitutes a virtuous woman (Bahia 1997; see also Dasgupta and Hedge 1988 and Rajan 1991 as sources of the following discussion). These include the characteristics of chastity, patience and selflessness, which are exemplified by the central woman, 'Maa', who, abandoned by her villainous husband, brings up her sons without straying from traditional boundaries. Her emblematic status is signified by her being dressed at all times in a respectable sari, which covers her body, having her hair tied back and always covering her head in the presence of a man as a mark of respect. In contrast, the 'evil' woman in the film is dressed in a bright multi-coloured sari and has her head uncovered.

Throughout the film it is Maa's role to bring up her sons in the correct and respectable way at whatever cost to herself. Indeed, since one son is kidnapped and becomes a villain while the other stays with her and becomes virtuous, the film signals the significance of the mother's place, whose sacrifices must be endured for personal honour and the social good. Despite her husband's lack of acknowledgement of her existence, Maa continues to keep her Gharbarchoth (a traditional sacrifice in which she goes without food for one day each year to enhance her husband's life) and later when he reappears subordinates herself to him despite his continual betrayal of her trust. Above all things she must seek to save her marriage without which she has no identity.

It is not that popular Hindi films have not tried to represent more independent and assertive women, but rather, that such women are frequently depicted as coming to undesirable ends. For example, in *Ek Hi Bhool*, the core character of Satanna is represented as assertive and unwilling to be mistreated by men. However, the subject position offered to the audience is one in which Satanna's self-reliance is cast as selfishness and vain ambition, which cause her to lose her husband. In time, Satanna comes to learn that she was fortunate to have married Ram who provided for her and was kind to her in ways not available to many other Indian women. Indeed, he later defends her honour when no one else will, causing her to beg at his feet for forgiveness thereby restoring their marriage and the natural order of the universe.

In a similar way, the film *Laadla* represents the independent factory-owning woman Shittel as a heartless character with a reprehensible disregard for tradition. She declares that even after marriage she will remain number one with her husband below her. These 'unnatural acts' are contrasted to benevolent women, for example Kajool, who is more passive and respectful of the position of women in Indian society as signified by her clothing (a sari that covers her body) and repression of her own feelings for Shittel's husband. Again, the independent woman must learn the errors of her ways and Shittel is rejected by her entire family before falling at her husband's feet to beg his forgiveness. In the final scene, dressed in a traditional sari serving her husband his lunch, she is a much happier and contented person.

However, not all representations of Indian women depict them as subordinate. For example, it is arguable that the popular Hindi film *Dilwale Dulhania Le Jayenge* offers us a young independently minded woman who is modern and self-reliant but treated sympathetically by the film. Although one can read the film in a way that ultimately returns her to male power, she is a departure from the stereotypes of *Ek Hi Bhool* and *Laadla*. Further, the British-made *Bahji on the Beach* offers an appreciative and subtle treatment of a group of British Asian women. Indeed, theorists have been interested not only in subject positions that seek to fix the character of femininity but also those which are argued to destabilize them.

Madonna's videos

Thus, Kaplan (1992), drawing on the work of Butler, explores the ambiguity of Madonna as a text that deconstructs gender norms. Her concern is not so much with the fabrication of fixed representations of women, but with the exploration of sex as an unstable but regulated performance, that is, a politics of the signifier.

Through analysis of her videos, frequently showcased on television in general and MTV in particular, Kaplan argues that Madonna is able to 'alter gender relations and to destabilize gender altogether' (Kaplan 1992: 273). Not only do Madonna's videos seek to empower women by exhorting them to take control of their lives, but they play with the codes of sex and gender to blur the boundaries of masculinity and femininity. Above all, Kaplan argues, Madonna's videos involve a continual shifting of subject positions, of stylized and mixed gender signs that question the boundaries of gender constructs. This, she argues, is a politics of representation that centres on sex and gender as unstable 'floating' signifiers.

For example, in the video 'Express Yourself' Kaplan argues that Madonna continually shifts the focus of the camera, and thus the audience, to adopt a variety of subject–viewer positions so that identification is dispersed and multiple. Body boundaries are violated and gender norms crossed, for example, Madonna mimes the male film maker Fritz Lang only to open her jacket to reveal a bra. Likewise, in 'Justify My Love', Madonna confuses the audiences as to the gender of a variety of lovers and couplings while 'Truth or Dare' not only pretends to reveal the 'truth' about Madonna, thus engaging in the politics of representation as truth, but also places her in a range of gendered identities. This includes a sequence where, as Cleopatra, Madonna simulates masturbation under the gaze of male eunochs sporting huge conical breasts. As Kaplan asks, 'Are the eyes male or female? Is it feminine to masturbate publicly, or does that action transgress feminine codes and reach over to masculinity? Such are the questions the performance provokes' (Kaplan 1992: 275).

During 1998 Madonna was again at the centre of controversy when she appeared at an awards ceremony dressed in a version of 'traditional' Indian clothing. Indeed, as reported by fashion magazines, the ethnic Indian 'look' had become chic within the USA, Britain and Australia. Madonna's appearance was met with protest from some Hindus for defiling sacred items by juxtaposing them with her bare nipples. On the one hand, Madonna could be criticized for commodifying ethnicity and offending the religious beliefs of some Hindus. On the other hand, the very performativity of the ethnic identity she enacted and resignified could be said to be supportive of anti-essentialist ideas that all ethnic identities are performances and none can lay claim to authenticity. Thus, Madonna was deconstructing ethnic identity. The potential for the incomensurability of interpretations here raises questions about whether a global feminism is possible. That is, can women and feminists from a variety of cultures across the globe be said to have the same fundamental interests at heart?

Global feminism?

Kaplan (1997) raises some of these issues in her discussion of the film *Warrior Marks*, directed by the African American Alice Walker and the Kenyan-born British Asian Pratibha Parmar. The film was a graphic critique of clitoridectomies in Africa, which aimed to dramatize the terror and pain involved and to educate women about the dangers of such practices. In doing so, the film makes appeal to the idea that clitoridectomies are a form of torture and child abuse in violation of universal women's rights (as affirmed by the 1995 Beijing Women's Conference). However, the adult African women in the film confidently defend clitoridectomies as a necessary part of their traditions and sacred practices. While sympathetic to the anti-clitoridectomy theme, Kaplan raises a number of potential criticisms of the film including the arguments that it:

- makes its points at the expense of the African women
- reproduces the imperialist tradition of teaching Africans a 'better' way of living
- relies on established stereotypes of Africans as exotic and savage
- assumes a global women's rights and is thus essentialist.

How can there be a global feminism when there is a difference that cannot be bridged between these Western African American and British Asian feminists and the African women in the film? There would appear to be no agreed rules or point of potential arbitration for coming to agreement as to what would constitute justice or women's rights and interests. By implication, universal women's rights are either impossible or, if declared, another version of the imperialist representation of western categories as applicable at all times and in all places. Consequently, Kaplan asks the question, can one ever know the other?

This is a complex debate within feminism about which I am not qualified to make definitive statements. However, I would suggest that questions about knowing the other are insufficiently specific about what knowing means. Of course we can never know any one if by knowing we mean total knowledge of the other that would require us to be the other and not ourselves. Further, since all knowledge is culture bound and positional cultures and political discourses can be incommensurable for there is no metalanguage of translation. However, we can all recognize each other as language users and rather than consider languages (as culture and knowledge) as constituted by untranslatable and incompatible rules we should see them as learnable skills. Incommensurable languages could only be unlearnable languages. This would encourage *dialogue* and the attempt to reach pragmatic agreements. There is no a priori reason why this should succeed, agreement may never be reached, but there is no a priori reason why it should fail either (Rorty 1991a). Given the poverty, inequality and violence that women across the globe endure it is difficult to believe that agreement could not be reached on a range of practical issues.

Soap opera as women's space

Thus far, we have concentrated on forms of textual analysis illustrating the subject positions that seek to fix readers. However, rather than regarding audiences as simply reproducing a core textual meaning, a range of new studies of television soap opera has stressed the way in which viewers construct, negotiate and perform a multiplicity of meanings and gendered identities. While soap opera does produce certain symbolic forms of gendered spectatorship, for example the subject position of 'ideal mother' (Modleski 1982), there is a difference between 'the analysis of spectatorship, conceived as a set of subject positions constructed in and through texts, and the analysis of social audiences, understood as the empirical social subjects actually engaged in watching television' (Ang 1996: 112).

It has been argued (Hobson 1982; Ang 1985; Geraghty 1991) that the central themes of soap opera – interpersonal relationships, marriages, divorces, children and so forth – chime with the traditionally domestic concerns of women so that soap opera is a space in which women's concerns and points of view are validated and from which women take pleasure. In her work on the British soap *Crossroads*, a much maligned programme regarded by many as the very definition of trash television, Hobson (1982) argued that it had a special place in the lives of its mainly female audience, whose very competencies in the interpersonal and domestic sphere, allied to various kinds of programme and genre knowledge, allowed them to take an active role as audience members.

Other studies of the soap opera audience confirm both the general genre competencies of the audience and a sense of a collective, collaborative network of viewing. Thus, in Seiter's (1989) study a network of women viewers used each other to keep track of the complex plot developments over a long period of time. This network is often family based – mothers and daughters – or neighbourhood centred and topics of discussion included speculation about future developments and moral-ideological judgements about characters and their actions. We must be concerned then not simply with textual devices that produce a variety of modes of femininity but with the extent to which textual subject positions are 'taken up' by concrete women and men (the subject of Chapter 5).

Summary and conclusions

Sex and gender, like race and ethnicity, are social constructions intrinsically implicated in matters of representation. They are matters of culture rather than nature. Though there is a strand of feminist thinking that stresses the essential differences between men and women, I have focused on, and argued for, that work which underpins the idea of the historically specific, unstable, plastic and malleable character of sexual identity. However, this does not mean that one can simply throw off sexual identities with ease and take on others for, while sex is a social construction, it is one which constitutes us both through the impositions of power and the identifications of the psyche. That is, constructions are regulated and have consequences.

Since sexual identity is not a universal biological essence, but a matter of how femininity and masculinity are spoken about, then feminism and cultural studies must be concerned with how women and men are represented. For example, cultural studies has explored the representation of women in popular culture and within literature to argue that women across the globe are constituted as the second-sex, as subordinated to men. That is, women have subject positions constructed for them which place them in the patriarchal work of domesticity and beautification or, increasingly within the west, of being a mother, having a career, being able to explore one's individuality and looking attractive. Women in post-colonial societies carry the double burden of having been subordinated by colonialism and native men. At the same time, we noted the possibility of destabilizing representations of sexed bodies.

While texts construct subject positions it does not follow that all women or men take up that which is offered; rather, reception studies have stressed the negotiations between subject and text, including the possibility of resistance to textual meanings. Indeed, such studies have often celebrated the values and viewing culture of women. This shift from text to audience, from image to talk, is the focus of Chapter 5, where, in a study of young British Asians, we can see the place of television as a textual resource for concrete persons who identify or otherwise with the ethnic and gendered subject positions that texts offer and, through talk, perform a range of ethnicities, femininities and masculinities.

Further reading

Geraghty, C. (1991) *Women and Soap Opera*. Cambridge: Polity Press.

Moi, T. (1985) *Sexual/Textual Politics: Feminist Literary Theory*. London and New York: Routledge.

Nicholson, L. (1995) Interpreting gender, in L. Nicholson and S. Seidman (eds) *Social Postmodernism*. Cambridge: Cambridge University Press.

Weedon, C. (1997) *Feminist Practice and Poststructuralist Theory*. Oxford: Blackwell.

5

AUDIENCES, IDENTITY AND TELEVISION TALK

The representations of race and gender discussed in previous chapters matter because they are intertwined with those ideologies, or forms of power/knowledge (Foucault 1980) that are constitutive of cultural identities. By power/knowledge is meant a mutually constituting relationship between power and knowledge so that knowledge is indissociable from 'regimes of power'. Knowledge is formed within and through the practices of power even as it contributes to the development, refinement and proliferations of new techniques of power. However, as was noted at the end of Chapter 4, while texts construct subject positions it does not follow that audiences 'take-up' that which is offered. In this chapter we shall be exploring the relationship between ideologies, representations and the meaning making powers of audiences.

Ideology as discourse

Ideologies as a form of power/knowledge are structures of signification, which constitute social relations in ways that are thoroughly saturated by power. If meaning is, as argued in Chapter 1, a matter of difference and deferral, then ideology can be understood as the attempt to fix meaning for particular purposes. That is, it is the practices of hegemonic power that seek to fix difference, to put closure around the unstable meanings of signifiers in the discursive field (Laclau and Mouffe 1985). For example, according to Barthes (1972), myth naturalizes that which is historically contingent making particular world-views appear unchangeable and God-given.

Ideologies as forms of power/knowledge are discourses which give meaning to both material objects and social practices, they define and produce the acceptable and intelligible way of understanding the world while at the same time excluding other ways of reasoning as unintelligible. No assumption is being made here (as in Althusserian Marxist versions of ideology) that 'ideology' is the counterpoint of a 'truth' waiting to be discovered; rather, the claim is that ideology is constituted by discourses or 'regimes of truth' which have specific *consequences* for relations of power. In Hall's interpretation of Gramsci, the concepts of ideology and **hegemony** do not suggest a single coherent unified dominant ideology but a complex field of competing ideas which have points of separation and break as well as those of juncture; 'in short, an ideological complex, ensemble or *discursive formation*' (Hall 1996c: 434). Ideologies are discourses which provide people with rules of practical conduct and moral behaviour and are thus equivalent 'to a religion understood in the secular sense of a unity of faith between a conception of the world and a corresponding norm of conduct' (Gramsci 1971: 349). Though ideology can be presented as coherent sets of ideas, it more often appears as the fragmented discursive meanings of common sense located intertextually in a variety of representations. It is through common sense that people routinely organize their lives and experience and this becomes a crucial site of ideological conflict. Thus, Gramsci is concerned with the character of popular thought and *popular culture* as the most significant site of ideological struggle.

It is important to see television and indeed all forms of popular culture as a site of *contestation* and not the simple injection of ideology into audiences because, as Chapter 4 argued, while representations construct subject positions it does not follow that all readers/viewers will take up that which is offered. Rather, reception studies have stressed the negotiations between subject and text. Consequently, no consideration of the relationship between global television and the constitution of cultural identities would be complete without exploring evidence provided by audience research. However, empirical evidence never simply 'speaks for itself' in an unambiguous way; rather, it is framed within particular theoretical perspectives. In this chapter the concentration is on the framework which has dominated audience research within the cultural studies tradition, namely (at least retrospectively) the **active audience** paradigm. This tradition suggest that audiences are not cultural 'dopes' but are active producers of meaning from within their own cultural contexts.

The chapter takes us through the main theoretical and empirical supports for the active audience approach before presenting a case study of young British Asians and Afro-Caribbeans talking about soap opera. This case study is illustrative of the constitutive place of television talk in the construction of cultural identity with specific reference to questions of ethnicity, hybridity and, above all, gender. That is, it suggests to us how some young British Asians and Afro-Caribbeans, as part of global diasporas, construct and enunciate their identities through talk about television.

The 'active' television audience

Watching television is a set of socially and culturally informed activities, a significant aspect of which is concerned with discursive *meaning*. Television audiences are active creators, they do not simply accept uncritically textual meanings but bring previously acquired cultural competencies to bear on them. Further, since texts do not embody one set of unambiguous meanings but are polysemic, that is, they are carriers of multiple meanings, differently constituted audiences will work with different textual meanings. In this context, there is now a good deal of mutually supporting work on television audiences within the cultural studies tradition from which the following conclusions can be drawn.

- The audience is conceived of as active and knowledgeable producers of meaning rather than effects of a structured text.

But

- Meanings are bounded by the way the text is structured and by the domestic and cultural context of the viewing
- Audiences need to be understood in the contexts in which they watch television both in terms of meaning construction and the routines of daily life
- Audiences are easily able to distinguish between fiction and reality; indeed they actively play with the boundaries
- The processes of meaning construction and the place of television in the routines of daily life alter from culture to culture and in terms of gender and class within the same cultural community.

Lest the 'active audience' paradigm be seen as 'Eurocentric', we should note McAnany and La Pastina's (1994) review of telenovelas audience studies which substantiates the importance of local cultural configurations in a Latin American context. They suggest that audiences are active, for example they recognize the fictional nature of the genre and the functioning of its rules, and derive a variety of meanings from telenovelas which they make relevant to their lives.

On the *theoretical* front two fields of study have proved to be particularly influential within cultural studies: Hall's (1981) encoding-decoding model and literary reception studies. Hall conceives of the process of television encoding as an articulation of linked but distinct moments – production, circulation, distribution, reproduction – each of which have their specific practices which are necessary to the circuit but which do not guarantee the next moment. Thus, though meaning is embedded at each level it is not necessarily taken up at the next moment in the circuit. In particular, the production of meaning does not ensure consumption of that meaning as the encoders might have intended because television messages, constructed as a sign system with multi-accentuated components, are polysemic.

To the degree that audiences share cultural frameworks with producers/ encoders, then the audience will decode signs in the same way, that is, a 'dominant' reading. However, where the audience is situated in different social positions (for example, of class and gender) with different cultural resources, the audience is able to decode the programmes in alternative ways, that is, a negotiated or oppositional reading. In short, television messages carry multiple meanings and can be interpreted in different ways. That is not to say that all the meanings are equal among themselves; rather, the text will be 'structured in dominance' leading to a 'preferred meaning', that is the one the text guides us to.

Work within the tradition of hermeneutics and literary reception studies further challenges the idea that there is one textual meaning associated with authorial intent and that texts are able to police meanings created by readers/audiences. For Gadamer (1976) and Iser (1978), the relationship between the text and the audience is an interactive one in which the reader approaches the text with certain expectations and anticipations, which are modified in the course of reading, to be replaced by new 'projections'. Thus, understanding is always from the position and point of view of the person who understands and involves not merely reproduction of secure textual meaning but its *production* by the readers. The text may guide the reader, but it cannot fix meanings that are the outcome of the oscillations between the text and the imagination of the reader. Wilson (1993) applies concepts consistent with the work of Iser to the small screen and argues that all readings of television are productive of new meaning as viewers attempt to construct coherent sense making narratives from the uncertainties of the text.

The active audience paradigm is part of a wider emphasis in cultural studies on the meaning oriented activity of consumers who become bricoleurs selecting and arranging elements of material commodities and meaningful signs. For example, Fiske (1987) argues that popular culture is constituted by the meanings that people create rather than those identifiable within the texts. While he is clear that popular culture is very largely produced by capitalist corporations, he 'focuses rather upon the popular tactics by which these forces are coped with, are evaded or are resisted' (Fiske 1989: 8). Fiske discusses television in terms of two separate economies – a financial economy of production and a cultural economy of consumption. The former is primarily concerned with money and the exchange value of commodities, while the latter is the site of cultural meanings, pleasures and social identities. Crucially, while the financial economy 'needs to be taken into account' in any investigation of the cultural, it does not determine it nor invalidate the considerable power that audiences have as producers of meaning at the level of consumption. Indeed, popular culture is seen as a site of semiotic warfare and of popular tactics deployed to evade or resist the meanings produced and inscribed in commodities by producers.

In reaction to this 'populist' position, McGuigan (1992) regards Fiske as representing a retreat from critical thinking and an abandonment of political economy leading to the acceptance of the free market and consumer capitalism. In a similar move, Curran (1991) has criticized the active audience paradigm for abandoning a critical edge towards the power of media corporations in favour of 'audience autonomy'. However, as Ang (1996) points out, recognition of the plural meanings that audiences produce is not an abandonment of the need to explore media institutions or texts but the sign for a new problematic, namely, the need to enquire about 'the way in which cultural contradiction, inconsistency and incoherence pervade contemporary, postmodern culture' (Ang 1996: 11).

Indeed, not only are multiple audience positions compatible with a wider consumer culture of niche marketing, but the take-up of any ideology or identity, be it critical or conservative, *requires* audiences to be actively engaged with texts. Audiences are *always active* and meaning always unstable and in flux; the critical questions surround where the 'cut' is made to stabilize and regulate meanings and identities. That is, how ideology, in the overdetermined and chaotic play of audience's discursive competencies and television's 'preferred meanings', seeks to fix and stabilize the representations with which audiences identify and thereby construct their identities. Again, identities are conceived here as the 'suture' between texts and identifications, the sedimented positionalities we have taken up and tried to live (Hall 1997b). In this context, watching television is both constitutive of and constituted by forms of cultural identity. That is, television forms a resource for the construction of cultural identity just as audiences draw from their own sedimented cultural identities and cultural competencies to decode programmes in their own specific ways.

Television audiences and cultural identity

For the purposes of establishing and popularizing the active character of audiences within cultural studies, the early work of Morley and Ang proved to be critical.

Nationwide

Morley's (1980) research into the audience for the 1970s British news magazine programme *Nationwide* was based on Hall's encoding/decoding model and confirms both a multitude of readings and a clustering around key decoding positions constituted by class. For example, dominant decodings were made by a group of conservative print managers and bank managers, while oppositional decodings were made by a group of shop stewards whose own political perspectives led them to reject wholesale the discourses of *Nationwide*.

It is both one of the strengths and weaknesses of the encoding/decoding model that, at least in its original form, *class* is the critical nodal point for structuring audience's interpretations and providing the point of resistance to what was seen as hegemonic class ideology. However, one of the central criticisms of Morley's *Nationwide* study was its reliance on discourses of class at the expense of gender or race. Gender, for example, is of equal significance and has been explored by a number of writers in relation to television.

Dallas

Ang's (1985) much discussed study of the US soap opera, *Dallas*, suggests that women viewers of *Dallas* are actively involved in the production of both meaning and pleasure and that these take on a range of manifestations which are not reducible to either the structure of the text, an 'ideological effect' or a political project. Watching *Dallas*, she says, is an experience which is mediated by the 'ideology of mass culture' which places *Dallas* in an inferior relationship to other cultural activities, leading viewers to adopt a range of viewing positions including

- feelings of guilt about watching *Dallas*
- an ironic stance used to stave off the contradiction of liking *Dallas* yet seeing it as 'trash'
- a sense that it was acceptable to watch the programme if you were 'aware of the dangers'
- an ideology of populism by which the women defended their right to like anything they wished.

During the 1980s, *Dallas* became a symbol for the globalization of American television and fears about cultural imperialism. In this context, Liebes and Katz's (1991) empirical study of *national* and *ethnic* cultural identity as mediating factors in the reception of television fiction is of particular interest. They explored the reception of *Dallas* among viewers from a range of cultural and ethnic backgrounds paying particular attention to the *cross-cultural* dimensions. The study was looking for evidence of different readings of *Dallas* in terms of understanding and critical ability and it was assumed that members of the focus groups would discuss the text with each other and develop interpretations based on mutual cultural understanding. Liebes and Katz argue that their study does indeed provide evidence of different readings of the narrative based in different cultural backgrounds.

In particular, they explore the differences between 'referential' and 'critical' approaches to the programme across different groups. By 'referential' they mean an understanding of *Dallas* which fundamentally takes the programme as referring to 'reality' and discusses the programme as if it were real. By 'critical' they mean an awareness of the fabricated character of the programme and a discussion in terms of the mechanisms of narrative construction and the economics of the television industry. Liebes and Katz argue that there were distinct differences between ethnic groups in the levels of each type of statement and conclude that Americans and Russians were particularly critical. However, the critical awareness displayed by Americans was centred on questions of form and production context, based on their greater understanding of the business of television. Americans were less critical in terms of content and tended to assume that *Dallas* has no themes and ideology but is merely entertainment. In contrast, the Russians were more critical of the 'politics' of *Dallas,* seeing it as a distorted representation of the capitalist west, while Arab groups had a high sensitivity to the 'dangers' of western culture and of western 'moral degeneracy'.

The Liebes and Katz research into *Dallas* suggests a number of important connections between global television and national/cultural identity. Most significantly, we can draw the conclusion that audiences use their own sense of national and ethnic identity as a position from which to decode programmes so that, for example, US programmes are not consumed by audiences uncritically with the destruction of indigenous cultural identities as the inevitable outcome. Indeed, the deployment of their own cultural identifications as a point of resistance also helps to constitute that very cultural identity through its enunciation.

The Young and the Restless

Miller's (1995) work on the US soap *The Young and the Restless* offers further evidence regarding the interpretation of global television in non-western contexts. He argues that we would be mistaken in regarding *The Young and the Restless* in Trinidad as simply the export and consumption of American culture or as the unproblematic carrier of modernity and consumer culture. Instead, he recounts the ways in which the soap opera is 'localized', made sense of and absorbed into local practices and meanings. He demonstrates the social and participatory nature of soap opera viewing alongside a sense of the relevance of the narrative content for moral issues in Trinidad. In particular, the gossip and scandal, specifically that of a sexual nature, which are core concerns of the soap opera's narrative resonate with the Trinidadian concept of Bacchanal which, according to Miller, is a deeply rooted folk concept which fuses ideas of confusion, gossip, scandal and truth. The concern of the soap thus 'colludes with the local sense of truth as exposure and scandal' (Miller 1995: 223). Further, *The Young and the Restless* provides models and talking points for the discussion and imitation of fashion which plays a significant part in the formation and maintenance of identity within Trinidad as an expression of the 'true' public self. Miller's work is significant because it suggests that the study of the formal characteristics of narratives is insufficient and stresses the need to understand local processes of absorption and transformation which, by their very nature, will be specific, contingent and unpredictable.

Neighbours

Gillespie (1995) provides us with useful evidence about the nature of television talk among young people of the Asian diaspora in Southall (London). For example, she discusses the way that the young people use *Neighbours* to articulate their own emergent norms and values. In particular, the rules surrounding male–female relationships and teenage romance are the subject of discussion, for, while *Neighbours* makes such relations a core part of its narratives, these relationships are taboo within the 'parent' culture. This is especially significant for girls, because *Neighbours* portrays young women with a far greater degree of freedom than many British Asian girls can themselves expect; the programme thus offers the pleasure of seeing more assertive women and provokes discussion about gender identities.

Television, space and identity

Watching television is a matter not only of textual meaning but also of the place of television within the rhythms and routines of everyday domestic life. In particular, watching television is something we commonly do in specific domestic spaces, for example the 'living room', with other people to whom we are often, though not always, connected by family relationship. Thus, writers have begun to take an interest in the domestic spaces in which television is watched and to suggest connection between spaces, activities and the construction of identities.

In this context, we shall be concerned with two particular aspects of television and everyday life. First, the manner in which broadcasting provides ritual social events wherein families or groups of friends watch together and talk before, during and after programmes. Second, the connection between such rituals, the spaces in which they are watched and the production of cultural identities with particular reference to questions of gendered identities.

Space as place

Space, as Massey (1994) argues, is not 'empty' but is produced culturally by social relations. That is, the spaces of home, nation, classroom, front room, and so on, are constructed in and through social relations and are invested with emotional commitment in order that space becomes place. Thus, the distinction between space and place is, according to Silverstone (1994), one marked by feeling. That is, places are spaces invested with human experiences, memories, intentions and desires which act as important markers of individual and collective identity.

Space then is a part of the 'ever shifting geometry of social/power relations' (Massey 1994: 4). In particular, the attempt to fix the meaning of space is an attempt to anchor it to specific identities which are claimed as one's own. For example, though space is a site of contestation and conflict, nationalists claim to locate spaces as those of exclusive national identities through attempts to name and fix their meaning. Likewise, gender identity is a site of potential conflict within the space defined as home which is commonly coded as feminine and underpinned with the ideology that women live more local, private and domestic lives than men.

Technology, television and gender in the home

As Silverstone (1994) argues, television provides a link between home and identity in a number of ways, both as a domestic object and through its mediation of images of domesticity (see Chapter 4). Here, we are primarily concerned with the first of these, namely, the place of television as a technological object in the home and its connections with domestic routines, spatial boundaries and gendered identities. That is, domestic routines and spaces are gendered together as social and cultural categories as, for example, when kitchens are coded female and garages coded male. In particular, the private world of the home, where the television is situated, is commonly coded female while public issues and public space are designated male.

Within these gendered spaces, technologies have particular *valences*, that is, they fit in with certain social/gender norms. Thus, A. Gray (1992) suggests that technologies 'used for one off jobs with a visible end product' (drill, sander, saw) are understood as masculine while those 'used in the execution of the day to day chores with an end product that is often immediately consumed' (cooker, washing machine, iron) are understood as feminine. However, we need to be clear that this is not an issue of technological complexity or otherwise but of the *absorption of technology into social relations*. Gray argues, via her ethnographic study of West Yorkshire households, that while the video cassette recorder (VCR) as a whole was seen as both masculine and feminine by women, the timer function was seen as male. In particular, the technology of setting the timer on the video was regarded by the women in the study as technologically difficult, and thus male, despite their routine use of equally complex washing machines.

Watching television in south London

What is being argued here is that both space and technology are gendered so that cultural identity may be both constituted by and constitutive of television as a technology watched in the home. Of relevance here is Morley's (1986) study 'Family television' in which he seeks to understand how television is interpreted and used by different families with a specific focus on power and gender. From his qualitative interviews with 18 south London working-class families he draws the following conclusions:

* Power and control over programme choice lies mostly with adult men
* Men have more attentive viewing styles than women, who are engaged in other domestic activities
* Men tend to plan their viewing more systematically than women, who tend to watch what is on at any given moment
* While men deny talking about television, women use it as a conversation piece
* The use of the video is controlled by 'Dad'
* Women express guilt over their viewing preferences, especially 'solo' viewing habits
* Drama and fiction feature more in the preferences of women than men for whom sport and news are more central
* Women prefer local to national news.

There are acknowledged limitations to this work in terms of the restricted range of families both in terms of number (only 18) and composition (exclusively white, London working class) but it is nevertheless suggestive of the kinds of work that can be done in relation to television in a domestic setting.

Watching television in Venezuela

Barrios's (1988) ethnographic exploration of a telenovelas audience, carried out in Venezuela among 13 families, focused on the mutually constituting way that television viewing and the organization of family life are inter-twined. Television viewing was integrated into the daily routines of life – getting up in the morning, meal times, homework times, returning from work and so forth. Of particular significance was the ritual sacred space created around the two blocs of telenovelas time in which interruption was frowned upon. This was especially important to women, whose lives centred on domestic labour, but also played a part in the lives of men and children. Indeed, questions about who watches what on television, when and where, were at the heart of family politics both encouraging and disrupting communication between family members.

Watching television in China

The connections between television, space and daily routines in a global context have been further explored by Lull (1991, 1997) in China where limited domestic space means that the introduction of a television set into a household has considerable impact. When the television is on it cannot be escaped so that watching television has to be a collective family experience; the family routines now include a specific time to watch TV. The arrival of television has altered family relationships including potential conflict over what is watched, when and by whom. The regulation of children's viewing was a particular issue.

Television as global space

In contrast to the stress above on the home as a place, Meyrowitz (1986) is concerned with global space and the way in which electronic media alter our sense of the 'situational geography' of social life so that we inhabit a virtual world-wide space in which new forms of identification are forged. The core of his argument is that electronic media break the traditional bonds between geographic place and social identity since mass media provide us with increasing sources of identification which are situated beyond the immediacy of specific places. For example, the way in which television brings the outside world into the home redefines the boundaries between the private and the public. This is of particular significance for women and children who are often 'house-bound' but who now have the 'masculine' public world brought by television into the 'feminine' private world of the home.

One space of particular interest to the study of global television and local identities and which is receiving increased attention within cultural studies (see Chapters 2 and 3) is that of ethnic diaspora. For example, the participants in Gillespie's study (discussed earlier) share membership of an Asian diaspora with most of the Birmingham (UK) based young people who contributed to my own research into talk about television soap operas (discussed below). In both instances, it is argued that talk about soap opera is constitutive of identity in that young people negotiate through talk shared understandings about how to 'go on' in their society as persons within social relationships.

Ethnicity, gender and hybridity: a case study of television talk

The purpose of this case study is to discuss qualitative research into the role of television soap opera as a resource employed by British Asian and Afro-Caribbean teenagers and thus to give a concrete example of how a specific group of persons deploy television as a resource for the construction of cultural identities. I shall be centrally concerned with the discursive production of multiple and gendered hybrid identities among British Asian and Afro-Caribbean girls and the stress will be on the formative nature of language as a resource in lending shape to ourselves and our world out of the contingent and disorderly flow of everyday talk and practice. Soap talk is an appropriate vehicle to explore these issues given that they are popular with young people and centre on interpersonal relationships intertwined with social issues (Buckingham 1987; Geraghty 1991).

The central methodological strategy of this case study was to enable young people to do the research themselves and involved recruiting young people, all in the 14–15-year-old age bracket, to carry out research among their peers on the theme of soap operas and relationships. The aim was to have young people talk about soaps within friendship groups without an adult presence. Each self-selected group of young people were given a tape recorder and asked to have a discussion on soap opera at a time and place of their choosing. Most carried out the activities in school at lunch times or with their teacher's permission in class time, though in private. The study involved 20 groups of young people and 77 individuals, most of whom, though not all, are British Asians. Of these 20 were male and 57 female (20 were white, 47 Asian and 10 Afro-Caribbean). Here I have concentrated, with one exception, on the British Asian girls. (The data collection aspects of this project were a collaborative effort with Julie Andre, then of the University of Birmingham, UK.)

British Asian-ness and British blackness

In my view, the stories told here about young British Asians and Afro-Caribbeans not only bring their life-worlds to the attention of others, but also contribute to the legitimation of the idea of British Asian-ness and British blackness through the redefinition of the very idea of what it means to be British. In this respect, the predominance of British Asian girls in the sample is significant. Their position is special by virtue of living across cultural boundaries – at its simplest Asian, Afro-Caribbean and white – and also, as girls, being somewhat marginalized within male dominated cultures. These girls need to be able to reflect across the range of their identity experiences to make sense of their lives and are arguably in a unique position to reflexively construct hybrid identities. They are aware of themselves as operating across discourses and sites of activity and offer some insights into their own circumstances.

While identities are always historically contingent, they are also subject to a process of structuration in that they are not random or freely chosen by agents. In this sense, research can produce retrospective narratives about the impress of history and culture on identity within specific cultural traditions. In this case, the narratives concern questions of diasporic identities in the context of late-twentieth-century accelerated globalization. Issues of globalization form a background to the study in two ways. First, soap opera is one of the prime genres of global television; there are few television systems that do not produce and/or import soap operas. Second, these girls are the second and third generation children of migrants from India, Africa and the Caribbean whose arrival in Britain is an aspect of global economic, cultural and political forces. What it means to be an Asian or black girl in contemporary Britain is a central focus of their talk.

They put Asians down so much

Questions of ethnicity as a form of cultural identity were prominent in the girls' discussions, particularly in reference to the representation of Asian and black people in soap operas. In this discussion, the girls complain about the inadequate representation of Asian and black girls in the Australian soap *Neighbours*.

   B: I think they put Asians down so much.
   A: Yeah.
   B: It's not like that.
   C: They also put blacks down as well.
   B: I know they do, they only keep the Australian thingy people high.

The girls complain that the representation of Asians is inadequate in both quantitative and qualitative terms since there are not enough Asians in *Neighbours* and they are treated in negative and stereotypical terms when they do appear. Thus the girls give expression to a sense that Asians are both 'in' and 'out' of Australian and British society, for the under-representation and stereotyping of Asians engender and maintain feelings that they are excluded from a full part in these societies. The girls assert their British-Asian-ness but in a way which underlines what they are not, that is fully recognized participants.

The kinds of Asian identities constructed by these girls are not 'pure' or essentialist Asian identities, rather, they are British Asian hybrids (Barker 1997a) cross-cut by considerations of gender.

> B: What about that thingy in *Neighbours*, Lahta.
> D: That is not a typical Asian girl, did you see her with a sari on?
> A: That is a joke.
> B: And going out with . . .
> C: That Brett.
> A: I know, that was taking the er [*pause*] mickey then, a typical Asian, they're always taking the piss of Asian or black people, or Chinese.

Thus Lahta, a rare Asian character in *Neighbours*, is seen as 'not a typical Asian girl' because, among other things, she had 'a sari on'. The girls infer that they are typical Asian girls but in a way that is different from Lahta. They do not wear saris and would not routinely expect to do so. Their experience of being Asian is unlike Lahta's, who has arrived in Australia directly from India, because they are British and live in the mixed traditions of a British-Asian context. In this way, the girls redefine what it means to be Asian appearing to suggest that it is they and not Lahta who 'really' represent Asian girls. Thus, Lahta is different from them because 'the girl came from India you know' whereas they live in Birmingham (UK). This is underlined by a different group of girls when they suggest:

> B: And the way her [Lahta] brother was over-controlling her life it's not on, it's not like that in our life.
> A: That does not happen.
> B: People aren't that strict.
> C: And I don't think that brothers act towards their sister like that.

The familial relationships experienced by these girls are not perceived to be the same as those of a traditional Indian family or the media representation thereof. Indeed, girl A appears to see the representation of 'a typical Asian' as 'taking the mickey' and 'taking the piss'. Depending on how one reads this line, we could also see them as claiming that Lahta's going out with

Brett, a white boy, is also 'taking the piss'. We could infer that for these girls, going out with a white boy is unlikely. Overall, the girls appear to invest in an Asian identity which incorporates an inclusive and traditional sense that you do not go out with white boys, combined with a post-traditional view of being Asian, you do not wear saris, you do not get controlled by your brothers. This can be described as a British-Asian hybrid form.

In addition to redefining what it means to be Asian, the discussions are also significant for the way in which ethnicity and gender are intertwined in the production of the identities of the speakers as Asians and girls. Here the girls discuss a sequence in *Neighbours* which centred on dancing and sexual activity at a party.

> B: You know Vikram, he's a hypocrite 'cos do you remember when it was that party, I can't remember when, and he was dancing with Philip's wife Julie and he can't talk that his daughter, I mean sister.
>
> A: No but he didn't fancy her.
>
> C: He didn't fancy her, that was just a normal dance.
>
> A: He doesn't mind her having friends like, normal friends, but not like you know, boyfriends and trying to have it off with them.
>
> B: Yes I think that's wrong, it's the influence of everybody around her, you know Lahta she doesn't want to feel, you know, left out.
>
> A: Yes that's why Asians do this stuff sometimes.
>
> B: Yeah, sometimes, yeah.
>
> C: Why not Asians, most girls.
>
> D: Get a bad reputation and that stuff.
>
> B: I mean most girls do it at our time, I mean I know for . . .

The question of what is acceptable dancing and sexual behaviour brings the girls' own sexual and emotional dilemmas to the fore. The feeling of being 'left out', contrasted to the dangers of getting a 'bad reputation', appears to be an emotional dilemma to which these girls orientate and which is structured by concerns of both gender and ethnicity. Vikram is a 'hypocrite' for the sexual implications of dancing with Julie while simultaneously trying to halt Lahta's relationship with Brett. The criticism can be regarded as directed at some aspects of traditional Asian masculinity. Though the other girls defend Vikram, 'he didn't fancy her, that was just a normal dance', and imply that dancing with sexual overtones is unacceptable, 'he doesn't mind her having friends like, normal friends, but not like you know, boyfriends and trying to have it off with them', there is sympathy for Lahta on the grounds that 'she doesn't want to feel, you know, left out'. This feeling of being left out is explained in terms of her ethnicity, 'yes that's why Asians do this stuff sometimes'. In other words, the experience of being Asian leads one to feel 'left out' and this is countered through relationships with boys which can, by implication, make one feel a part of things. However, this is seen by another girl as not simply to do with being Asian but to do with being female, 'why not Asians, most girls'. Thus, the dangers of getting a 'bad reputation' appear to be overdetermined by the conjunction of ethnicity and gender. Yet, some of the girls maintain a degree of distance from the traditions of gender and Asian culture since, in practice, they seek out hidden space to pursue their sexuality, 'I mean most girls do it at our time', and go on to name participants who are claimed to be sexually active.

The coming together of ethnicity and gender in a way which involves identification, but results in exclusion, is further underlined in a sequence in which the girls discuss Rick from *Neighbours* as being attractive. Thus, Rick is viewed in sexual terms, he is 'the best looking one', a perception confirmed by the other girls, and routinely repeated by the white girls in the sample. However, this sexual and gendered orientation is undercut for the girls by the shock of learning (from one of the participants) that the actor has appeared on television and said that 'he wouldn't go out with an Asian girl'. Significantly, the structure of the discourses deployed by the girls during much of the discussions were ones in which Asians and girls are inactive. The girls use generic sentences like 'they're always taking the piss out of Asian or Black people', which construct Asians as a collectivity to whom things are done by others. There are few sentences in which Asians are active and do things to others. The exception is Vikram, a man who, through 'over-controlling', 'dancing' and 'fancying', does things to and with women.

As I describe it, the girls are producing multiple and hybrid identities complicated by relations of gender. They see themselves as Asian yet distance themselves from aspects of tradition by virtue of their participation in other domains of British culture. They are both in and out of British society and Asian culture.

Black, British and working class

In this section, we concentrate on one particular participant, who I have called Sandra, and designated as A in the extracts. Rather than focusing on issues of Asian-ness cross-cut by gender, we are now focusing on the diaspora of the 'Black Atlantic' (Gilroy 1993) and the construction of blackness inflected by discourses of class. Consider the following extract.

A: Right, I think we'll start off by talking about *EastEnders*.
B: *Eastenders*.
A: Yeah.

B: I think its erm, I think its the most realistic programme I see on TV nowadays.

C: It's got a lot to do with us right.

B: Yeah, it talks about racism, relationships, erm women, not getting jobs and really everything.

A: What's going on in *EastEnders* lately, I cannot relate to at all 'cos for a start my mum does not own a pub.

B: Yeah but . . .

A: Secondly, I do not live in a square.

C: The majority of people, you know, live in that kind of a place, you know, middle-class people.

A: No, *EastEnders* is not a middle-class programme.

C: Working class I mean.

A: It's for the working class, the majority, and most people who live in the, actually in the East End, think it's not realistic of life at all, but frankly I think some of the subjects in there are quite good, they deal with today, ones like Mark being HIV positive and his wife.

B: Wanting kids, Ruth.

A: Wanting kids Ruth, right. But she's stupid if you think about it. If she wanted kids why did she marry Mark.

B: Yeah she knew she wouldn't be able to have them.

A: 'Cos she knew that if she had unprotected sex with Mark there's not just a chance that she'll become pregnant, but she'll actually be infected with the HIV virus, so, I think she should have thought about it before she leapt and married him.

Two of the girls in the above sequence, including Sandra, are Black, of Afro-Caribbean lineage. The third is British Asian. Speakers C and B assert that *EastEnders* is realistic because it is about 'us'. The group 'us' is constituted in terms of shared identifications with being black and women. However, Sandra dissents on the grounds of class. She identifies with being working class and considers the representation of working-class people as being as inadequate. She speaks from a position constituted by class which, for an instant, overrides questions of ethnicity and gender. In addition, she quickly introduces another facet of her identity, a concern with serious 'subjects' on which she can elaborate and speak from a position of moralist. *EastEnders* is regarded as 'good' because of the 'subjects' it covers. For Sandra, Ruth really 'should have' given more thought to marrying Mark. Sandra's serious moral tone, her definition of her self as concerned with such issues, is a recurrent theme of the discussion. Two further examples will suffice. Talking about another female character, Cindy, Sandra declares that,

> A: Yeah, if you think about it she shouldn't have allowed herself to get into the situation 'cos she must remember that it was Ian who took her out of the gutter.

Sandra of course does think about such things. That is part of her self-identity. Further, such thinking leads her to adopt fairly robust moral positions as indicated by the words 'shouldn't have' and 'she must remember'. She connects this moral position with her previous concern with class. Ian is valorized as having lifted Cindy 'out of the gutter'. That this is a contestable interpretation of the narrative underlines the significance to her identity of the specific interpretation she puts on it. At another moment the girls are about to discuss a sexual encounter. In other conversations involving different girls from the same school the term 'shag' or 'have it off' were the most frequently used descriptors for sex. However, our subject prefers, in this context, to use and identify with respectable and officially sanctioned language.

> B: I heard right that, I've read in a magazine that them two are gonna have erm.
> A: That they're gonna have sexual intercourse.

We may note that she uses the vernacular 'they're gonna' but adopts the authorized and approved term 'sexual intercourse'. Sandra's use of 'sexual intercourse' could be read as recognition of the tape recorder in the corner. However, even if this were the case it illustrates Sandra's awareness of 'approved' language since she is sensitive to the kind of words she might be expected to use by those in authority. Sandra is caught in something of a dilemma. She has already established herself a working-class identity, yet she also identifies with the language, work ethic and social position of a sector of the middle class, the professionals. Later she again underlines this by an awareness of sanctioned language, 'Cos don't you think she's quite a slut, sorry pardon my language'.

Sandra reinforces her class ambivalence in a later discussion of the Australian soap *Heartbreak High*. On the one hand she affirms her working-class sensibility,

> A: Don't you know money just drops out of thin air in *Heartbreak High*.

But on the other she identifies with the social aspirations of those who work hard at school. There is a collective complaint that the students represented in *Heartbreak High* mess around too much in school. This is unacceptable to Sandra.

> A: If I messed around like that I wouldn't even be in school.

B: I know.

A: There's some kids in school right, the half of them in class are always willing to work whereas in *Heartbreak High* they don't show even half of them like that.

The significance of the place of school work in her aspirant identity is made clearer when she explains why she likes the American programme *Fresh Prince of Bel Air*.

A: . . . what I like about *Fresh Prince* is that they're not just showing a load of black people who live in the Bronx or in the ghetto, who like have to steal and sell drugs for a means of living, they're actually showing that there are some successful blacks in America.

B: True.

A: Who do well, who do not use drugs or violence to get their own way and I think it actually shows a good representation of some of the blacks in America now who are doing really well in professions and everything and it's quite good because it's, it's unfair to say that all blacks live in ghettos and everything 'cos we know that is totally untrue.

B: Yeah.

A: That's why I really like that programme 'cos it shows a positive image, but even though it's mainly a black programme I think that more people can relate to erm *Fresh Prince*, I think some Asians can relate to *Fresh Prince* as well.

Sandra clearly identifies with 'successful blacks' which she regards as a 'positive image'. She resents the continued racist depiction of black people as drug-dealing thieves. She prefers to identify with the professionals. This remains something of a problem for her in that Britain is a country with severe structural racism and limited black professionals. It is therefore no surprise that she does not cast off her black working-class identity in favour of a middle-class one. She remains acutely aware of herself as black and of the inadequacy of representations of blacks and Asian on television. Sandra not only adopts a discursive position of 'blackness' but drives the discussion forward. She recognizes the essentially racist implications of representations in *Heartbreak High*.

A: And why did they decide to totally write out Jack her boyfriend, he only comes into it occasionally now.

B: I know, it's because he's Asian, if he was black same thing, Asian same thing – they only keep their own thingy people in that.

A: Yeah and in *Heartbreak High* right even though they try to show people from many ethnic . . .

B: They put them down all the time.

A: Even though they try to show people from many ethnic minorities you only see blacks and Asians, I mean Orientals, in the background they're none of the main characters, like Alex he's white, he's Caucasian and all the rest of the characters are Caucasian and everything, . . . [edit] . . . I think it's about time even though it says that *Heartbreak High* is quite realistic, I think they should have some blacks and Asians being the main characters.

One might assume that her awareness of inequality based on ethnicity might prevent her from identifying in any way with Britain as a nation. That, of the range of identity positions she articulates, national identity would not be one of them. Though it is a rare instance, she does later identify with a notion of 'this country', which carries at least some element of positive accent. Further, she does not deploy the self-defining argot of Afro-Caribbean culture in Handsworth, Birmingham (UK) but favours a more 'standard' English inflected with Birmingham working-class idioms.

These shifting and multiple identifications are an outcome of positioning herself within a variety of discourses. Indeed, Sandra illustrates the multiplying global resources for the construction of self-identity for, as Pieterse has suggested,

> Multiple identities and the decentring of the social subject are grounded in the ability of individuals to avail themselves of several organisational options at the same time. Thus globalisation is the framework for the amplification and diversification of 'sources of the self'.
>
> (Pieterse 1995: 52)

Sandra deploys a range of resources drawn from a variety of times and spaces. The most obvious resources she draws on are local and personal. They include her mother, her friends and her school life. They also include her experiences of multi-ethnic Handsworth. She is talking with an Asian girl and draws parallels between black and Asian experience in Britain. However, she also draws on resources of a more globalized nature. *East-Enders*, *Neighbours*, *Heartbreak High* and *Fresh Prince of Bel Air* are television programmes that originate from Britain, Australia and America and which circulate around a good part of the planet including the 'Black Atlantic', that exchange of cultural resources within the black diaspora of Britain, America, the Caribbean and Africa.

In summary, I have argued that Sandra has a number of different identifications and identities which are in tension with each other. Her self-identity is a multiple and shifting one. She is fiercely working class and yet also identifies with the language and social aspirations of middle-class professionals. Living in a post-traditional society in which all life-worlds are subject to discursive scrutiny, she does not simply accept the inferior social position of black people but critiques it. She wants to be a *successful* person but is aware of, and resents, the limitations that being black in Britain involves. This is expressed through a critique of the representation of black and Asian people on television. Sandra can be regarded as a black British hybrid. She identifies with *this country* but also with being black. She wants the promised mobility offered to those who work hard but knows that, as a black woman, she is not able to avail herself of all the resources or opportunities available to others, such as white men. This leads her to identify with others who are similarly placed. She recognizes the similarity of experience shared by blacks and Asians. She is black, British, working class, with professional aspirations and a mastery of a discourse of high ground morality.

Soap talk and the construction of femininity

In many respects, the young people in the study were both an 'active' audience and implicated in the production and reproduction of ideology. They were 'active' in that they moved easily between discussions centred on the plots, as if it was the 'real world', to recognition of the constructed nature of the text within a television production context. However, this did not prevent many of them from constructing ideological stereotypes of gender and family roles.

Grant

The significance of gender in the girls' discussions emerged most clearly in relation to their favourite characters (Barker and Andre 1996), one of whom was *EastEnders'* Grant Mitchell, as the following extract reveals.

> B: I like *EastEnders* best, I like Grant.
> C: Grant in *EastEnders*.
> A: I love Grant our [sister] fancies Grant like mad.
> B: . . . I like all the Dickheads.
> D: Oh I really liked Grant. I didn't want him to go, even though he was the violent type. I didn't like him before, in like, before, but once he came out of jail, I *really* liked him.

For these girls, Grant stands in a tradition of rebellious men characterized by strength, energy, self-assurance and independence. Indeed, Grant's 'wayward' status as a 'Dickhead' is admired. These are characteristics which, as we shall see later, were less tolerated in women. A contrasting approach adopted by girls was to express a growing interest in Grant as he became more embroiled in plots centred on romantic, marital and interpersonal themes. While girl D formally disapproves of the 'violent type', the character is 'really liked' later when his altered position in the text makes it more acceptable. It is relevant to say that this girl was especially committed to the conventions of love and the 'quest romance'. Most soap pairings were allowable 'as long as they love each other' and Grant's positioning in story lines that connect with this theme make him more agreeable.

The fact that girls appropriate Grant in different ways, on the one hand as a symbol of rebellion and on the other as a more sensitive figure located in discourses about love, expresses a tension in this British Asian 'girl culture' between attraction to the traditional private world of interpersonal relationships, traditional both to women and soap opera, and the desire to take up more assertive characteristics in the public sphere.

Natalie and Bianca

Some of the tensions within 'girl culture' manifested themselves in discussions that centred on two other *EastEnders* characters, Natalie and Bianca.

> B: I like Natalie, I think her and Ricky should get together.
> A: Yeah well, they, they can like relate to each other and Natalie's a much nicer person, she cares for other people, she doesn't just think about herself and, I don't know, she's been there for Ricky more than Bianca has.
> C: What about Bianca's dress [*laughter*] did you see that [*laughter*]?
> A: Bianca's Bianca's dress it was pink it clashed with her hair.
> C: She makes me laugh she's so stupid.
> B: She's so stupid.

Natalie is constructed as a 'nice person' in contrast to Bianca. Natalie is a 'nicer person', she can 'relate to' Ricky, she 'cares for other people' and 'doesn't just think about herself'. These qualities are constitutive of the traditional identity of women, skilled in the private world of interpersonal relationships, but excluded from more assertive roles in the public domain. This is an identity to which these particular girls seem to be orienting towards. For these are the very same girls for whom all is forgiven 'if you do love the person'.

Bianca was universally disliked by the participants. She was described by one group of girls as 'a right slag' and 'a bit of a cow'. In describing Bianca in these terms the girls appear to be attacking her in two ways: first, for being over-assertive, pushy and self-centred; second, for her confident sexuality. The term 'slag' suggests the perception of what they regard as inappropriate sexual behaviour for women. Given the apparent sexual nature of the assault on Bianca it is significant that some speakers attack her appearance. 'Urm, what do you think of her walking into the pub like that, she's practically wearing a slip'. Many of these girls do not accept assertive women in the same way as they warm to Grant as an assertive men.

Cody, Helen and Beverley

While there are other examples of what might be seen as traditionally sexist judgements, Cody from *Neighbours* was criticized (by girls) for having 'a weird voice', 'a deep voice' and 'a rough voice', we would be mistaken to see these discussions as simply reinforcing traditional gender identities. The tension to which I have already alluded, between 'tradition' and a desire to be more assertive, continues to manifest itself. Thus, one girl criticized Helen, also from *Neighbours*, for her apparent commitment to domesticity. 'All Helen does is sit there baking casseroles, giving advice'. In a not dissimilar vein, Beverley from *Brookside*, having been criticized for her social pretensions, was praised for her assertive past. 'But she's changed, remember when she first, she came in, she was like, urm, sort of like, urm, a man-eater [*laughter*]'. One could interpret 'man-eater' as a derogatory term. However, in this context, I see it as a form of praise for her self-assurance and sexual confidence.

Exploring sexual identity

Soap talk provides young people with a forum for discussion about topics that are difficult or embarrassing, including sexual identity, and in particular homosexuality that falls outside the heterosexual imperative. As the conversations develop, a range of positions are taken regarding sexuality with some speakers trying to secure themselves a fixed heterosexual identity while others, adopting a more flexible position, are open to the plasticity of sexual identity.

Beth, Della and Binny

During the early part of the research the lesbian characters, Beth in *Brookside* and Della and Binny in *EastEnders*, were involved in prominent story lines and appeared in almost all the conversations. Through discussions about these characters the young people explored their ideas of what constitutes lesbianism. Among girls there was little outright hostility towards gays and lesbians, though there was a degree of ambivalence as they sought to understand what for them lesbianism 'is'. The main tension occurred between those who needed to produce *explanations* for the character being a lesbian and those who accepted it as a given.

> B: I think the lesbian thing, Beth and all that, I think, I suppose it could be real life. I wouldn't really know. I don't know any lesbians.
>
> C: Well, I don't think I don't know any lesbians anyhow but you never know, but anyway.
>
> B: And I don't know if it's real life, but I suppose, yeah, well you can understand why because of what happened to her, the rape and all that it's probably made her feel that way about men, but she isn't admitting that she's just saying that's how it is. In *EastEnders* I think that Della and Binny they make me laugh. Anyway I think they're good for each other in a way. I don't think Della is that much into it. I think she should have just gone off with Steve or gone with another fella. Binny is more, like into their relationship, but Binny she is just like, no, now I've got confused, no Della, she's just like, she I don't think she's a fully, what do you call it, like a whole hearted lesbian, if there is such a thing as a whole hearted lesbian, but I know what I mean.
>
> D: That programme really [*pause*] showed what I feel really angry about because people just expect people to be different if they're gay and I don't think that's right, that people should expect people to be different because they're not, and that really bugs me when people treat people differently 'cos it [*raises voice*] really gets on my nerves.

In distancing herself from lesbianism by questioning its reality and denying any personal knowledge speaker A expresses the ambivalence found among these girls. Indeed, she questions whether there is such a thing as a 'whole hearted lesbian'. Confusion over Della's sexuality arose from her friendship with the male character Steve and, elsewhere, they sought to clarify whether Della was 'going out' with Steve or still 'going out' with Binny. The reading of doubt into the character's sexuality arose because of her friendship with a heterosexual male, something they may have perceived as not constituting homosexual feeling or behaviour which was used to confirm the correct normative solution (for these young women) of heterosexuality.

In another discussion, made possible by the audience's knowledge of her childhood experiences, the participants needed to explore 'reasons' why Beth from *Brookside* was a lesbian and spoke of 'being able to understand' why she 'became' a lesbian. A consensus developed that Beth became a lesbian because of the sexual abuse she had suffered as a child, at the hands of her father, and because she had slept with a boyfriend who was subsequently accused of rape. Clearly assumptions are being made about her (and lesbians in general) alleged hostile feelings towards men. Even though the speaker acknowledges Beth's explanation that 'she is just how she is', she still needs to maintain that there is a 'reason' behind Beth's sexuality, of which the character is unaware.

At the same time, the girls are supportive of the relationship between Della and Binny. They are seen as 'good for each other', in the same terms that the girls discussed the appropriateness of heterosexual relationships – whether, for example, as we saw earlier, Ricky is best suited to Natalie or Bianca. Indeed, girl D clearly uses the conversation to express her support for the right to freely choose one's sexuality. Further, she took a positive view of a kiss between two (male) friends in the serial *Byker Grove*: 'I know people that, that's happened to and I, I think that they should let, they should let them carry on like that'.

Morality, ethics and soap talk

One of the striking aspects of the performance of gender in relation to television 'soap talk' is the strong position occupied by the concerns of morality and ethics. Soap talk is one of the ways in which the young British Asians in this study seek to make intelligible and manageable the moral and ethical dilemmas that face them (C. Barker 1998). For Foucault, ethical reflection constitutes one of the ways in which the subject is 'led to focus attention on themselves, to decipher, recognise and acknowledge themselves as subjects of desire' (Foucault 1987: 5). This concern with self-production or 'techniques of the self' is centred on the question of ethics as a mode of 'care of the self' which, in contrast to the notion of 'docile bodies', reintroduces agency and the possibility of resistance and change.

According to Foucault, morality is concerned with systems of injunction and interdiction and formed in relation to formalized codes. Ethics, in contrast, is concerned with practical advice as to how one should concern oneself with oneself in everyday life: for example, what it means to be a 'good' person, a self-disciplined person, a creative person and so forth (Foucault 1979, 1984, 1986, 1987). Foucault contrasts morality, which operates through a set of imposed rules and prohibitions (associated with Christianity), with ethics, which is concerned with the actual practices of subjects in relation to the rules which are recommended to them which they enact with varying degrees of compliance and creativity. In particular, he points to an ethics of self-mastery and 'stylization' which is drawn from the character of relationships themselves rather than from external rules of prohibition.

This more dynamic conception of the self suggests a route by which ethics can be seen as the site of a form of self-fashioning activity. For example, the girls' discussions (below) are significant for the way in which they are concerned both to morally discipline characters from soaps and to 'make themselves' through a concern for ethics as the 'care of the self'. The conversations explored both formal moral injunctions which derive from British Asian cultural life and a mode of concern with oneself centred on sexuality and fulfilment in personal relationships. Thus do the girls attempt to forge new languages of morality, ethics and action as they seek to make intelligible and manageable the moral and ethical dilemmas that face them.

Moral condemnation and explanation

Within the girls' discussions of sexual morality two key themes emerge which are in tension with each other. The first is the condemnation of inappropriate sexuality both in terms of its representation (where it is regarded as too explicit) and the verbal disciplining of characters who act in 'immoral' ways. This strong line of moral *condemnation,* which shows a concern with purity and austerity, lays blame on individuals. However, this is mitigated by a second strand, that of *explanation,* by which the acts of characters can be understood and forgiven so that the absolute morality of condemnation gives way to the relativizing of morality by recontextualizing it within a framework of social relationships. For example, the girls discuss *Heartbreak High*:

A: And did you watch when Zachery was having it off?
B: Do you mean a few weeks before? I mean it's so embarrassing, those programmes shouldn't be shown in the day, you know that.
A: Why not?
C: I mean think about it, nowadays it's a normal day thing.
A: You don't exactly see a teacher having it off with a student.
B: But it does happen.
C: Yes it does happen, it's realistic, that sort of thing really does happen in real life around the world.
A: But every week all they show is someone having sex every week.
B: That's true.

A: If it's Nick and Jody, Nick and Daniel or anyone, they go from one room to another.

B: It doesn't happen like that in real life, I don't think it does, not that easily.

A: No, not that often anyway.

C: That's fantasy, that's fantasy.

Speaker B complains that the representation of sexuality is 'so embarrassing' that the programmes shouldn't be shown. This line of argument is confirmed and supported by speaker A: 'all they show is someone having sex every week'. The rhetorical devices of this line are interesting. First, there is clear exaggeration: sex is 'all they show'. Second, it is a kind of anonymous sex performed by 'someone' which 'they' broadcast. Third, there is the implicit condemnation of the frequency of the representation of sex which conflates sex being 'shown every week' and sex being 'enacted' every week. This moral absolutism is mitigated, undercut and relativized by the argument put by C that 'nowadays it's a normal day thing'. Though this is challenged by A, 'you don't exactly see a teacher having it off with a student', both speakers B and C reassert its 'reality', 'it does happen' and 'it's realistic'. By implication moral questions are consensual questions. If 'it' happens, if 'it' is realistic, then 'it' is acceptable to be shown on television. Indeed, it is possible to read this conversation as implying the relativity of all moral judgements, that is to say, if 'it' happens, if 'it' is normal, then it is acceptable. Certainly moral truth seems to be closely linked to epistemological judgements about realism.

The complexity and contradictory nature of the moral logic deployed by the girls can be seen even more clearly by tracing the inputs of individual speakers. Thus speaker A is the first to challenge B's assertion that 'those programmes shouldn't be shown in the day' by asking 'why not?' However, speaker C, whose assertion that 'it's a normal day thing' would appear to be in support of A's 'why not?', now finds that A challenges the realist claim, 'you don't exactly see a teacher having it off with a student'. Later, A agrees with the original sentiments of girl B by suggesting that 'but every week all they show is someone having sex every week' which, elsewhere, was not regarded as realistic. Speaker B, who had suggested that the sex was so embarrassing, also agrees that too much sex is shown but is unsure about how realistic such depictions are. The line 'but it does happen' would suggest the realism of depicting sexual activity as widespread but this is contradicted by 'it doesn't happen like that in real life, I don't think it does, not that easily'. C is equally contradictory. What to begin with is regarded as 'a normal day thing' and 'realistic' has become 'fantasy' by the end of the sequence.

Sharon, Phil and Cindy

To this complex mix is added a gender dimension in which women often take the blame. For example, the girls discuss characters in *EastEnders*:

A: Yeah but how come they always have to, you know, go and have an affair with people in their family.
C: That is true.
A: Sharon had an affair with Phil.
All: Cindy.
B: Look at Cindy.
E: Cindy's a slag.
B: Cindy's had oh, Wicksy, she's had Ian.
C: And Wicksy's brother.
B: And Wicksy's brother, all three of them are pigs.
A: That's so unrealistic that is.
B: Wicksy and David are brothers and their Dad is Pete and Ian's Dad is Pete.
C: And she's slept with all three of them.
C: I know.
E: No, God, I hate Ian.
D: I bet they're not his kids, I bet they're that Tricky Dicky's kids.
E: Did she give it him?
D: No but he said she did.

The moral tone is set at the start of the sequence by the disavowal of having affairs 'with people in their family'. The judgement is confirmed and made more explicit ('They' becomes Sharon, Phil, Cindy, and so on) by the other girls and Cindy is declared 'a slag'. These actions are deemed reprehensible on two linked grounds. They are immoral, 'Cindy's a slag', and unlikely/untrue, 'that's so unrealistic that is'. As in the previous sequence, this involves a regime of moral-reality-truth claims that conflates the allegedly factual with the moral and the normal. Facts, norms and morals, classifications which western philosophical thinking takes to be separate categories, are rolled up in to mutually supporting claims. Morality thus embodies truth, where truth is seen as social commendation rather than epistemological statements about an independent world (Rorty 1989).

Further, it was Sharon who had an affair with Phil and not vice versa. She is held responsible as the initiator of the already condemned affair. It is Cindy who is 'a slag' and 'Cindy who had oh Wicksy, she's had Ian'. It is women who 'have' men. Under some circumstances the agency attributed to women could be seen as a positive reversal of the more common discursive position in which men are active and women the objects of their attention. However, in this case the agent is one to be morally blamed. Though the men are not liked, 'all three of them are pigs', nevertheless it is Cindy as the primary active agent who is held responsible since 'she's slept with all three'. She is the person who does things and sex is something for her to bestow, 'did she give it to him?'

Here individual agents are held to be the source of morality, it is a question of individual choice which depends implicitly on a unified and coherent self which is able to make independent moral judgements. This is in contrast to those moments when the girls contextualize moral choices within an explanatory and mitigating set of social relationships. Morality talk thus embodies the paradox that morality is a *social* resource which constructs the self as *individually* responsible. Morality is about what I should do, it is part of what Foucault calls the 'steering mechanism of the self', but originates in, and refers to, social relationships expressed through the social resource of language.

Katie and Carl

The socially constructed language-game of western morality frequently places responsibility for moral action on individuals and the sequence below (about *Brookside)* continues this line of thinking.

C: Katie, don't she see that she's trying to steal her man.

B: I know.

A: Cos don't you think she's quite a slut, sorry pardon my language, but if you think about it she's like throwing herself on all these men and like he's not refusing either, like look at her and Carl they had sex on the beach – it was just disgusting. Did you watch that one?

B: I didn't know that.

A: It was disgusting and now she sees that Katie's going out with someone she's trying to make that man say oh Katie's looking for a deep relationship when that's totally untrue, cos she actually wants him for herself and she's actually going to her friend, oh do you really think I'd do something like that, but if your friend's going out with somebody who you really fancy you should just ignore . . .

B: And if you're a real friend . . .

A: Your feelings.

B: And if you're a real friend you wouldn't hurt her feelings.

A: Yeah you should just ignore your feelings and that's it really.

'She' (Jackie) is reprehensible 'for trying to steal her man' and because 'she's quite a slut' for 'throwing herself on all these men'. Furthermore, *she* is deceiving her friend *Katie* by lying to and about her. The girls make it clear that 'if your friend's going out with somebody who you really fancy you should just ignore [your feelings]' and 'if you're a real friend you wouldn't hurt her feelings'. Girls should both be loyal to each other and not get involved in 'throwing themselves at men'. In contrast to this, the behaviour of 'a slut', the concept of a 'deep relationship' is implicitly preferred. In this case, and the one that preceded it, we should remind ourselves that these are girls talking and positioning themselves in discourses of morality which are gendered in ways detrimental to women. Girls discipline themselves through a particular 'regime of the self' which brings together discourses of truth, reality and morality.

However, such self-disciplining remains contradictory and full of tension since the absolute moral arguments that the girls had previously constructed are mitigated and relativized by an implicit recognition that morality is a social phenomenon and that moral action needs to be understood in context. For example, though 'affairs' are broadly condemned, circumstances may make them more understandable and acceptable. Thus, for one girl, the behaviour of Philip's (from *Neighbours*) wife Julie is such that 'I wouldn't blame him if he went off and had an affair with someone else'.

Ian and Cindy

The extract below (about *EastEnders*) illustrates the way the girls put moral judgements in a social context which offers explanation and a degree of understanding and sympathy.

A: I think if they're gonna start an affair they might as well get started, it's getting very obvious by the way they're both behaving around each other.

B: I know, but you know Ian, I think he's not worth it anyway because it's not even his, the twins are his, innit, they're his children.

A: Yeah.

B: But if you think about it the other son isn't his and he's been dissed by her so many times he should just get up and leave.

A: But in a way I think Cindy's trapped in it because she can't look after three children on her own with no money coming in and he really owns her.

B: But did you watch it though [*unclear*] cos Phil went round the house to talk about why, you know, they're sneaking up on him, but he also mentioned, you know, Cindy shouldn't be made to do all of the housework and everything but I know, I know where she's coming from because I wouldn't wanna, you know, she was so career-minded when she was younger.

A: Precisely.

B: Everything's just falling apart for her.

A: And Sharon well, I don't know what she's playing at.

B: I think she's being kinda stupid because, if you think about it though, she was doing all right with Grant, I know he hit her and everything, he hit her a few times eh, but I think both of them need each other, cos like you know, it's like good and bad together innit.

A: Mmm.

B: She needs him and he needs her.

A: I think that everyone's being cruel to Sharon, they seem to forget that Phil was also part of the affair.

B: Yeah that's what I think, me too.

A: And it's like Sharon's to blame, Sharon's been kicked out of her only home, everything's been taken away from her and they don't seem to care at all.

It is suggested that since 'they' (Cindy and David) seem to be preparing for an affair 'they might as well get started'. This is a rather pragmatic and non-judgemental approach compared to the moral absolutism of earlier condemnations. There is a certain sympathy expressed for Ian, Cindy's husband, and for Cindy herself. Thus Ian has been 'dissed by her so many times he should just get up and leave'. While this sympathy for Ian (who is otherwise disliked by the girls) might imply condemnation of Cindy, in fact explanations of Cindy's behaviour are supplied which mitigate her moral responsibility and deflect blame. Thus, Cindy is deemed to be 'trapped' by the need to look after three children and do all the housework.

Sharon and Grant

Moral responsibility is thereby shifted from the individual to the social and the tension and movement between moral responsibility as located in individuals and/or social relationships comes to the fore in the discussion of Sharon. At first she is held responsible for the break up of the marriage between herself and Grant, 'Sharon well, I don't know what she's playing at'. Speaker B agrees, indeed, Sharon is expected to tolerate male violence for which they are somehow both held responsible: 'I know he hit her and everything, he hit her a few times eh, but I think both of them need each other'. However, girl A holds a different view. Her 'mmm' suggests ambiguity and polite disagreement, which is made more explicit with 'I think that everyone's being cruel to Sharon, they seem to forget that Phil was also part of the affair'. The girl who had opened the Sharon sequence by not knowing what she was 'playing at' now defends her and suggests in the final line that Sharon should not have to shoulder the blame. Interestingly girl B, who had even suggested that Sharon should tolerate violence, now agrees that Sharon is getting a bad deal, 'Yeah, that's what I think, me too'. Moral judgements about Sharon are thus redirected from the individual to the social by recontextualizing her actions with particular reference to the place of women in social and domestic life.

Summary and conclusions

It has been suggested that audiences are active creators of meaning and not 'cultural dopes' who consume uncritically everything television has to offer. Rather, global television is a resource which we draw on to construct our identities in a variety of different ways. Thus, we should talk not of an audience so much as audiences who use television to construct a range of meanings in the context of the wider circumstances of their lives.

It was also suggested that watching television is situated within the social practices of daily life, particularly domestic practices, so that the meanings generated by audiences in relation to television are not confined to meaningful viewing but are generated and sustained by the rhythms and routines of everyday life. In particular, it was argued that the domestic space of the home is a site for the construction and contestation of wider cultural identities including those of gender.

In our case study we explored some examples of the way in which young girls from within the Asian and Afro-Caribbean diaspora enunciated identities in the context of talk about television soap operas. In doing so, it was suggested that many of the girls defined themselves as Asian or black at the same time as they redefined the meaning of those terms to encompass their own British Asian and black British hybrid identities. It was argued that conceptions of ethnicity as identity were cross-cut by questions of class and, above all, gender. Thus, the girls enact multiple, hybrid and fragmented identities.

Television soap opera is a resource for discussions about favourite characters, gender identifications and personal-sexual morality. In this study, the girls enacted multiple and contradictory identities which are constituted in the movement between traditional and post-traditional discourses of gender and ethnicity. Thus, they appear to position themselves as traditionally 'feminine' yet also take up more assertive forms of womanhood.

It was argued that television soap talk illustrates the centrality of morality and ethics for self-identity and constitutes a set of tools and guides to action within social relationships. Not only may we conclude that the morality of relationships is crucial in the identity formation of young people but also that the central importance of ethics and morality for self-identity undercuts the idea that we live in an amoral society. Far from being without moral resources these girls place such considerations at the centre of their lives and identities. Within these discourses moral responsibility is sometimes attached to individuals, while at other times and places individuals are disinvested of blame by dint of the social circumstances in which they act. Thus, the girls move between the individualistic and social poles of moral discourses. Here, the girls used television soap opera as a stimulus for discussions about ethics which form the basis of a self-fashioning project.

Further reading

Ang, I. (1996) *Living Room Wars: Rethinking Media Audiences for a Postmodern World*. London and New York: Routledge.

Buckingham, D. (1987) *Public Secrets: EastEnders and its Audience*. London: British Film Institute.

Gillespie, M. (1995) *Television, Ethnicity and Cultural Change*. London and New York: Routledge.

Liebes, T. and Katz, E. (1991) *The Export of Meaning*. Oxford: Oxford University Press.

Morley, D. (1992) *Television, Audiences and Cultural Studies*. London and New York: Routledge.

6 | TELEVISION AND THE CULTURAL POLITICS OF IDENTITY

Cultural studies is, and always has been, a multidisciplinary field of inquiry which blurs the boundaries between itself and other disciplines. And yet, cultural studies cannot be said to be 'anything'; it is not literary studies, it is not sociology and it is not linguistics, though it draws upon these subject areas. Thus, for cultural studies to differentiate itself from other subject areas there must, as Hall (1992b) argues, be something at stake. Here, Hall is pointing us to cultural studies' affiliation with contexts outside of the academic, specifically to social and political movements. That is, cultural studies has made claims for its connections to matters of power and politics, to the need for social change and to representations of and 'for' marginalized social groups, particularly those of class, gender and race (but also of age, disability, nationality, and so on).

In this sense, cultural studies is not only a body of theory but also a set of political stances including the production of theory as a political practice (indeed, its pre-eminent practice). Here, knowledge is never a neutral or objective phenomenon, but a matter of *positionality*, of the place from which one speaks, to whom, and for what purposes. However, Hall (1992b) also points out the need to maintain due modesty about what theoretical cultural studies can practically achieve in the face of overwhelming indifference to it. Nevertheless, this does not mean that one should not keep pointing to the insights theory can offer.

In general, cultural studies seeks to play a demystifying role. That is, it points to the constructed character of cultural texts and to the myths and ideologies which are embedded in them in the hope of producing subject positions, and real subjects, who are enabled to oppose subordination.

Indeed, as a political theory, cultural studies has hoped to organize disparate oppositional groups into an alliance of cultural politics. Broadly speaking, such a cultural politics is organized around

- the power to name
- the power to represent common sense
- the power to create 'official versions'
- the power to represent the legitimate social world.

(Jordan and Weedon 1995: 13)

For example, to describe British Asians as full human beings and citizens with equal social rights and obligations is quite a different matter from regarding them as a sub-human pool of colonial labour. That is, to use the language of **citizenship** to describe British Asians is a different representation of common sense and official ideology from one in which they are described as 'wogs', 'pakis' and 'aliens'. Further, the language of citizenship legitimizes the place of British Asians in business and politics while the language of the 'alien presence' denies this place and seeks to exclude them from the public affairs of the nation.

In particular, the cultural politics of identity involves the power to describe ourselves in what Rorty (1989) calls 'new languages'. These questions of cultural power translate into the practical purposes of identity politics when African Americans challenge the invisibility of black people on television or their representation as marginal and criminalized; when women redescribe themselves as citizens of equal standing with men, when class elite notions of the educational curriculum are expanded to include popular culture as well as Shakespeare; when the 'grey wolves' voice the discontents of forgotten and excluded older people and when gays and lesbians stage 'Pride'.

Thus, what is being argued is that issues of identity, which are themselves issues of language (see Chapter 1), are 'political' because they are intrinsically bound up with questions of power for, as we have seen, power is *productive* of the self. Power, as social regulation, enables some kinds of knowledge and identities to exist while denying it to others. Consequently, it matters whether we are described as black or white, male or female, African or American, rich or poor, because of the differential cultural resources by which we will have been constituted and the regulation to which we are 'subjected'.

This chapter is organized around four issues which relate to the politics of cultural identity.

- The first issue is concerned with the questions of *agency* and identity. That is, if identity and subjectivity are discursive constructions and the outcome of disciplinary determinations, in what sense can subjects have the kind of self-motivated activity required for any politics of identity to be possible? For example, some feminists have been critical of Foucault for the fashion in which his characterization of persons as 'docile bodies' appears to undercut the grounds of a feminist politics based on human agency.

- The second issue relates to the difficulty of *founding* or justifying any politics when we acknowledge that there is no access to a universal truth which could be the basis for political action. This problem I shall approach through the work of Richard Rorty and his version of postmodern pragmatism, in which he suggests that we do not require universal foundations as the basis for political action.
- The third issue concerns the space within which the cultural politics of identity can operate, that is, the issue of the *public sphere* as a site for cultural and political debate and the place of television within it.
- The fourth issue centres on the forms of cultural politics which surround *television,* including the attempt to find the institutional space to make 'transgressive' or 'alternative' programmes.

Identity and the question of agency

Though the argument that identities are discursive constructions is now widely held within cultural studies, it is not without its problems. In particular, if subjects and identities are the product of discursive and disciplinary practices, if they are social and cultural 'all the way down', how can we conceive of persons as able to act and engender change in the social order? Since subjects can appear within these arguments to be 'products' rather than 'producers', how shall we account for the human *agency* which would seem to be the basis of political action?

The concept of agency has commonly been associated with notions of freedom, free will, action, creativity, originality and the very possibility of change through the acts of free agents. However, we need to differentiate between a 'mystical' or metaphysical notion of free agency in which agents are self-constituting (that is bring themselves into being out of nothingness) and a concept of agency as *socially produced* and enabled by differentially distributed social resources giving rise to various degrees of the ability to act in specific spaces. That is, there is a conceptual difference between acts considered to have been made by agents who are free in the sense of 'not determined' and agency as the *socially constituted capacity to act.* For example, that an aspect of the identities of the girls discussed in Chapter 5 is centred on 'Asian-ness' is not something they simply chose, but is the outcome of the values and practices of the global Asian diaspora and British culture, which in turn enable them to perform British Asian-ness as agents.

The notion that agents are free in the sense of undetermined is untenable for two reasons:

- In what could an undetermined or uncaused act consist? Such an idea assumes that something is created from nothing, that being and acting can appear from nowhere. Such a notion must be metaphysical in its thrust and rely on some God-like form of original creation.
- There is enough historical and sociological work available, not least from Foucault, Giddens, Hall and other writers deployed in this book, to show that subjects are determined, caused and produced, by social forces which lie outside of themselves as individuals (see Chapter 1).

Thus, it is possible, and more tenable, to argue that agency consists of acts which make a pragmatic difference so that agency means the ability to enact X rather than Y course of action. Of course, precisely because agency is socially and differentially produced some actors have more options and domains of action than others. Thus, those who have been acculturalized as male or white may have more socially constituted and regulated options for action than others.

A notion of agency based on the idea of 'could have acted differently' avoids some of the problems of the metaphysical 'free as undetermined' because the pathways of action are themselves socially constituted. However, on what basis can actors 'choose' one act instead of another and what are the causes of such choice? Since we have no practical way of comparing the future outcomes of actions we face a series of contingent choices which can be made only on the basis of culturally specific *value judgements,* values in which we have been previously socially constituted. In other words, the basis for our choice does not spring out of thin air but has been determined or caused by the very way we are constituted as subjects, by where, when and how we came to be who we are. For example, that the subjects of postmodern globalized culture value choice and are presented with an array of lifestyle options is precisely the consequence of the globalization of consumer capital-ism and the constitution of subjects at a specific moment in time and space.

In short, what is being argued is that *agency is determined*, that it is itself a *social construction* and that agents are *not free in the sense of undeter-mined.* However, agency, understood as our ability to act, is a culturally *intelligible* way of understanding ourselves and we clearly have the existen-tial experience of facing and making choices, we do act even though those choices and acts are determined by social forces, particularly language, which lie beyond us as individual subjects. Indeed, the existence of social structures, and of language in particular, *enables* action so that neither human freedom nor human action can consist of an *escape* from social determinants (Giddens 1984).

Freedom and determination

It is felicitous to consider freedom and determination as *different modes of discourse* and discursively constructed experience (Wolff 1981). That is, discourses of freedom and discourses of determination are different, socially produced, narratives about human beings which have different purposes and are applicable in different ways. For example, while we might accept the notion of determination 'all the way down' this has no bearing on existential experience; in other words, it plays no part in our everyday practices. Further, since discourses of freedom and discourses of determination are socially produced for *different purposes* in different realms it makes sense to talk about freedom from political persecution or economic scarcity without the need to say that agents are free in some metaphysical undetermined way.

To regard the self and identities as both contingent and determined does not mean that we are not *original*. While cultural identity is a social accomplishment, our individuality can be understood in terms of the specific ways in which the social resources of the self are arranged. That is, while we are all subject to the 'impress of history', the particular form that we take, the specific arrangements of discursive elements, is unique to each individual for we have all had unique patterns of gendered relations, class structures, ethnic cultures, friends and family as discursive resources. Here, a reading of Freud can be useful since the symbolic productions of the unconscious are unique to each individual operating with very particular resources, associations and identifications (Rorty 1989). Thus, the self is 'original' like the moving elements of a kaleidoscope or like a snowflake constructed from the common ingredients that make up snow.

Innovation and change

Nor does the determined or caused contingency of the self make the question of *innovative acts* especially problematic since

- creativity can be seen as the ability to utter sentences which do not fit into old language games but serve to modify them and create new ones (Rorty 1991a)
- innovation can be understood as the practical outcomes of unique combinations of social structures, discourses and psychic arrangements.

Innovation as such is *not a quality of the act,* nor a question of intentionality, but is a retrospective judgement by us on the form and outcomes of that act made in relation to other acts in specific historical and cultural conjunctures. Further, innovative acts can be regarded as the consequence of discourse formed in one sphere of cultural life transported into another. For example, discourses of individuality and creativity formed in and through artistic practice or in the domain of leisure activities may have disruptive and disturbing consequences in the context of discipline oriented work organizations, schools or in families structured round an ideology of parental authority and control.

Innovation and change are therefore possible both because we are unique interdiscursive individuals and because the discourses which constitute society are themselves contradictory. In the context of contemporary western societies, it is intelligible to us to say that we can 'rearticulate' ourselves, re-create ourselves, form ourselves anew in unique ways. This does not mean that we are not caused or determined but that we *make ourselves singular by making new languages*, new metaphors to describe ourselves with, which expand the repertoire of alternative descriptions (Rorty 1989).

Social change

In so far as this applies to individuals, so it applies also to social formations. Social change becomes possible through rethinking the articulation of the elements of 'societies', of redescribing the social order and the possibilities for the future. Of course, as Wittgenstein (1953) argued, there is no such thing as a private language, so that rethinking is a social and political activity. Thus, social change is connected to rethinking, redescribing and to the material practices that it organizes. Rethinking ourselves, which emerges through social practice and more often than not through social contradiction and conflict, brings new political subjects and practices into being. For example, in relation to Rastafarians in Jamaica, Hall has argued that

> Rasta was a funny language, borrowed from a text – the Bible – that did not belong to them; they had to turn the text upside-down, to get a meaning which fitted their experience. But in turning the text upside-down they remade themselves; they positioned themselves differently as new political subjects; they reconstructed themselves as blacks in the new world: they *became* what they are. And, positioning themselves in that way, they learned to speak a new language. And they spoke it with a vengeance . . . they only constitute a political force, that is, they *become* a historical force in so far as they are constituted as new political subjects.
> (Hall 1996b: 143–4)

However, even if we accept the possibility of an agency based politics we are left with a problem of justification, for post-Enlightenment philosophy from Nietzsche to Derrida has pointed to a loss of faith in the universal foundational schemes that have justified the rational, scientific, technological and political projects of the western world. This is what Lyotard (1984) describes as 'incredulity toward metanarratives'; that is, doubt about the certainties that traditional explanations of the world have offered us. This is particularly so in the context of globalization, which in opening up all cultural traditions to scrutiny has decentred western notions of progress and correct solutions to problems. For example, the grand narratives (big guiding stories) of Marxism, white civilization or Christianity have sought to assure us about the direction of politics/history or morality respectively. Once we no longer believe in grand narratives we are left with a problem, namely, on what basis can we justify our political values and activities if there is no universal truth with which to underpin them? As one possible answer to this question I now turn to the pragmatist philosopher Richard Rorty.

Politics without foundations

Rorty (1980, 1989, 1991a, 1991b) has consistently spelled out a philosophy of language, self and political action which combines an anti-representational view of language with a description of the self as a centreless weave of beliefs and attitudes. He argues that we do not require universal foundations to pursue a pragmatic improvement of the human condition on the basis of the values of our own traditions. Indeed, we cannot escape values anymore than we can ground them in metaphysics so that a historically and culturally specific value based politics is an inevitable and inescapable condition of human existence.

Under the influence of Darwin's evolutionary story, Rorty holds to a naturalistic and holistic description of human beings as animals who adapt and change in the context of their environment. Such adaptation has no telos, or inevitable historical point to which it is unfolding; rather, human 'development' is the outcome of numerous acts of chance and environmental adaptation which make the 'direction' of human evolution contingent so that 'progress' or 'purpose' can be given meaning only as a *retrospectively* told story.

For Rorty, the relationship between language and the rest of the material universe is one of causality and not of adequacy of representation or expression. That is, we can usefully try to explain how human organisms come to

act or speak in particular ways but we cannot usefully see language as representing the world in ways which more or less correspond to the material
world. For Rorty, '*no* linguistic items represent *any* non-linguistic items'
(Rorty 1991a: 2), that is, no chunks of language line up with or correspond
to chunks of reality. Above all, there is no archimedian vantage point from
which one could verify the 'truth' of any correspondence between the world
and language. Thus, while we can describe this or that discourse, chunk of
language, as being more or less useful and as having more or less desirable
consequences, we cannot do so by reference to its correspondence with an
independent reality but only in relation to our *values*.

Truth as social commendation

Rorty argues that most of the beliefs that we hold to be 'true' are indeed
'true', though truth is not an epistemological statement about correspondence between language and reality but a consensual term referring to
degrees of agreement and coordination of habits of action. To say that something is not necessarily true is now to suggest that someone has come up
with a better way of describing things where 'better' refers to a value judgement about the consequences of describing the world in this way (including
its predictive power).

It follows that truth, knowledge and understanding can be only from
within particular language-games, that is, from within particular kinds of
acculturalization. As Rorty puts it,

> no description of how things are from a God's-eye-view, no skyhook
> provided by some contemporary or yet-to-be developed science, is
> going to free us from the contingency of having been acculturated as we
> were. Our acculturation is what makes certain options live, or momen-
> tous, or forced, while leaving others dead, or trivial, or optional. We
> can only hope to transcend our acculturation if our culture contains (or,
> thanks to disruptions from outside or internal revolt, comes to contain)
> splits which supply toe holds for new initiatives. . . . So our best chance
> for transcending our acculturation is to be brought up in a culture
> which prides itself on not being monolithic – on its tolerance for a plu-
> rality of subcultures and its willingness to listen to neighbouring cul-
> tures.
>
> (Rorty 1991a: 13–14)

I take Rorty to be arguing that it is desirable to open ourselves up to as many
possible descriptions and redescriptions of our globalized world as possible.
For Rorty, the contingency of language and the irony which follows from

this (irony here means holding to beliefs and attitudes which one knows are contingent and could be otherwise, that is they have no universal foundations) leads us to ask about what kind of human beings we want to be (for no transcendental truth and no transcendental God can answer this question for us). This takes the form of questions about us as individuals – who we want to be – and questions about our relations to fellow human beings: how shall we treat others? For Rorty, these are political and pragmatic questions bringing forth political-value responses rather than metaphysical or epistemological issues. Further, acceptance of the legitimacy of a range of truth claims is in itself a political position, and not an abandonment of politics as some critics have suggested, since it signals support for cultural pluralism and a multitude of cultural identities.

The consequences of pragmatism

In this context, the desirability of cultural and political pluralism, and of describing the self and identity in terms of a centreless weave of beliefs and attitudes, is not the outcome of epistemological claims about what the world or the self are 'really' like but is based on an evaluation of the pragmatic consequences of adopting this view. Continued redescription of our world is a pragmatically desirable thing to do because it offers the possibility both of an enlargement of the self and the improvement of the human condition through comparison between different actual practices. For example, one of the consequences of multiple descriptions of the world is the greater likelihood of finding useful ways of adapting to and shaping our environment. A second consequence is to adopt the image that

> our minds gradually growing larger and stronger and more interesting by the addition of new options – new candidates for belief and desire, phrased in new vocabularies. The principal means for such growth . . . is the gradual enlargement of our imagination by the metaphorical use of old marks and noises.
>
> (Rorty 1991a: 14)

A third significant consequence is that of listening to the voices of others who may be suffering where the avoidance of suffering is taken to be the paramount political virtue. This entails a commitment to the politics of democratic cultural pluralism. In other words, both individual identity projects and the cultural politics of collectivities require us to forge new languages, new ways of describing ourselves, which recast our place in the world. *The struggle to have new languages accepted in the wider society is the realm of cultural politics.* For example, Rorty argues that feminism represents the redescription of women as subjects. The critical point of his argument is that

> injustices may not be perceived as injustices, even by those who suffer them, until somebody invents a previously unplayed role. Only if some-body has a dream, a voice, and a voice to describe the dream, does what looked liked nature begin to look like culture, what looked liked fate begin to look like a moral abomination. For until then only the lan-guage of the oppressor is available, and most oppressors have had the wit to teach the oppressed a language in which the oppressed will sound crazy – even to themselves – if they describe themselves as oppressed.
>
> (Rorty 1995: 126)

The politics of new languages

Thus, the language of feminism brings oppression into view and expands the logical space for moral and political deliberation. In this sense, feminism (and all forms of identity politics) does not need essentialism or **foun-dationalism** at all; what is required is 'new languages' in which the claims of women do not sound crazy but come to be accepted as 'true' (in the sense of a social commendation). Thus, *feminism does not involve less distorted per-ception, but is a language with consequences which serve particular pur-poses and values*. The emergence of such a language is regarded not as the emergence of universal truth but as a part of an evolutionary struggle which has no predetermined destiny. Rorty regards feminism as creating 'women's experience' by creating a language rather than finding what it is to be a woman or unmasking truth and injustice. As such, feminism is a form of 'prophetic pragmatism' which imagines, and seeks to bring into being, an alternative form of community. Feminism forges a moral identity for women as women by gaining semantic authority over themselves and not by assum-ing that there is an universal essential identity for women waiting to be found.

In her discussion of Rorty's arguments, Fraser (1995a) agrees with the pragmatism which he propounds but argues that he locates the redescrip-tions involved exclusively in *individual* women. In contrast, she suggests that such redescriptions are to be seen as a part of a *collective* feminist poli-tics and further, that such a politics must involve argument and contestation about which new descriptions will count and which women will be empowered. Thus, Fraser links feminism to the best of the democratic tra-dition and to the creation of a 'feminist counter sphere' of collective debate and practice.

In sum, what is being argued is that *we do not need universal foundations* to validate political values or political action. Rather, political projects can be justified in terms of pragmatism related to our values. Knowledge is not a matter of getting a true or objective picture of reality, but of learning how best to cope with the world. We produce various descriptions of the world and use those which seem best suited to our purposes. We have a multiplicity of vocabularies because we have a multiplicity of purposes. The crucial questions are, which descriptions best achieve our purposes, what are our purposes and whose descriptions came to count as 'true'? The conflict over each of these questions constitutes core concerns of cultural politics including the relationship between personal identity projects, the need for social solidarity and the organization of the public sphere.

Private identities, democratic citizenship and the public sphere

When, as Rorty argues, no science or religion can found moral or political views, a tension may arise between our individual identity projects and a collective politics of social solidarity. On the one hand, the contemporary concern with 'identity' has something in common with the 'romantic' notion of self-invention and enlargement whose moral imperative is to continually add to and enrich descriptions of oneself. On the other hand, a commitment to social solidarity might imply acceptance of, and subjection to, the discipline of a collective morality and/or identity. As Butler has argued, even the identity categories of feminism can 'limit and constrain in advance the very cultural possibilities that feminism is supposed to open up' (Butler 1990: 147), not least through the 'policing' of what it means to be a 'woman'. The same argument would apply to ethnic identities. That is, commitment to a particular ethnic identity as a form of solidarity can constitute a collective and essentialist disciplining of private identities and projects.

Private vs public

While private projects are necessarily social in that identity is constructed with public language, and some *cultures* value individualism while others do not, and are therefore causes of individual projects, there is no necessary reason why a commitment to an individual project *must* involve any particular political project. Though the distinction between the 'public' and the 'private' is a culturally contingent one, nevertheless, if one accepts that there are benefits from maintaining this distinction for practical purposes, then one may argue for a global culture which will 'make it easy as possible for people to achieve their wildly different private ends without hurting each other' (Rorty 1991b: 196).

Not only may private projects be set within larger social and historical narratives (for example diaspora stories) which give coherence to individual lives, but also it is consistent to forge social institutions which best allow for different and diverse private identity projects to prosper. Thus, while such a politics must accept that we all have our private, contingent, identity projects to pursue, that we have a right to 'make ourselves' as we see fit and to pursue our own 'originality', at the same time, our own identity projects depend on the development of a *collective* cultural space and a collective politics since, as Bauman argues, 'Survival in the world of contingency and diversity is possible only if each difference recognises another difference as the necessary condition of the preservation of its own' (Bauman 1991: 256).

This is not simply an abstract philosophical or epistemological issue but a pragmatic one concerning the ability of people to live together. Although languages and ways of life can be said to have no common foundation – there is no exact and direct correspondence between languages – nevertheless, we can *learn* other languages and take practical steps to communicate with each other (Rorty 1991a). This suggests the need for dialogue and underpins the procedural arguments for a diverse and plural public sphere of *citizens* where citizenship as a form of identity provides the grounds for a shared polity. That is, the best chance of pursuing a private identity project may be to live in a culture which prides itself on being heterogeneous.

Identity of citizenship

We can, as Dahlgren (1995) argues, see citizenship as a form of identity, one aspect of our multiple identities, so that a civic 'identity of citizenship' holds together the diversity of values and life-worlds within a democratic framework. The identity of citizenship may be the only thing we have in common, but a commitment by diverse groups to the procedures of democracy, and to intersubjectively recognized rights and duties of citizenship in the social, civil and political domains, advances democracy and provides the conditions for particularistic identity projects. This involves what Mouffe (1992) calls the 'hegemony of democratic values'. Such a view does not require us to accept all current versions of what democracy means but seeks to extend its reach from formal governmental procedures to include economic, organizational and domestic democracy. There are, of course, no universal foundations for radical democracy though there is the historically contingent grounds of the democratic political tradition which values justice, tolerance, solidarity and difference. The concept of citizenship is a mechanism for linking the micro-politics of cultural identities with the official macro politics of institutional and cultural rights. As Mercer argues, 'the concept of citizenship is crucial because it operates in the hinge that articulates civil society and the state in an open-ended and indeterminate relationship (Mercer 1994: 284). From within the British Asian context Parekh suggests what a stress on citizenship and cultural rights might mean for the politics of 'new ethnicities'.

> First, cultural diversity should be given public status and dignity. . . . Second, minorities can hardly expect to be taken seriously unless they accept the full obligations of British citizenship. . . . Third, the minority communities must be allowed to develop at their own pace and in a direction of their own choosing. . . . Fourth, like individuals, communities can only flourish under propitious conditions. . . . Fifth, the distinct character of ethnic communities needs to be recognized by our legal system.
>
> (Parekh 1991: 197–9; cited in McGuigan 1996: 151)

McGuigan (1996) comments that Parekh's limitation of his discussion of citizenship to the nation-state may be outdated in the context of globalization, which has dislocated the taken-for-granted modern nexus of culture, ethnicity, state and citizen. He cites Turner (1994) to the effect that we may need to develop an idea of global human rights not tied to any specific nation-state, but concludes that while global citizenship is a fine ideal, local struggles in the context of national formations will remain the key sites of action. Here, the notion of the public sphere retains considerable leverage.

The public sphere

For Habermas (1989), the public sphere is a realm which emerged in a specific phase of 'bourgeois society'. It is a space that mediates between civil society and the state, in which the public organizes itself, and in which 'public opinion' is formed. Within this sphere individuals are able to develop themselves and engage in debate about the direction of society.

Habermas attempts to ground the public sphere in the notion of an 'ideal speech situation' in which competing truth claims are subject to rational debate and argument. Thus, the public sphere is conceived as a space for debate based on conversational equality. Yet, as Fraser (1995b) has argued, no such conditions exist in practice. Rather, social inequality means that not only are citizens denied equal access to the public sphere, but also subordinate groups are denied participatory parity and the space to articulate their own languages, needs and demands. According to Fraser, a modern conception of the public sphere such as Habermas's requires interlocutors to bracket status differences, to confine discussion to questions of the public good (barring private concerns) and to create only one, because common, public sphere. However, given that social inequality cannot be bracketed, that many private issues are public (e.g. domestic violence) and there are competing versions of the public good, she argues that a postmodern conception of the public sphere should accept the desirability of multiple publics and multiple public spheres while at the same time working to reduce social inequality. For example, she argues that feminism represents a 'counter public sphere' of debate and political activity.

Though I think Habermas is mistaken in his attempt to construct a universal and transcendental rational justification for the public sphere, as a *normative* position the concept retains political leverage. That is, it can be justified on the value based pragmatic grounds of cultural pluralism rather than on epistemological grounds. Hence, the objective of the movement towards radical democracy within the public sphere might be then taken as

> A society where everyone, whatever his/her sex, race, economic position, sexual orientation, will be in an effective situation of equality and participation, where no basis of discrimination will remain and where self-management will exist in all fields.
>
> (Mouffe 1984, cited Best and Kellner 1991: 196)

Diversity and solidarity

These abstract principles can be made more concrete and relevant to television through the values of diversity and solidarity. The concept of *diversity* suggests that pluralistic media are expected to represent the full range of public opinion, cultural practices and social and geographical conditions. *Solidarity* suggests forms of sharing and cooperation which are genuine and not enforced, that is it implies supportive tolerance and solidarity rather than control. In this context, television *could* act as cultural and social interpreter and promote an arena of solidarity in which to present diverse values. This then is the realm of the cultural politics of television.

The cultural politics of television

Television is at the centre of public life and cultural debate within most cultures under contemporary global conditions. Indeed, while Habermas (1989) bemoans the decline of the public sphere, other commentators (Giddens 1990; Thompson 1995) have argued that modern societies have witnessed the *enlargement* of the public sphere by the media as they bring greater visibility to public discourses and action. Indeed, the public sphere is

now arguably a media saturated one in which the visual has gained in prominence over the verbal and mediated relationships are more conspicuous than
face-to-face encounters. In this mediated sphere, not only does 'the public'
enter the domestic sphere via the television set but also the boundaries
between the public and the private are blurred. This is also, paradoxically, a
public sphere in which entertainment is as significant as news and the language of advertising and commercial interests is ensconced in the public
domain.

Nevertheless, television can contribute to the cultural politics of identity
by expanding the range of voices and identities seen and heard in the public
sphere. That is, we should seek from television a *diversity of representations,*
which, in turn, suggests the need to produce 'transgressive' programmes
which offer competing ways of looking at the world. By 'transgressive' or
'alternative' I mean the production and dissemination of those redescriptions of the social order and of cultural identities which were earlier referred
to as 'new languages'. As such, a cultural politics for television implies the
need to press against the limitations of the regulated representations which
television currently offers and to assist in the development of alternative discursive resources, that is, other voices which might destabilize cultural
hegemony.

Although a cultural politics of television can take a number of forms I
would suggest that most fall into one of the following categories.

- *Analysis of television programmes which contributes to alternative critical discursive resources for audiences.*

Thus, Eco (1986) has argued that what is required is a form of 'semiological guerrilla warfare' in which audiences become better equipped to decode
programmes in a variety of ways and be aware of how television polices the
boundaries of meaning. Indeed, the deconstruction of television from within
cultural studies could be said to contribute to just such a strategy. For
example, in Chapters 3 and 4 we encountered analysis of the representation
of race and gender which arguably contribute to a deconstruction of racist
and sexist practices.

Such analytical deconstruction is especially useful where it informs the
creation of educational materials. For example, semiotics has underpinned
the production of a number of teaching packs by the British Film Institute
(BFI) and the Society for Education in Film and Television (SEFT). Others,
for example Masterman (1980), have argued for a sustained strategy of
'teaching television' in schools and collages with a particular emphasis upon
its language and grammar. Of course, whether such a strategy is effective or
not must be a moot point; indeed some commentators (e.g. Fiske 1989) suggest that audiences for popular programmes carry out such semiological

warfare in any case. Accordingly, media and cultural studies is torn between positions which argue on the one hand for the necessity of critical media education and on the other for a sense that audiences already have acute deconstructive skills.

- *Attempts to change the organizational configurations of television leading to greater diversity.*

Many commentators have argued for a restructuring of the political economy of television in order to allow outside voices into the mainstream. In particular, this has been the bottom line defence of public service television (as part of the public sphere) which, it is argued, is able to produce programmes that television funded from advertising could not. In Britain, much consultation went into the launch of Channel Four which many hoped would act as a publisher for a variety of alternative projects. While Channel Four has indeed widened the scope of television in the UK, its financial base, allied to government policy, has given it a much more mainstream flavour than its original supporters had hoped for. Further, in the USA and Australia, the Public Broadcasting Service (PBS) and Special Broadcasting Service (SBS) respectively pick up only 2–5 per cent of the audience with programming which, though not screened on the networks, is not necessarily providing space for 'new languages'. Indeed, right across the globe, the successful lobbyists for change have not been supporters of public service television, but the advocates of commercial and market led television (see C. Barker 1997b).

- *The production of 'transgressive' programmes from outside of established television organizations.*

Despite the overwhelming predominance of transnational corporate control of production and distribution there are signs of alternative productions taking place outside the domains of mainstream television organizations, albeit on a rather limited scale (Dowmunt 1993). Thus, Batty (1993) describes the development of 'alternative' television in Ernabella, a remote Aboriginal community located in the semi-arid regions of northern South Australia. The project began as a small-scale undertaking producing video programmes for the Ernabella community but, as the members became more confident, they began to stitch together locally produced programmes with some from the national ABC network which they accessed via a satellite dish. The success of this venture, argues Batty, is based on the adaptation of international technology by local people for local needs and funded from local sources.

While Ernabella television was in the remote Australian outback, 'Deep Dish' was a project conceived in the heartland of the USA. Lucas and Wallner

(1993) describe how, in the midst of the Gulf War, a group of media activists became discontented with the lack of serious discussion or questioning in the mainstream US media. In response they launched the *Gulf Crisis TV Project* with the express purpose of producing alternative programmes. They were then able to persuade a number of access cable channels and PBS stations to screen the programmes, which were distributed nationally by hiring satellite time. Thus, the very commercial availability of television technology was being put to a quite different purpose. However, though such projects may be welcome, they are difficult to achieve and always open to the charge that they attain small audiences of the 'already converted'.

- *The production of 'transgressive' programmes from within established television organizations.*

A more traditional approach to the politics of television has been to seek to produce 'transgressive' or 'alternative' programmes for mainstream television. For example, during the 1970s, playwright Trevor Griffiths (1976) coined the phrase 'strategic penetration' for his attempt to write 'radical' drama for British television. His argument was that plays which exploited and subverted the conventions of mainstream television and reached a mass audience were very much more effective than those films or plays which were produced outside of those conventions or in a different medium. Indeed, during the 1970s and 1980s, Griffiths was successful in having a string of works broadcast by British television, some of which were exported to the USA and Australia. Similarly, in the USA some film makers have attempted to produce socially critical films for television such as the acclaimed *Bitter Harvest*.

However, it is unclear whether the conditions still exist within television to pursue such a strategy. For example, the evidence in Britain is that the cultural space within television which allowed such works to be broadcast has all but disappeared so that Griffiths has retreated from television and returned to the theatre. Nor is television in the USA renowned for its radicalism. However, given that the overwhelming characteristic of television is its ability to consistently draw a huge audience, albeit one that is showing signs of fragmenting into more specialist niches, the strategy of producing challenging programmes for mainstream television is the one which perhaps offers the greatest rewards, though it may also be the hardest to achieve.

Institutional dimensions of power

Since any politics of television needs to be multidimensional, there is no reason to suggest that any one of the above strategies for intervention should be privileged to the extent of excluding the others. Different strategies may be more or less viable at distinct moments of time, under particular social, economic and political circumstances with divergent audiences in mind and in the context of a range of institutional and funding arrangements. Of course, which ever strategy is pursued, a crucial issue is the need to secure the material *resources and institutional space* without which 'new voices' cannot be heard.

Thus, Bennett (1992) argues that the textual politics which much cultural studies produces ignores the institutional dimensions of cultural power. Consequently, he urges cultural studies to adopt a more pragmatic approach, to work with cultural producers and to 'put policy into cultural studies'. In particular, if we are to expand the range of representations on television through the production of programmes which give voice to the 'new languages' of cultural identity, we face the difficulties of securing the necessary resources from *within* television organizations. This necessarily involves a politics of television organizations.

The politics of television organizations

The possibilities of producing 'transgressive' programmes within mainstream television organizations will differ from country to country depending, at least in part, on the institutional arrangements that exist in each context. However, in general terms, the constraining and enabling aspects of the organization of television as they relate to the production of transgressive programmes centres on its funding and regulation.

The funding arrangements of television

Television production is an expensive business, for example, an episode of a popular US series can cost in excess of $1.5 million, and these costs are escalating by the minute. Consequently, no television organization, whether public service or commercial, can afford to produce programmes which do not have a significant payback. Alternative voices, or new languages, if they are to be heard, will have to find leverage either in terms of profits, audience share or prestige (which for public service organizations in particular may act as a buffer against straightforward profit taking).

In US television, a system dominated by ratings and advertisers, a great deal of time and effort goes into testing pilot programmes before they go into full production since, for both the networks and the programme makers, profit is associated with either audience maximization or niche markets made up of persons with high disposable income. In Britain, the BBC and ITV companies have traditionally had more scope to produce programmes which do not have to maximize their ratings as evidenced by the tradition of single drama and documentaries which are absent from the US scene. Accordingly, at least in Europe and Australia, it has been argued that public funding and regulation allows for a greater diversity of programming and representations of cultural identity.

Public service television

Though the particular arrangements for public service television vary, it is marked, according to Brants and Siune (1992), by an element of public finance and a degree of protection from competition, combined with some form of accountability to political representatives of the public via administrative organization. These elements of a public service model give rise to structural and institutional arrangements which were intended to offer accountability, access and adequacy or quality of programming. In particular, it was argued that whereas commercial television must seek the largest possible audience in order to sell viewers to advertisers, public service television can afford to produce programmes which cater for minority tastes and whose prime concern is aesthetic and political values. In terms of what Blumler (1992) calls 'vulnerable values', public television aims to offer a universal and comprehensive service with balanced, impartial, accurate, diverse and quality programming.

Commercial television

However, the political direction of television right across the globe is away from public service television and towards commercialization. Consequently, though a defence of public television is one strategy for maintaining and expanding cultural pluralism (see C. Barker 1997b), pragmatic cultural politics requires that one work with existing arrangements and consider what the potential for intervention is within current commercial systems. Two possibilities present themselves within even the most commercially oriented of television set-ups.

First, the requirement to attract audiences does mean that commercial companies are susceptible to market/audience opinion and the lobbying of pressure groups, perhaps even more so than the rather institutionally sealed and protected public television companies. For example, long-term cultural changes combined with the lobbying of the African American community (and its not inconsiderable spending power) have meant that the overt racism of *Amos 'n Andy* is simply unacceptable on US television. As we saw in Chapter 4, racism remains within US television but it would be churlish and stubborn not to acknowledge that change has taken place.

The second possibility concerns the development of niche marketing and segmented audiences. On the one hand, the decline of universalism (a television service in which all persons can get all channels) means that audiences can avoid the full range of programmes if they so wish. Thus, a probing drama or cultural documentary can be condemned to the sidelines of a specialist television channel. However, the challenge of cable television, combined with the growth of niche marketing, has led mainstream networks to seek forms of quality 'cable resistant' programming which attracts audiences with high disposable incomes. For example, the ground breaking *Hill Street Blues* and *NYPD Blue* were viable in a US context not because they were immediately able to attract a massive audience, but because they were watched by an educated and relatively well off section of the audience attractive to advertisers. Finally, the development of cable television and niche marketing has allowed the emergence of channels dedicated to particular cultural groups. For example, both Telemundo and Univision, the Spanish language channels in the USA, cater for the Latino diaspora while the Black Television Network has sought to attract the African American community. Both have been successful and are surviving, though it is open to doubt whether the programming they offer is markedly different from mainstream television (dominated as they are by telenovelas and music video receptively) though the audience composition may be.

Regulation and censorship

While funding is one issue for the cultural politics of television, another relates to the question of state regulation and censorship. The ability to expand the diversity of voices and representations within the public sphere through the production of transgressive programmes must overcome the potential barrier of state regulation and censorship. No state allows a complete free for all in relation to the regulation of content on television. Even the USA, where financial considerations and the US constitution combine to limited state regulation, has rules which curtail what one can be said and shown. This, plus the power of advertisers, has led internal 'standards' departments to monitor the acceptability of programme content.

BBC
In Britain, though the BBC has a long tradition of independence from direct state intervention, it is subject to pressure from politicians, who control the long-term levels of the licence fee which, along with the BBC's charter, is subject to periodic renewal. Indeed, the history of the BBC is marked by a series of controversies and conflicts with politicians which have shaped the internal climate of the organization indicating what can and cannot be done.

For example, during the 1980s the BBC was subject to a series of attacks by Conservative politicians who claimed the organization's coverage was unbalanced. Perhaps the most famous of these interventions led to the banning of a programme about Northern Ireland, *At the Edge of the Union*.

Despite its system of hierarchical control, producers in the BBC do still retain a degree of autonomy greater than that found in many television systems. However, self-censorship has continued to curtail the expansion of the boundaries of the sayable on television. For example, the BBC has long had a referral-up system whereby decisions about controversial material have to be taken by higher management. This reflects both the concern about state intervention and the activities of such pressure groups as the 'conservative' National Viewers' and Listeners' Association.

Professionalism

In the context of liberal democratic states, the most severe restrictions on the range of representations which television produces do not come from state intervention or journalistic conspiracy but from the operation of *professionalism* based on the hegemonic values of a given culture. Professionalism can be seen as a strategy for controlling an occupation through a system of self-government which operates in the interests of its members. As such, professionalism is a market strategy operating through restriction of entry, control of training and definitions of standards (which exclude outsiders). In addition, professionalism has a moral and normative element by which a self-referential world claims a mandate to judge itself based on its control of knowledge and expertise. This leads to the development of house styles and working practices by which judgements are made in reference to already existing programmes (Elliott 1977). For example a good deal of the racism and sexism of television news, for example the association of young black men with crime remarked on in Chapter 3, is the outcome of 'normal' professionalism and the reproduction of a hegemonic common sense (Hall *et al.* 1978).

Extending the boundaries of representation

In sum, any attempt to extend the boundaries of representation faces the limitations of finance, state influence and professional values which mark the business of television. This is not to deny that the representations which television produces cannot and have not changed nor that television is not able to produce challenging material. Rather, it is to suggest that change in television is a slow business bound up with the wider values and *longue durée* of a given social formation. Consequently, it is the pressure brought to bear by feminists, gay activists, black organizations and that discursive construction 'public opinion' (as measured and constituted through ratings and market information about consumers' spending patterns) which are likely to yield the best hope of change. The wider politics of cultural identity are thus of direct relevance to the representations which television produces and circulates. It is the cultural politics of civil society which provides the coherence, vision and motivation for pragmatic organizational change.

Having said that, questions remain as to what kinds of programmes *do* widen the range and diversity of representations. What kinds of programmes are 'transgressive'? If the politics of identity are constituted by the invention and circulation of 'new languages' then questions arise regarding the *form* and *accessibility* of those languages.

The problem of realism

There has been a long-running debate about the domination of *realism* in television and the degree to which this represents a limitation, or opportunity, for 'new languages'. Thus, some writers have argued that the very naturalist/realist form of television precluded its use as a vehicle of 'radical democracy' because it fails to deconstruct the way that television works, offering instead simply another 'authoritarian' account of the world. In contrast, other critics have suggested that realism remains the most effective mode of communication under contemporary conditions being the only shared language with which to communicate with large television audiences.

According to Abercrombie *et al.*

> There seem to be three main parameters of realism: (1) realism offers a window on the world; (2) realism employs a narrative which has rationally ordered connections between events and characters; (3) realism conceals authorship and disguises the production process of a text.
>
> (Abercrombie *et al.* 1992: 119)

Though it may appear to do so, television does not offer a 'window-on-the-world'; rather, it constructs representations using realist *conventions* which suggests a picture of an independent world. For MacCabe (1981), there are two problems with these realist conventions:

- that they purport to 'show things as they really are' rather than acknowledging that television is a constructed representation from a particular perspective
- that the narrative structures of realism are organized by a 'metalanguage' of truth which privileges and disguises the editorial position rather than

letting different discourses about the world 'speak for themselves' and compete for allegiances.

Thus,

> The narrative discourse simply allows reality to appear and denies its own status as articulation. . . . The narrative prose achieves its position of dominance because it is in the position of knowledge and this function of knowledge is taken up in the cinema by the narration of events.
>
> (MacCabe 1981: 218)

For MacCabe, along with other anti-realists, what is required is not realism but practices which reveal their own techniques and allow for reflection upon the very processes of signification, a filmic and televisual work of deconstruction. Such effects are said to have been achieved through the modernist techniques of directors like Jean-Luc Godard, which show the operation of cameras and refuse the smooth flow of realist narrative by jumping without 'motivation' from place to place or time to time. In this vein, stories do not follow the established convention of linear causality or the 'ordinary' flow of everyday time.

The politics of representation

MacCabe's anti-realism chimes in many respects with Hall's (1996d) call for a 'politics of representation', which explores the power relations embedded in the processes of signification and representation. As we saw in Chapter 3, the demand for realistic and positive images of black people is problematic because it rests on untenable essentialist conceptions of identity and a reflectionist (realist) epistemology. Hence Hall's wish for representations that acknowledge the arbitrariness of signification and deconstruct a black–white binary. Likewise, in Chapter 4, we saw how feminism has moved from an 'images of women' approach premised on a notion of representational adequacy to a 'politics of the signifier' in which 'woman' is a constitutive effect of representation. Here, we noted Kaplan's (1992) discussion of Madonna as exemplifying the destabilizing of gender through shifting signifiers and codes of sexuality.

However, the deconstructive work is, ironically, a construction itself. It is a language of its own. The problem is that large numbers of people do not speak that language and transgressive performances may not be read as such by audiences who do not already understand the 'rules' being violated and the purposes of the performance. For example, Madonna's performance of Indian identity (see Chapter 4) can be read as a deconstruction of all ethnic identities, but was also understood as an offence to Hindu beliefs and practices. To speak to audiences in difficult and unintelligible (to parts of the audience) ways may be to deny oneself the possibility of communication. Consequently, as Wolff (1981) has argued,

> The techniques and styles of cultural intervention are . . . closely connected to the context and conditions of its occurrence. It is not possible to say, in the abstract, that realist and naturalist modes of representation are always wrong-because realism may be the only possible language of communication for a particular audience.
>
> (Wolff 1981: 93)

More recently, it is claimed that postmodernism challenges the domination of realism in television, but, unlike modernism, does this through accessible *popular culture*. Thus, Hutcheon (1989) argues that postmodernism makes the whole idea of representation problematic, even as it is complicit with it. That is, postmodernism challenges the 'reality' of representation even as it also makes representations. Hutcheon argues that, in general terms, postmodernism 'takes the form of self-conscious, self-contradictory, self-undermining statement. It is rather like saying something with inverted commas around what is being said' (Hutcheon 1989: 1). In other words, postmodernism is a form of ironic knowingness, ironic because it understands the very limitations and conditions of its own knowing.

As was noted in Chapter 2, the markers of postmodern form are aesthetic self-consciousness/self-reflexiveness, juxtaposition/montage, paradox, ambiguity, uncertainty and the blurring of the boundaries of genre, style and history. Ironically, while postmodernism in the arts is seen as reaction against modernism, postmodern television seems to take on and make popular those very *modernist* techniques such as montage, rapid cutting, non-linear narrative techniques and the decontextualization of images. Postmodernism in television is more a reaction against realism in a medium where modernism never really took hold (Kellner 1992).

Miami Vice

Kellner identifies *Miami Vice* as postmodern in two fundamental ways:

- its aesthetic style – montage, genre blurring, the spectacle.
- its polysemic character involving shifting identities, meanings and ideologies.

Kellner (1992) argues that the identities of the two main detective protagonists, Crokett and Tubbs, are 'unstable, fluid, fragmentary, disconnected, multiple, open and subject to dramatic transformation'. This is signified through their constantly changing looks, styles and appearances, together with their interchanging of identities as cops with undercover roles as rich drug runners and hip buyers. In assuming those roles, Crokett and Tubbs slip in and out of various identities, suggesting that identity is a construction not a given, that it is a game and a matter of style and choice. Postmodern identities are thus signalled as being both unstable and constructed more from the images of leisure and consumption than from the world of work and occupation.

The Simpsons

Also arguably postmodern is *The Simpsons*, which has made a 'dysfunctional' American family the ironic heroes of a series which is on the one hand simply a cartoon and on the other a set of subtle reflections on American life and culture. It is surely not coincidental that the centre of the Simpsons' life is the television set and that the programme makes a series of intertextual references to other television programmes and genres. Thus, *Itchy and Scratchy*, a cartoon watched by the Simpson children, both parodies *Tom and Jerry* and mocks the double standard by which we seem to condemn television violence even as we lap it up. Further, *The Simpsons* requires us to have a self-conscious awareness of television and film genres so that, for example, the ending of one episode is entirely a reworking of the final sequence of *The Graduate*.

South Park

Also a cartoon, *South Park* parallels *The Simpsons* in its use of irony and intertextuality. In particular, it presents us with a series of 'politically incorrect', racist, sexist and small minded characters. In fact, *South Park* is constituted by a series of parodies of stereotypes. As we laugh at these parodic characters we arguably insinuate the need for anti-racism and anti-sexism. At the same time, *South Park* ironically mocks the very language of 'political correctness' as inadequate. The replacement of one authoritarian language by another. Are we to condemn the representation of the African-American 'Chef' as the sexy 'Barry White' figure, or does it lead us to critique the stereotyping of African-Americans as sexy macho singers? As with *Miami Vice* and *The Simpsons*, it must be a moot point as to whether audiences read postmodern television in 'critical' terms or simply as 'playfulness', or indeed whether 'playfulness' is 'critical'.

Summary and conclusions

Throughout this book it has been argued that identities are *discursive constructions*; indeed, there can be no identity, experience or social practice which is not discursively constructed since we cannot escape language. In this sense, identities are social and cultural 'all the way down', by which it is meant that identities are wholly social constructions and cannot 'exist' outside of cultural representations. None of these arguments need efface the languages of human agency provided that one understands agency as itself a socially constructed narrative and differentially distributed set of capabilities to act. Though we may conceive of agents as being able to act reflexively, such narratives of the self are socially constituted resources. Nor do anti-essentialist arguments preclude identity politics, provided that such a politics is seen in terms of redescription and the development of 'new languages' along with the building of temporary strategic coalitions of people who share at least some values.

It was argued that while it is not possible to construct universal foundations for political projects, it is, nevertheless, possible to undertake political activity which seeks improvement of the human condition on the basis of the values of specific and particular traditions. Cultural politics was conceived in terms of redescriptions of the social world, value judgements about the pragmatic consequences of action and the formation of coalitions centred on the hegemony of democratic values. It was argued that an expanded public sphere and a notion of common civic citizenship could provide the shared values around which a coalition identity politics can form.

It was further suggested that any attempts to extend the boundaries of representation on television face the limitations of finance, state influence and professional values. While the representations which television produces can and have changed, this was seen as bound up with the contestation of wider social values in which the cultural politics of identity play a part. Finally, it was argued that the domination of the television screen by realism poses particular problems for the cultural politics of representation. On the one hand, realism can be seen to uphold the status quo through its ideological illusion of representing the world 'as it is' rather than exploring its own conditions of production, a feat which both modernism and postmodernism strive towards. On the other hand, realism may be the language with which television can best communicate with particular audiences.

Further reading

Abercrombie, N., Lash, S. and Longhurst, B. (1992) Popular representation: recasting realism, in S. Lash and J. Friedman (eds) *Modernity and Identity*. Oxford: Blackwell.

Dahlgren, P. (1995) *Television and the Public Sphere*. Newbury Park, CA and London: Sage.

Dowmunt, T. (1993) *Channels of Resistance*. London: British Film Institute.

Jordan, G. and Weedon, C. (1995) *Cultural Politics: Class, Gender, Race and the Postmodern World*. Oxford: Blackwell.

Rorty, R. (1989) *Contingency, Irony and Solidarity*. Cambridge: Cambridge University Press.

Woodward, K. (ed.) (1997) *Identity and Difference*. London and Thousand Oaks, CA: Sage.

TELEVISION, GLOBALIZATION AND CULTURAL IDENTITIES: A SUMMARY

Some while ago I came across a greetings card entitled 'True Self'. The card depicts a radical young man called Stanley, in walking attire, stubble and a Ying-Yang T-shirt, who has climbed the mountains of Tibet in search of his true self. High up on a ledge he finally discovers what he has been looking for, only to find that the object of his inquiry is a conservatively dressed businessman armed with a brief case and an umbrella. The joke of course lies in the contrasting images of the young man; the Stanley who searches is identifiable as the stereotype of the 'cultural left' while the Stanley he finds is of the 'conservative right'. Thus the caption read 'Stanley was deeply disappointed when, high in the Tibetan mountains, he finally found his true self'.

The card works, that is to say it is intelligible to us, because it draws from, and plays with, a cultural repertoire of the self with which most of us in the western world are familiar. Thus, we tend to assume that we have a true self, an identity which we possess and which can become known to us. Further, identity is intelligible, both by ourselves and by others, through forms of representation so that, at least in this case, identity is signified through the signs of dress which connote conservative businessman and radical hippie. These signs are social markers of taste, beliefs, attitudes and lifestyles. Thus identity is deemed to be personal and social, marking us out as both the same as and different from other kinds of people.

This book has sought to examine some of the debates in cultural studies about subjectivity and cultural identity and in doing so to explore the assumptions of the cultural repertoire which the card deploys. It was argued that identity is indeed concerned with sameness and difference, with the personal and the social and with forms of representation. However, we questioned the assumption that identity is something we possess, a fixed thing to be found.

Thus, Stanley may be both relieved and disappointed to learn that identity is not best understood as a fixed entity that we possess, but as a description of ourselves which marks a process of becoming. Overall, it was argued that:

- Identities are discursive constructions, that is descriptions of ourselves with which we identify and in which we emotionally invest.
- Identities are social and cultural 'all the way down', by which is meant that identities are wholly social constructions and cannot 'exist' outside of cultural representations.
- We do not *have* an identity, rather we *are* a fractured self made up of a multiple weave of attitudes and beliefs.

In this context, it was argued that race, ethnicity and nationality are forms of identity which do not refer to fixed entities but are shifting and unstable discursive constructions. Likewise, sexual identity was argued to be a matter of how femininity and masculinity are spoken about and not universal biological essences. Thus, while there are differences between identities of race and gender, both are social constructions intrinsically implicated in matters of representation. That identities are matters of culture rather than nature does not mean that one can simply throw off those ethnic or sexual identities into which one has been acculturalized and take on others for, while identities are social constructions, they are ones that constitute us through the impositions of power and the identifications of the psyche.

Television in the era of globalization is vital to the construction of cultural identities because it circulates a bricolage of representations of class, gender, race, age and sex with which we identify or struggle against. That is, television is a proliferating and globalized resource for the construction of cultural identity and a site of contestation over meanings. We explored a number of representations of people of colour in British and US television and noted a range of different stereotypes. However, while television does still produce and circulate racist discourses, it was also argued that representations of black people on television are frequently ambiguous and ambivalent. Such ambiguities are the site of *cultural struggles* over meaning rather than the fixing of definitive meanings for audiences, and likewise with questions of sex and gender. For while television may represent women as the second sex, placing them in the patriarchal work of domesticity and male oriented sexuality, some sites or representations are able to destabilize gender constructions. For example, both drag and the videos of Madonna arguably suggest the performative and changeable character of all sexual identities.

While global television is a form of cultural power it was suggested that audiences are active creators of meaning and not 'cultural dopes'. While texts construct subject positions it does not follow that we all take up that which is offered, rather, reception studies have stressed the negotiations between subject and text, including the possibility of resistance to textual meanings. Consequently, representations, of for example race and gender, are, like identity itself, the site of struggles over meaning. Of course, any position of 'resistance' is itself a discursive construct drawn from another site. Cultural politics involves the play, juxtaposition and conflict between discourses.

Thus, global television does not simply reproduce a dominant or hegemonic culture with its associated identities in any clear and straightforward fashion. Rather, the relationship between globalization, television and cultural identities is a complex one in which a whole range of competing identities are in play from absolutist ethnic or religious identities to hybrid cross-cultural identities. Indeed, it was suggested that, in the context of globalization, both the physical movement of peoples and the electronic distribution of 'culture' contribute to the development of just such hybrid identities. Indeed, this conception of hybrid cultural identities is central to the arguments that television does not operate as a hypodermic injection of meaning (because audiences are active) and that global television is not best thought of as a form of cultural imperialism. Rather, in contributing to the dislocation of cultural identities from specific places, television is a resource for increasingly complex multiple identities and competing discourses of power.

Finally, it was argued that regarding identities as discursive-performative constructions need not undermine the language of human agency and the politics of identity, provided that one understands agency as itself being socially constructed. Nor does seeing truth as a historically contingent social commendation or 'regime of truth' constituted by power (rather than a transcendental universal category) prevent us acting politically to improve the human condition. In this context, and given that identities are fundamentally descriptions in language with which we identify, then the cultural politics of identity can be conceived in terms of redescriptions of the social world. That is, the development of 'new languages', as guides to action, have desirable pragmatic consequences.

The struggle to produce new languages and to have them heard and subsequently accepted as 'true' is the domain of a cultural politics. Cultural studies, it was argued, has seen itself as an intellectual project concerned with politics, where politics is understood in its broadest terms as anything to do with *power*. This is because, within cultural studies, power is regarded as pervading every level of social relationships. Power is not simply a coercive force which subordinates one set of people to another, though it certainly is this, but also a set of processes that generates and enables any form of social action, relationship or order. In this sense, power, while certainly constraining, is also enabling.

Having said that, cultural studies has shown a specific concern with subordinated groups, at first with class, and later with races, genders, nations, age groups, and so on. In particular, it has explored how subordination is not simply a matter of coercion but of consent. Here culture, and particularly *popular culture* (with which cultural studies has been especially though not exclusively concerned), was the ground on which consent was won or resisted. For example, such a cultural politics takes place in and around the institutions and representations of television and centres on

- putting pressure on television organizations to accept the legitimacy of a range of cultural identities
- the ability to secure resources to make programmes
- the production of a diversity of representations
- the attempt to win the hearts and minds of an active audience through a politics of representation.

All of this matters provided one is supportive of cultural diversity, difference and pluralism, that is, solidarity with a whole range of cultural differences. Thus, cultural studies and cultural politics is never a matter of neutral knowledge; rather, both are premised on historically contingent value traditions. Thus, to end this book we might reflect on Hall's argument that:

> the work that cultural studies has to do is to mobilize everything that it can find in terms of intellectual resources in order to understand what keeps making the lives we live, and the societies we live in, profoundly and deeply antihuman in their capacity to live with difference. Cultural studies' message is a message for academics and intellectuals but, fortunately, for many other people as well. In that sense, I have tried to hold together in my own intellectual life, on the one hand, the conviction and passion and the devotion to objective interpretation, to analysis, to rigorous analysis and understanding, to the passion to find out, and to the production of knowledge that we did not know before. But, on the other, I am convinced that no intellectual worth his salt, and no university that wants to hold up its head in the face of the twenty-first century, can afford to turn dispassionate eyes away from the problems of race and ethnicity that beset our world.
>
> (Hall 1997d: 343)

Simunye – we are one

GLOSSARY OF KEY CONCEPTS

Acculturalization: a set of social processes by which we learn how to 'go on' in a culture including the acquisition of language, values and norms.

Active audience: the capability of audiences to be creators and producers of meaning rather than being passive receptors of texts.

Agency: the socially determined capability to act and make a difference.

Anti-essentialism: since words do not refer to essences, identity is not a fixed universal 'thing'. Cultural identity is not an essence but a 'cut' or a snapshot of unfolding meanings.

Articulation: a temporary unity of discursive elements which do not have to 'go together' so that an articulation is the form of the connection that *can* make a unity of two different elements, under certain conditions. Articulation suggests both expressing/representing and a joining together so that, for example, questions of gender may connect with race but in context specific and contingent ways.

Citizenship: a form of identity by which individuals are granted social rights and obligations within political communities.

Convergence: breaking down barriers between technologies and industrial sectors, for example, the super information highway.

Cultural identity: a temporary stabilization of meaning, a becoming rather than a fixed entity. The suturing or stitching together of the discursive 'outside' with the 'internal' processes of subjectivity. Points of temporary attachment to the subject positions which discursive practices construct for us.

Cultural imperialism: the domination of one culture by another usually conceived of in terms of the ascendancy of specific nations or global consumer capitalism.

Culture: (a) Maps of criss-crossing discursive meaning (b) a zone of shared and contested values (c) a whole way of life (d) signifying practices.

Diaspora: dispersed networks of ethnically and culturally related peoples.

Differance: after Derrida, 'difference and deferral'. Meaning is unstable and never complete since the production of meaning is continually deferred and added to (or supplemented) by the meanings of other words.

Discourse: language and practice, regulated ways of speaking which define, construct and produce objects of knowledge.

Discursive formation: a pattern of discursive events which refer to, or bring into being, a common object across a number of sites.

Epistemology: concerned with the source and status of knowledge. The question of truth is an epistemological issue.

Essentialism: essentialism assumes that words have stable referents, that is, social categories reflect an essential underlying identity. By this token there would be stable truths to be found and an essence of, for example, femininity because words refer to fixed essences and thus identities are regarded as fixed entities.

Ethnicity: a cultural term for boundary formation between groups of people who have been discursively constructed as sharing values, norms, practices, symbols and artefacts and are seen as such by themselves and others. Closely connected to the concept of race.

Foundationalism: the attempt to give absolute universal grounds or justifications for the truth of knowledge and values.

Gender: see sex and gender.

Globalization: increasing multidirectional economic, social, cultural and political global connections and our awareness of them including the global production of the local and the localization of the global. Often associated with the institutions of modernity and time–space compression or the shrinking world.

Hegemony: a temporary closure, which seeks to fix meaning through the operation of power. The process of making, maintaining and reproducing the governing sets of meanings of a given culture. For Gramsci, hegemony implies a situation where a 'historical bloc' of ruling-class factions exercise *social authority* and *leadership* over the subordinate classes through a combination of force and, more importantly, consent.

Hybridity: the mixing together of different cultural elements to create new meanings and identities. Hybrids destabilize and blur cultural boundaries in a process of fusion or creolization.

Identity politics: forging 'new languages' of identity and acting to change social practices usually through the formation of coalitions where at least some values are shared.

Ideology: the attempt to fix meanings and world-views by power. Maps of meaning which, while they purport to be universal truths, are historically specific understandings which obscure and maintain the power of social groups (for example, class, gender, race).

Knowledge: see power/knowledge.

Modernity: a post-traditional historical period marked by industrialism, capitalism, the nation-state and forms of surveillance.

Multiple identities: the assumption of different and potentially contradictory identities at different times which do not form a unified coherent self.

National identity: a form of imaginative identification with that nation-state as expressed through symbols and discourses. Thus, nations are not only political formations but also systems of cultural representation so that national identity is continually reproduced through discursive action.

Performativity: discursive practice which enacts or produces that which it names through citation and reiteration of the norms or conventions of the 'law'. Thus, the discursive production of identities through repetition and recitation.

Political economy: concerned with power and the distribution of economic resources. Political economy is concerned with who owns and controls the institutions of television.

Postmodernism: (a) Cultural style marked by intertextuality, pastiche, genre blurring and bricolage (b) philosophical movement which rejects 'grand-narratives' (that is, universal explanations of human history and activity) in favour of *irony* (the recognition of the contingent character of beliefs, values, knowledge, and so on).

Postmodernity: (a) A historical period after modernity marked by the centrality of consumption in a postindustrial context (b) a cultural sensibility which rejects 'grand-narratives' in favour of local truths within specific language-games.

Power/knowledge: after Foucault, knowledge is not neutral but always implicated in questions of social power. Power and knowledge are mutually constitutive.

Public sphere: a space for democratic public debate and argument which mediates between civil society and the state, in which the public organizes itself, and in which 'public opinion' is formed.

Race: categories of people based on alleged biological characteristics including skin pigmentation. A 'racialized group' would be one identified and subordinated on the grounds of race as a discursive construct.

Representation: by which signifying practices appear to stand for or depict another object or practice in the 'real' world. Better described as a 'representational effect' since signs do not stand for or reflect objects in a direct 'mirroring' mode, but constitute them.

Self-identity: the way we think about ourselves and construct unifying narratives of the self.

Semiotics: the study (or 'science') of signs and signification.

Sex and gender: sex has been taken to refer to the biology of the body while gender concerns the cultural assumptions and practices which govern the social construction of men and women. After Butler, sex and gender are both taken to be discursive-performative social constructions and indissociable.

Signification: the process of generating meaning through a system of signs (signifying system).

Social identity: our social obligations and relationships with others. How others see us.

Stereotype: vivid but simple representations which reduce persons to a set of exaggerated, usually negative, character traits. A form of representation which essentializes others through the operation of power.

Strategic essentialism: acting as if identities were stable for specific political reasons. For example, accepting the category of 'woman' to be a stable unity for the purposes of mobilizing women in feminist political action.

Subject position: that regulated set of discursive meanings from which the text makes sense. The subject which must be identified with in order for a discourse to be meaningful.

Synergy: the bringing together of previously separate activities to produce higher profits often leading to the formation of multinational, multimedia corporations.

BIBLIOGRAPHY

Abercrombie, N., Lash, S. and Longhurst, B. (1992) Popular representation: recasting realism, in S. Lash and J. Friedman (eds) *Modernity and Identity*. Oxford: Blackwell.

Alcoff, L. (1989) Cultural feminism versus post-structuralism: the identity crisis in feminist theory, in M. Malson, J. O'Barr, S. Westphal-Wihl and M. Wyer (eds) *Feminist Theory in Practice and Process*. Chicago: University of Chicago Press.

Althusser, L. (1971) *Lenin and Philosophy and Other Essays*. London: New Left Books.

Anderson, B. (1983) *Imagined Communities: Reflections on the Origins and Spread of Nationalism*. London: Verso.

Ang, I. (1985) *Watching Dallas: Soap Opera and the Melodramatic Imagination*. London: Methuen.

Ang, I. (1996) *Living Room Wars: Rethinking Media Audiences for a Postmodern World*. London and New York: Routledge.

Ang, I. and Hermes, J. (1996) Gender and/in media consumption, in I. Ang, *Living Room Wars*. London and New York: Routledge.

Appadurai, A. (1993) Disjuncture and difference in the global cultural economy, in P. Williams and L. Chrisman (eds) *Colonial Discourse and Post-Colonial Theory*. London: Harvester Wheatsheaf.

Ashcroft, B., Griffiths, G. and Tiffin, H. (1989) *The Empire Writes Back: Theory and Practice in Post-Colonial Literatures*. London and New York: Routledge.

Bahia, K. (1997) An analysis of the representation of femininity in popular Hindi film of the 1980s and 1990s. Unpublished dissertation. University of Wolverhampton.

Ballard, R. (ed.) (1994) *Desh Pardesh: The South Asian Presence in Britain*. London: Hurst.

Barker, C. (1997a) Television and the reflexive project of the self: soaps, teenage talk and hybrid identities. *British Journal of Sociology* 44(4).

Barker, C. (1997b) *Global Television: An Introduction*. Oxford: Blackwell.

Barker, C. (1998) 'Cindy's a slut': moral identities and moral responsibility in the 'soap talk' of British Asian girls, *Sociology*, 32(1).

Barker, C. and Andre, J. (1996) Did you see? Soaps, teenage talk and gendered identity, *Young: Nordic Journal of Youth Research*, 4(4).

Barker, M. (1982) *The New Racism*. London: Junction Books.

Barrios, L. (1988) Television, telenovelas, and family life in Venezuela, in J. Lull (ed.) *World Families Watch Television*. Newbury Park, CA and London: Sage.

Barth, F. (1969) *Ethnic Groups and Boundaries*. London: Allen & Unwin.

Barthes, R. (1972) *Mythologies*. London: Cape.

Batty, P. (1993) Aboriginal television in Australia, in T. Dowmunt (ed.) *Channels of Resistance*. London: British Film Institute.

Bauman, Z. (1991) *Modernity and Ambivalence*. Cambridge: Polity Press.

Bennett, T. (1992) Putting policy into cultural studies, in L. Grossberg, C. Nelson and P. Treichler (eds) *Cultural Studies*. London and New York: Routledge.

Best, S. and Kellner, D. (1991) *Postmodern Theory: Critical Interrogations*. London: Macmillan.

Bhabha, H. (ed.) (1990) *Nation and Narration*. London and New York: Routledge.

Blumler, J. (ed.) (1992) *Television and the Public Interest*. Newbury Park, CA and London: Sage.

Bogle, D. (1973) *Toms, Coons, Mulatoes, Mammies and Bucks: An Interpretative History of Blacks in American Films*. New York: Viking Press.

Bordo, S. (1993) *Unbearable Weight: Feminism, Western Culture and the Body*. Berkeley, CA: University of California Press.

Bottomore, T. and Rubel, M. (eds) (1961) *Karl Marx: Selected Writings in Sociology and Philosophy*. Harmondsworth: Pelican.

Brah, A. (1996) *Cartographies of Diaspora*. London: Routledge.

Bramlett-Solomon, S. and Farwell, T. (1996) Sex on soaps: an analysis of black, white and interacial couple intimacy, in V. Berry and C. Manning-Miller (eds) *Mediated Messages and African American Culture*. Thousand Oaks, CA and London: Sage.

Brants, K. and Siune, K. (1992) Public broadcasting in a state of flux, in K. Siune and W. Truetzschler (eds) *Dynamics of Media Politics: Broadcasting and Electronic Media in Western Europe*. Newbury Park, CA and London: Sage.

Buckingham, D. (1987) *Public Secrets: EastEnders and its Audience*. London: British Film Institute.

Butler, J. (1990) *Gender Trouble*. New York and London: Routledge.

Butler, J. (1991) Imitation and gender subordination, in D. Fuss (ed.) *Inside/Out: Lesbian Theories, Gay Theories*. London: Routledge.

Butler, J. (1993) *Bodies that Matter*. London and New York: Routledge.

Campbell, C. (1995) *Race, Myth and the News*. Thousand Oaks, CA and London: Sage.

Cantor, M. and Cantor J. (1992) *Prime Time Television: Content and Control*. Newbury Park, CA and London: Sage.

Carby, H. (1984) White women listen, in Centre for Contemporary Cultural Studies, *The Empire Strikes Back*. London: Hutchinson.

Chambers, I. (1986) *Popular Culture: The Metropolitan Experience*. London: Methuen.

Chodorow, N. (1978) *The Reproduction of Motherhood*. Berkeley, CA: University of California Press.

Chodorow, N. (1989) *Feminism and Psychoanalytic Theory*. Cambridge: Polity Press.

Clarke, D. (1996) *Urban World/Global City*. London: Routledge.

Clifford, J. (1992) Traveling cultures, in L. Grossberg, C. Nelson and P. Treichler (eds) *Cultural Studies*. London and New York: Routledge.

Collard, A. with Contrucci, J. (1988) *Rape of the Wild*. London: The Women's Press.

Collins, J (1992) Postmodernism and television, in R. Allen (ed.) *Channels of Discourse, Reassembled*. London and New York: Routledge.

Commission for Racial Equality (CRE) (1984) *Report into Ethnic Minorities on Television*. London: CRE.

Connell, R. W. (1995) *Masculinities*. Cambridge: Polity Press.

Cowie, E. (1978) Women as sign. *M/F* 1.

Crofts, S. (1995) Global *Neighbours*?, in R. Allen (ed.) *To Be Continued . . . Soap Opera Around the World*. London and New York: Routledge.

Curran, J. (1991) Rethinking the media and the public sphere, in P. Dahlgren and C. Sparks (eds) *Communication and Citizenship*. London and New York: Routledge.

Dahlgren, P. (1995) *Television and the Public Sphere*. Newbury Park, CA and London: Sage.

Daly, M. (1987) *Gyn/Ecology*. London: The Women's Press.

Daniels, T. and Gerson, J. (eds) (1989) *The Colour Black*. London: British Film Institute.

Dasgupta, D. and Hedge, R. (1988) The Eternal Receptacle: a study of mistreatment of women in Hindi films, in R. Ghandially (ed.) *Women in Indian Society*. London and Newbury Park: Sage.

Deleuze, G. and Guattari, F. (1988) *A Thousand Plateaus*, trans. B. Massumi. Minneapolis, MN: University of Minnesota Press.

Derrida, J. (1974) *Of Grammatology*. Baltimore, MD: Johns Hopkins University Press.

Derrida, J. (1980) *La Carte postale*. Chicago: University of Chicago Press.

Dowmunt, T. (ed.) (1993) *Channels of Resistance*. London: British Film Institute.

Dyer, R. (1977) *Gays and Film*. London: British Film Institute.

Dyer, R. (1997) Seeing white, *Times Higher Educational Supplement*, 27 June.

Dyson, K. and Humphries, J. (eds) (1990) *Political Economy of Communications*. London and New York: Routledge.

Eco, U. (1986) *Travels in Hyper-reality*. London: Picador.

Elliott, P. (1977) Media organisations and occupations, in J. Curran, M. Gurevitch and J. Woollacott (eds) *Mass Communication and Society*. London: Edward Arnold with the Open University.

Entman, R. (1990) Modern racism and the images of blacks in local television news, *Critical Studies in Mass Communication*, 7(4): 332–45.

Evans, M. (1997) *Introducing Contemporary Feminist Thought*. Cambridge: Polity Press.

Featherstone, M. (1991) *Consumer Culture and Postmodernism*. Newbury Park, CA and London: Sage.

Featherstone, M. (1995) *Undoing Culture: Globalisation, Postmodernism and Identity*. Newbury Park, CA and London: Sage.

Ferguson, M. (1990) Electronic media and the redefining of time and space, in M. Ferguson (ed.) *Public Communication: The New Imperatives*. Newbury Park, CA and London: Sage.

Fiske, J. (1987) *Television Culture*. London and New York: Routledge.

Fiske, J. (1989) Everyday quizzes, everyday life, in J. Tulloch and G. Turner (eds) *Australian Television: Programs, Pleasures and Politics*. London and Sydney: Allen & Unwin.

Foucault, M. (1970) *The Order of Things*. London: Tavistock.

Foucault, M. (1972) *The Archaeology of Knowledge*. New York: Pantheon.

Foucault, M. (1973) *The Birth of the Clinic*. London: Tavistock.

Foucault, M. (1977) *Discipline and Punishment*. London: Allen Lane.

Foucault, M. (1979) *The History of Sexuality Vol. 1: The Will to Truth*. London: Allen Lane.

Foucault, M. (1980) *Power/Knowledge*. New York: Pantheon.

Foucault, M. (1984) On the genealogy of ethics: an overview of work in progress, in P. Rabinow (ed.) *The Foucault Reader*. New York: Pantheon.

Foucault, M. (1986) *The History of Sexuality Vol. 3: The Care of the Self*. Harmondsworth: Penguin.

Foucault, M. (1987) *The Uses of Pleasure*. Harmondsworth: Penguin.

Fraser, N. (1995a) From irony to prophecy to politics: a response to Richard Rorty, in R.S. Goodman (ed.) *Pragmatism*. New York: Routledge.

Fraser, N. (1995b) Politics, culture and the public sphere: towards a postmodern conception, in L. Nicholson and S. Seidman (eds) *Social Postmodernism*. Cambridge: Cambridge University Press.

Gadamer, H-G. (1976) *Philosophical Hermeneutics*. Berkeley, CA: University of California Press.

Gallagher, M. (1983) *The Portrayal and Participation of Women in the Media*. Paris: UNESCO.

Gardner, K. and Shukur, A. (1994) I'm Bengali, I'm Asian, and I'm living here, in R. Ballard (ed.) *Desh Pardesh: The South Asian Presence in Britain*. London: Hurst.

Geraghty, C. (1991) *Women and Soap Opera*. Cambridge: Polity Press.

Giddens, A. (1984) *The Constitution of Society: Outline of the Theory of Structuration*. Cambridge: Polity Press.

Giddens, A. (1989) *Sociology*. Cambridge: Polity Press.

Giddens, A. (1990) *The Consequences of Modernity*. Cambridge: Polity Press.

Giddens, A. (1991) *Modernity and Self-Identity: Self and Society in the Late Modern Age*. Cambridge: Polity Press.

Giddens, A. (1992) *The Transformation of Intimacy: Sexuality, Love and Eroticism in Modern Societies*. Cambridge: Polity Press.

Giddens, A. (1994) Living in a post-traditional society, in U. Beck, A. Giddens and C. Lash, *Reflexive Modernisation*. Cambridge: Polity Press.

Gillespie, M. (1995) *Television, Ethnicity and Cultural Change*. London and New York: Routledge.

Gilligan, C. (1982) *In a Different Voice*. Cambridge, MA: Harvard University Press.

Gilroy, P. (1987) *There Ain't No Black in the Union Jack*. London: Unwin Hyman.

Gilroy, P. (1993) *The Black Atlantic*. London: Verso.

Gilroy, P. (1997) Diaspora and the detours of identity, in K. Woodwood (ed.) *Identity and Difference*. Thousand Oaks, CA and London: Sage.

Gramsci, A. (1971) *Selections from the Prison Notebooks*, edited by Q. Hoare and G. Nowell-Smith. London: Lawrence & Wishart.

Gray, A. (1992) *Video Playtime: The Gendering of a Leisure Technology*. London: Routledge.

Gray, H. (1996) Television, Black Americans, and the American dream, in V. Berry and C. Manning-Miller (eds) *Mediated Messages and African American Culture*. Thousand Oaks, CA and London: Sage.

Griffiths, T. (1976) An interview with Trevor Griffiths, *The Leveller*, November.

Gurevitch, M., Levy, M. and Roeh, I. (1991) The global newsroom: convergence and diversities in the globalisation of television news, in P. Dahlgren and C. Sparks (eds) *Communication and Citizenship*. London and New York: Routledge.

Habermas, J. (1989) *The Structural Transformation of the Public Sphere*. Cambridge, MA: MIT Press.

Hall, S. (1977) Culture, the media and the ideological effect, in J. Curran, M. Gurevitch and J. Woollacott (eds) *Mass Communication and Society*. London: Edward Arnold with Open University Press.

Hall, S. (1981) Encoding/decoding, in S. Hall, D. Hobson, A. Lowe and P. Willis (eds) *Culture, Media, Language*. London: Hutchinson.

Hall, S. (1990) Cultural identity and diaspora, in J. Rutherford (ed.) *Identity: Community, Culture, Difference*. London: Lawrence & Wishart.

Hall, S. (1992a) The question of cultural identity, in S. Hall., D. Held and T. McGrew (eds) *Modernity and its Futures*. Cambridge: Polity Press.

Hall, S. (1992b) Cultural studies and its theoretical legacies, in L. Grossberg, C. Nelson and P. Treichler (eds) *Cultural Studies*. London and New York: Routledge.

Hall, S. (1996a) Who needs identity?, in S. Hall and P. Du Gay (eds) *Questions of Cultural Identity*. London: Sage.

Hall, S. (1996b) On postmodernism and articulation: an interview with Stuart Hall, edited by L. Grossberg, in D. Morley and D-K. Chen (eds) *Stuart Hall*. London: Routledge.

Hall, S. (1996c) Gramsci's relevance for the study of race and ethnicity, in D. Morley and D-K. Chen (eds) *Stuart Hall*. London: Routledge.

Hall, S. (1996d) New ethnicities, in D. Morley and D-K. Chen (eds) *Stuart Hall*. London: Routledge.

Hall, S. (1997a) The work of representation, in S. Hall (ed.) *Representation: Cultural Representations and Signifying Practices*. London and Thousand Oaks, CA: Sage.

Hall, S. (1997b) The centrality of culture: notes on the cultural revolutions of our time, in K. Thompson (ed.) *Media and Cultural Regulation*. London: Sage.

Hall, S. (ed.) (1997c) The spectacle of the other, in S. Hall (ed.) *Representation: Cultural Representations and Signifying Practices*. London and Thousand Oaks, CA: Sage.

Hall, S. (ed.) (1997d) Race, culture and communications, in J. Storey (ed.) *What is Cultural Studies?* London: Routledge.

Hall, S., Critcher, C., Jefferson, T., Çlarke, J. and Roberts, B. (1978) *Policing the Crisis: Mugging, the State and Law and Order*. London: Macmillan.

Hamelink, C. (1983) *Cultural Autonomy in Global Communications*. New York: Longman.

Harvey, D. (1989) *The Condition of Postmodernity*. Oxford: Blackwell.

Hebdige, D. (1990) Fax to the future, *Marxism Today*, January.

Henriques, J., Holloway, W., Urwin, C., Venn, C. and Walkerdine, U. (1984) *Changing the Subject*. London: Methuen.

Hobson, D. (1982) *Crossroads: Drama of a Soap Opera*. London: Methuen.

hooks, b (1986) *Ain't I a Woman: Black Women and Feminism*. London: Pluto.

hooks, b. (1990) *Yearning: Race, Gender, and Cultural Politics*. Boston, MA: South End Press.

Hoskins, C., McFadyen, S., Finn, A. and Jackel, A. (1995) Film and television co-productions: evidence from Canadian-European experience, *European Journal of Communication*, 10(2).

Hutcheon, L. (1989) *The Politics of Postmodernism*. London and New York: Routledge.

Irigaray, L. (1985a) *Speculum of the Other Women*, trans. G. Gill. Ithaca, NY: Cornell University Press.

Irigaray, L. (1985b) *This Sex Which Is Not One*, trans. C. Porter and C. Burke. Ithaca, NY: Cornell University Press.

Iser, W. (1978) *The Act of Reading: A Theory of Aesthetic Responses*. London and New York: Routledge & Kegan Paul.

Jencks, C. (1986) *What is Post-Modernism?* London: Academy.

Jhally, S. and Lewis, J. (1992) *Enlightened Racism: The Cosby Show, Audiences, and the Myth of the American Dream*. Boulder, CO: Westview Press.

Jones, J. (1996) The new ghetto aesthetic, in V. Berry and C. Manning-Miller (eds) *Mediated Messages and African American Culture*. Thousand Oaks, CA and London: Sage.

Jordan, G. and Weedon, C. (1995) *Cultural Politics: Class, Gender, Race and the Postmodern World*. Oxford: Blackwell.

Kaplan, E. (1992) Feminist criticism and television, in R. Allen (ed.) *Channels of Discourse, Reassembled*. London and New York: Routledge.

Kaplan, E. (1997) *Looking for the Other: Feminism, Film and the Imperial Gaze*. London and New York: Routledge.

Kellner, D. (1992) Popular culture and the construction of postmodern identities, in S. Lash and J. Friedman (eds) *Modernity and Identity*. Oxford: Blackwell.

Kerner Commission (1968) *Report of the National Advisory Committee on Civil Disorders*. New York: E.P. Dutton.

Krishnan, P. and Dighe, A. (1990) *Affirmation and Denial: Construction of Femininity on Indian Televisions*. New Delhi, Newbury Park and London: Sage.

Kristeva, J. (1986) Women's time, in T. Moi (ed.) *The Kristeva Reader*. Oxford: Blackwell.

Lacan, J. (1977) *Ecrits: A Selection*. London: Tavistock.

Laclau, E. (1977) *Politics and Ideology in Marxist Theory*. London: New Left Books.

Laclau, E. and Mouffe, C. (1985) *Hegemony and Socialist Strategy: Toward a Radical Democratic Politics*. London: Verso.

Lash, S. (1990) *Sociology of Postmodernism*. London: Routledge.

Lash, S. and Urry, J. (1987) *Disorganised Capitalism*. Cambridge: Polity Press.

Leab, D. (1975) *From Sambo to Superspade: The Black Experience in Motion Pictures*. New York: Houghton Mifflin.

Liebes, T. and Katz, E. (1991) *The Export of Meaning*. Oxford: Oxford University Press.

Lopez, A. (1995) Our welcomed guests: telenovelas in Latin America, in R. Allen (ed.) *To Be Continued . . . Soap Opera Around the World*. London and New York: Routledge.

Lucas, M. and Wallner, M. (1993) Resistance by satellite, in T. Dowmunt (ed.) *Channels of Resistance*. London: British Film Institute.

Lull, J. (1991) *China Turned On: Television, Reform and Resistance*. London: Routledge.

Lull, J. (1997) China turned on (revisited): television, reform and resistance, in A. Sreberny-Mohammadi, D. Winseck, J. McKenna and O. Boyd-Barrett (eds) *Media in Global Context*. London: Arnold.

Lyotard, J-F. (1984) *The Postmodern Condition*. Minneapolis, MN: University of Minnesota Press.

McAnany, E. and La Pastina, A. (1994) Telenovela audiences, *Communication Research*, 21(6).

MacCabe, C. (1981) Realism and the cinema: notes on some Brechtian themes, *Screen*, 5(2).

McClintock, A. (1995) *Imperial Leather*. London: Routledge.

McGuigan, J. (1992) *Cultural Populism*. London: Routledge.

McGuigan, J. (1996) *Culture and the Public Sphere*. London: Routledge.

Mackinnon, C. (1987) *Feminism Unmodified*. Cambridge, MA and London: Harvard University Press.

Mackinnon, C. (1991) Difference and domination, in K. Bartlett and R. Kennedy (eds) *Feminist Legal Theory*. Boulder, CO and London: Westview Press.

McNay, L. (1992) *Foucault and Feminism*. Cambridge: Polity Press.

McQuail, D., De Mateo, R. and Tapper, H. (1992) A framework for analysis of media change in Europe in the 1990s, in K. Siune and W. Truetzschler (eds) *Dynamics of Media Politics: Broadcasting and Electronic Media in Western Europe*. Newbury Park, CA and London: Sage.

Maddox, B. (1977) Women and the switchboard, in I. de Sola Pool (ed.) *The Social Impact of the Telephone*. London: Hutchinson.

Martin-Barbero, J. (1988) Communication from culture, *Media, Culture, Society*, 10.

Martin-Barbero, J. (1993) *Communication, Culture and Hegemony: From Media to Mediations*. London and Thousand Oaks, CA: Sage.

Martin-Barbero, J. (1995) Memory and form in Latin American soap opera, in R. Allen (ed.) *To Be Continued . . . Soap Opera Around the World*. London and New York: Routledge.

Martindale, C. (1986) *The White Press in Black America*. Westport, CT: Greenwood Press.

Massey, D. (1994) *Space, Place and Gender*. Cambridge: Polity Press.

Masterman, L. (1980) *Teaching about Television*. London: Macmillan.

Mattelart, M. and Mattelart, A. (1992) *The Carnival of Images*. New York: Bergin & Garvey.

Medhurst, A. (1989) Laughing matters: introduction, in T. Daniels and J. Gerson (eds) *The Colour Black*. London: British Film Institute.

Meehan, D. (1983) *Ladies of the Evening: Women Characters of Prime-Time Television*. Metuchen, NJ: Scarecrow Press.

Mercer, K. (1994) *Welcome to the Jungle – New Positions in Black Cultural Studies*. London and New York: Routledge.

Meyrowitz, J. (1986) *No Sense of Place: The Impact of Electronic Media on Social Behaviour*. New York and Oxford: Oxford University Press.

Miller, D. (1995) The consumption of soap opera: *The Young and the Restless* and mass consumption in Trinidad, in R. Allen (ed.) *To Be Continued . . . Soap Opera Around the World*. London and New York: Routledge.

Mishra, U. (1985) Toward a theoretical critique of Bombay cinema, *Screen*, 26 (3–4).

Mitchell, J. (1974) *Psychoanalysis and Feminism*. London: Allen Lane.

Modleski, T. (1982) *Loving with a Vengeance: Mass-Produced Fantasies for Women*. London: Methuen.

Moi, T. (1985) *Sexual/Textual Politics: Feminist Literary Theory*. London and New York: Routledge.

Morley, D. (1980) *The Nationwide Audience*. London: British Film Institute.

Morley, D. (1986) *Family Television: Cultural Power and Domestic Leisure*. London: Comedia.

Morley, D. (1992) *Television, Audiences and Cultural Studies*. London and New York: Routledge.

Morley, D. and Robbins, K. (1995) *Spaces of Identity: Global Media, Electronic Landscapes and Cultural Boundaries*. London and New York: Routledge.

Mouffe, C. (1992) Democratic citizenship and the political community, in C. Mouffe (ed.) *Dimensions of Radical Democracy*. London: Verso.

Mouffe, C. (1984) Towards a theoretical interpretation of 'New Social Movements', in S. Hanninen and L. Palden (eds) *Rethinking Marx*. New York and Bagnolet: International General/IMMRC.

Murdock, G. (1990) Redrawing the map of the communications industries: concentration and ownership in the era of privatisation, in M. Ferguson (ed.) *Public Communication: The New Imperatives*. Newbury Park, CA and London: Sage.

Murdock, G. and Golding, P. (1977) Capitalism, communications and class relations, in J. Curran, M. Gurevitch and J. Woollacott (eds) *Mass Communication and Society*. London: Edward Arnold with Open University Press.

Nicholson, L. (ed.) (1990) *Feminism/Postmodernism*. London: Routledge.

Nicholson, L. (1995) Interpreting gender, in L. Nicholson and S. Seidman (eds) *Social Postmodernism*. Cambridge: Cambridge University Press.

Oakley, A. (1974) *Housewife*. London: Allen Lane.

Parekh, B. (1991) British citizenship and cultural difference, in G. Andrews (ed.) *Citizenship*. London: Lawrence & Wishart.

Pieterse, J. (1995) Globalisation as hybridisation, in M. Featherstone, S. Lash and R. Robertson (eds) *Global Modernities*. Newbury Park, CA and London: Sage.

Porter, V. (1989) The re-regulation of television: pluralism, constitutionality and the free market in the USA, West Germany, France and the UK, *Media, Culture and Society*, 11.

Rabinow, P. (ed.) (1986) *The Foucault Reader*. New York: Pantheon.

Rajan, S.R. (1991) *Ideal and Imagined Women*. London: Routledge.

Rich, A. (1986) *Of Women Born*. London: Virago.

Robertson, R. (1992) *Globalisation*. Newbury Park, CA and London: Sage.

Robertson, R. (1995) Globalization: time–space and homogeneity–hetrogeneity, in M. Featherstone, S. Lash and R. Robertson (eds) *Global Modernities*. Newbury Park, CA and London: Sage.

Robins, K. (1991) Tradition and translation: national culture in its global context, in J. Corner and S. Harvey (eds) *Enterprise and Heritage: Crosscurrents of National Culture*. London: Routledge.

Rorty, R. (1980) *Philosophy and the Mirror of Nature*. Cambridge: Cambridge University Press.

Rorty, R. (1989) *Contingency, Irony and Solidarity*. Cambridge: Cambridge University Press.

Rorty, R. (1991a) *Objectivity, Relativism, and Truth: Philosophical Papers Vol. 1*. Cambridge: Cambridge University Press.

Rorty, R. (1991b) *Essays on Heidegger and Others: Philosophical Papers Vol. 2*. Cambridge: Cambridge University Press.

Rorty, R. (1995) Feminism and pragmatism, in R.S. Goodman (ed.) *Pragmatism*. New York: Routledge.

Rose, J. (1997 edn) *Sexuality in the Field of Vision*. London: Verso.

Rowbotham, S. (1981) The trouble with patriarchy, in R. Samuel (ed.) *People's History and Socialist Theory*. London: Routledge.

Said, E. (1978) *Orientalism*. New York: Pantheon Books.

Sanchez-Tabernero, A. (1993) *Media Concentration in Europe*. Hamburg: European Institute for Media.

Saussure, F. (1960) *Course in General Linguistics*. London: Peter Owen.

Scannel, P. (1988) Radio times: the temporal arrangements of broadcasting in the modern world, in P. Drummond and R. Paterson (eds) *Television and its Audiences*. London: British Film Institute.

Scannel, P. (1989) Public service broadcasting and modern public life, *Media, Culture and Society*, 11.

Schiller, H. (1969) *Mass Communications and the American Empire*. New York: Augustus M. Kelly.

Schiller, H. (1985) Electronic information flows: new basis for global domination?, in P. Drummond and R. Patterson (eds) *Television in Transition*. London: British Film Institute.

Scott, J. (1990) Deconstructing equality vs difference, in M. Hirsch and E. Fox Keller (eds) *Conflicts in Feminism*. New York and London: Routledge.

Seiter, E. (1989) Don't treat us like we're stupid, in E. Seiter, H. Borchers, G. Kreutzner and E.-M. Warth (eds) *Remote Control: Television, Audiences, and Cultural Power*. London and New York: Routledge.

Sepstrup, P. (1989) Research into international television flows: a methodological contribution, *European Journal of Communication*, 4.

Shotter, J. (1993) *Conversational Realities*. Newbury Park, CA and London: Sage.

Silverstone, R. (1994) *Television and Everyday Life*. London and New York: Routledge.

Smith, A.D. (1990) Towards a global culture?, in M. Featherstone (ed.) *Global Culture*. Newbury Park, CA and London: Sage.

Smith, K. (1996) Advertising discourse and the marketing of *I'll Fly Away*, in V. Berry and C. Manning-Miller (eds) *Mediated Messages and African American Culture*. Thousand Oaks, CA and London: Sage.

Spivak, G.C. (1993) Can the subaltern speak?, in P. Williams and L. Chrismaw (eds) *Colonial Discourse and Postcolonial Theory*. London: Harvester Wheatsheaf.

Straubhaar, J. (1992) What makes news: western, socialist, and Third World television newscasts compared in eight countries, in F. Korzenny and S. Ting Toomey (eds) *Mass Media Effects across Cultures*. Newbury Park, CA and London: Sage.

Straubhaar, J. (1997) Distinguishing the global, regional and national levels of world television, in A. Sreberny-Mohammadi, D. Winseck, J. McKenna and U. Boyd-Barrett (eds) *Media in Global Context*. London: Arnold.

Thompson, J. (1995) *The Media and Modernity*. Cambridge: Polity Press.

Tomlinson, J. (1991) *Cultural Imperialism*. London: Pinter Press.

Tomlinson, J. (1997) Internationalisation, globalisation and cultural imperialism, in

K. Thompson (ed.) *Media and Cultural Regulation*. London and Thousand Oaks, CA: Sage.

Turner, B. (1994) Postmodern culture/modern citizens, in B. Van Steenbergen (ed.) *The Condition of Citizenship*. London and Newbury Park: Sage.

Varis, T. (1974) Global traffic in television. *Journal of Communication* 24.

Varis, T. (1984) International flow of television programmes, *Journal of Communication*, 34(1).

Vink, N. (1988) *The Telenovela and Emancipation: A Study on Television and Social Change in Brazil*. Amsterdam: Royal Tropical Institute.

Wallace, M. (1979) *Black Macho*. London: Calder.

Wallerstein, I. (1974) *The Modern World System*. New York: Academic Press.

Waterman, D. (1988) World television trade: the economic effects of privatisation and new technology, *Telecommunications Policy*, June.

Watson, J. (ed.) (1977) *Between Two Cultures*. Oxford: Blackwell.

Weedon, C (1997) *Feminist Practice and Poststructuralist Theory*. Oxford: Blackwell.

Weeks, J. (1990) The value of difference, in J. Rutherford (ed.) *Identity: Community, Culture, Difference*. London: Lawrence & Wishart.

Wernick, A. (1991) *Promo Culture*. Newbury Park, CA and London: Sage.

West, C. (1992) The postmodern crisis of the Black intellectuals, in L. Grossberg, C. Nelson and P. Treichler (eds) *Cultural Studies*. London and New York: Routledge.

West, C. (1993) *Keeping Faith*. London and New York: Routledge.

Williams, R. (1981) *Culture*. London: Fontana.

Williams, R. (1983) *Keywords*. London: Fontana.

Wilson, T. (1993) *Watching Television: Hermeneutics, Reception and Popular Culture*. Cambridge: Polity Press.

Winship, J. (1981) Sexuality for sale, in S. Hall, D. Hobson, A. Lowe and P. Willis (eds) *Culture, Media, Language*. London: Hutchinson.

Wittgenstein, L. (1953) *Philosophical Investigations*. Oxford: Basil Blackwell.

Wolff, J. (1981) *The Social Production of Art*. London: Macmillan.

Woodward, K. (1997) Motherhood: identities, meanings and myths, in K. Woodward (ed.) *Identity and Difference*. London and Thousand Oaks, CA: Sage.

INDEX